Nietzsche: Life as Literature

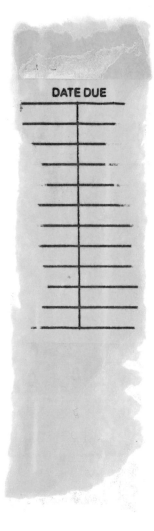

DATE DUE

Nietzsche

LIFE AS
LITERATURE

Alexander Nehamas

Harvard University Press
Cambridge, Massachusetts
London, England

Library of Congress Cataloging in Publication Data

Nehamas, Alexander, 1946–
 Nietzsche, life as literature.

 Includes index.
 1. Nietzsche, Friedrich Wilhelm, 1844–1900.
I. Title.
B3317.N425   1985   193   85–5589
ISBN 0–674–62435–1 (cloth)
ISBN 0–674–62426–2 (paper)

For Christine and Albert Nehama

PREFACE

Reading Nietzsche was a matter of course for intellectually inclined high school students when I was growing up in Greece. I am convinced today that almost none of us understood much of what we read, and I suspect that almost none of us enjoyed it very much either. At least in that respect, therefore, it was a relief to arrive in America as a college student in the mid-sixties, for I soon realized not only that no one expected me to bring Nietzsche's name up at judicious points in my conversation but also that I could not have even if I had wanted to, since I could find no connections between his concerns and the topics that were a matter of course in my new situation.

It was, then, with serious misgivings that, as a graduate student at Princeton University, I found that I had been assigned, quite by chance, to assist the late Walter Kaufmann in a course he offered on Nietzsche and existentialism. But my misgivings soon gave way to a new interest, mixed at the same time with a deep sense of bewilderment. On the one hand, I found that there were parts of Nietzsche which I liked, admired, and wanted to think about. On the other, there were parts which seemed to me at best incomprehensible and at worst embarrassing and better forgotten, or at least tactfully overlooked.

At that stage, still suspicious of my new interest, I read two important books. Kaufmann's *Nietzsche: Philosopher, Psychologist, Antichrist* showed me that being interested in Nietzsche was not being interested simply in a raving, ranting anti-Semitic, pro-Aryan irrationalist. Not all my doubts were removed, and some, particularly about Nietzsche's views of women, still disturb me after all these many years. Nevertheless, Kaufmann's book convinced me that Nietzsche *could* be read. At the same time, Arthur Danto's *Nietzsche as Philosopher* convinced me that Nietzsche *should* be read. I still recall the heady enthusiasm with which, in Danto's book, I recognized an author with ideas of great importance for the problems with which I was engaged at the time. To both these books, and to their authors personally, I am deeply indebted and grateful.

The Department of Philosophy at the University of Pittsburgh, which was considering me for a position in 1971, was scheduled to offer an undergraduate course on existentialism, though it was having some difficulty finding someone to teach it. This was an appointment I was eager to have, and so I expressed the willingness (though I did not, in so many words, claim the ability) to take that assignment. Devoting most of my attention, and most of the semester, to Nietzsche, I was able to teach the course in good conscience and with some success. This allowed me to keep my interest in Nietzsche alive while I was mostly concerned with problems in the history of ancient Greek philosophy. This combination made it possible, and in fact necessary, for me to apply to Nietzsche's texts the same approaches to reading which I had been taught, and continued, to apply to the texts of Plato or the pre-Socratics. The practice and the content of what follows may occasionally make my background apparent. For it, though he may find this preface a peculiar place to see himself acknowledged, I want to express my thanks to Gregory Vlastos.

More recently an interest in questions of literary theory caused me to read a number of German and, particularly, French authors on Nietzsche. I found Gilles Deleuze's *Nietzsche et la philosophie* and Sarah Kofman's *Nietzsche et la métaphore* particularly important for me, and I have tried to engage with the views of these and other writers from France in the body of this work. In general, I found that my questions were often similar to theirs. Though my answers have been different on many occasions, they have, I think, been no more different from theirs than they have been from the answers given to such questions by authors writing in England and America.

In 1978–79 I was a visiting fellow at Princeton University while on sabbatical leave from the University of Pittsburgh, and had the additional financial aid of the National Endowment for the Humanities.

During that year I wrote an essay on the eternal recurrence, which is now incorporated in this book. I am grateful to all three institutions for their support.

Richard Rorty's ideas about which aspects of that essay to bring into the foreground and which to put aside were crucial to my conception of the general project of which this book is the product. Rorty continued to talk to me about issues connected, directly or indirectly, with Nietzsche, and his suggestions about the penultimate draft of the book were invaluable. David Carrier and David Hoy, who have discussed Nietzsche with me on many occasions as well, also read the complete manuscript and generously gave me their ideas for improving it, as did my colleague Shelly Kagan.

Many other friends have listened to me go on about Nietzsche. These include Annette Baier, Donald Baxter, Paul Bové, Donald Crawford, Margreta de Grazia, Paul Guyer, Gilbert Harman, Jane Katselas, Richard Schacht, Hans Sluga, Robert Solomon, Tracy Strong, Charles Taylor, James Van Aken, and Kate Wininger. Thomas Laqueur and Bernd Magnus have been particularly generous with their time, ideas, and good will. All these friends have been patient and kind. Many of them also often proved me wrong. But I suppose that even in a book about Nietzsche I can be Socratic enough to believe that they thereby made the book, and myself, better than we would otherwise have been.

Susan Glimcher, who was the first to read the completed manuscript, not only also proved me wrong but, in addition, persuaded me that, every now and then, I might conceivably be right. This is a different benefit, but it is equally crucial. I don't know what I would have done without it.

The main bulk of this text was written during the academic year 1983–84, while I was a visiting scholar at the University of Pennsylvania, with the generous support of the John Simon Guggenheim Memorial Foundation, which I would like gratefully to acknowledge.

I must finally thank Lindsay Waters of Harvard University Press for his long-standing interest in my writing and for his encouragement of my work.

Versions of Chapters 5 and 6 originally appeared in *The Philosophical Review*, after receiving generous comments from that journal's editors. An article that was published in *Nietzsche-Studien* and an essay that will appear in the *Proceedings* of the Fifth Jerusalem Philosophical Encounter, held in 1983, contain material that has been included in Chapter 2. I am grateful for permission to reproduce these writings in what follows. Grateful acknowledgment is made to Random House, Inc. for permission to quote from the copyrighted works of Friedrich Nietzsche, translated by Walter Kaufmann and R. J. Hollingdale. Acknowledgment is also made to Viking Penguin, Inc. for lines quoted from *The Portable Nietzsche,* edited and translated by Walter Kaufmann. Copyright 1954 by The Viking Press, Inc. Copyright renewed © 1982 by Viking Penguin, Inc. Reprinted by permission of Viking Penguin, Inc.

CONTENTS

And I understood that all these materials for a work of literature were simply my past life.

Marcel Proust, *Time Regained*

ABBREVIATIONS

Works are cited in the text by abbreviation and by volume and/or section number; "Pref." refers to Nietzsche's prefaces, and "Epi." to his epilogues. Full bibliographical data can be found in A Note on Texts and Translations, pages 237–238.

A	*The Antichrist*
BGE	*Beyond Good and Evil*
BT	*The Birth of Tragedy*
CW	*The Case of Wagner*
D	*Daybreak*
EH	*Ecce Homo*
GM	*On the Genealogy of Morals*
GS	*The Gay Science*
HH	*Human, All-Too-Human*
KGW	*Werke: Kritische Gesamtausgabe*
MOM	*Mixed Opinions and Maxims*, in *HH*, vol. 2
NCW	*Nietzsche Contra Wagner*
PTG	*Philosophy in the Tragic Age of the Greeks*
TI	*Twilight of the Idols*
UM	*Untimely Meditations*
WP	*The Will to Power*
WS	*The Wanderer and His Shadow*, in *HH*, vol. 2
Z	*Thus Spoke Zarathustra*

INTRODUCTION

Nietzsche inevitably confronts his readers with two sets of paradoxes. One set is contained within his writing. It belongs to the content of his work, and it includes, for example, his view of the will to power, the eternal recurrence, the nature of the self, and the immoral presuppositions of morality. This set of paradoxes is part of what interpretations of Nietzsche's work aim to understand. The other set is generated by his writing. It is a product of his work, and it puts the very effort to understand him, to offer an interpretation of his views, including the first set of paradoxes, into question. This book, which is an effort to offer such an interpretation, is therefore also an effort to come to terms, so far as this is possible, with both sets of paradoxes.

These paradoxes are not unrelated to one another. On the contrary, a single view that Nietzsche holds straddles both kinds and shows that the distinction between what his writing contains and what it produces can be at best provisional. This view is perspectivism, Nietzsche's famous insistence that every view is only one among many possible interpretations, his own views, particularly this very one, included. But if the view that there are only interpretations is itself only an interpretation, and therefore possibly wrong, it may seem to follow that not every view is after all an interpretation and that Nietzsche's position undermines itself.

Perspectivism is a particular view which Nietzsche holds and which he discusses explicitly in his works. The paradox it presents is therefore part of the content of his writing, and as such it must be addressed by all attempts to interpret his thought. It is part of the object at which the interpretation of Nietzsche is directed. At the same time, however, perspectivism generates two problems that seem also to undermine the very attempt to produce such an interpretation. Perspectivism, thus, is both something that must be understood and something that suggests that understanding may be impossible.

The first problem is that Nietzsche, as I have said, holds a number of positions which he seems to accept in all seriousness. Does he or does he not, then, think that his views of the self, of morality, or of history, many of which are themselves at least apparently paradoxical, are true? If he does, how can this possibly be consistent with his view that all views are only interpretations? If he does not—that is, if he does not think that his views are true—why does he make the effort to present them in the first place?

Faced with this dilemma, some authors choose to emphasize what they consider Nietzsche's "positive" views and to overlook his perspectivism and its apparent implications. Others, by contrast, concentrate on the perspectivism and ignore such views or construe them negatively, as efforts, that is, merely to undermine the positions of others. In either case, perspectivism presents a serious challenge to the principles according to which an interpretation that aims to proceed coherently and to attribute a coherent position to Nietzsche must be presented.

But there is also a second and perhaps more difficult problem. If every view is only an interpretation, and if, as perspectivism holds, there are no independent facts against which various interpretations can be compared, what is the object at which the many interpretations that we consider interpretations *of* Nietzsche are directed? How can we even know that all these discussions and texts are interpretations of the same thing? And what relationship do they bear to one another? If perspectivism is correct, and, as it seems to claim, every interpretation creates its own facts, then it may seem impossible to decide whether any interpretation is or is not correct. And if there is nothing of which all these are the interpretations, then the very idea of interpretation, which seems to require at least that there be something there to be interpreted, begins to appear itself suspect. Finally, a serious question is raised about the status of Nietzsche's own writing, which often consists explicitly of interpretations of phenomena which, like morality, he thinks we have taken too long for granted.

Each of the chapters that follow examines one of the paradoxical positions that Nietzsche holds. Their titles are all quotations from Nietzsche's texts. Each chapter, therefore, is an interpretation of its title, and as such it aims to constitute an instance of the sort of interpretation which, as the chapters collectively try to show, is consistent with Nietzsche's perspectivism, and which is mainly directed at making his views plausible. The question of their truth is left to further interpretation.

I accept Nietzsche's view that there are no facts that are independent of interpretation and that are therefore capable of providing the common object of which all interpretations are interpretations. I also accept his view that there is, accordingly, no neutral standard which determines in every case which of our interpretations is right and which wrong. But I also think—and so, I believe and argue, does Nietzsche—that some interpretations are better than others and that we can even know sometimes that this is the case. This is one of the two themes that are central to the interpretation of Nietzsche which I develop in this book.

The second central theme around which my reading revolves concerns what I will call Nietzsche's aestheticism. Aestheticism is connected with perspectivism in two ways. First, it provides at least part of the motivation for perspectivism. Nietzsche, I argue, looks at the world in general as if it were a sort of artwork; in particular, he looks at it as if it were a literary text. And he arrives at many of his views of the world and the things within it, including his views of human beings, by generalizing to them ideas and principles that apply almost intuitively to the literary situation, to the creation and interpretation of literary texts and characters. Many of his very strange ideas appear significantly more plausible in this light. The most obvious connection, of course, is supplied by our common view that literary texts can be interpreted equally well in vastly different and deeply incompatible ways. Nietzsche, to whom this currently popular idea can in fact be traced, also holds that exactly the same is true of the world itself and all the things within it. This view, as we shall see, motivates his perspectivism as well as aspects of his doctrine of the will to power, of the eternal recurrence, of the nature of the self, and of his objections to morality.

Nietzsche's aestheticism is also connected with perspectivism in another way. The philology of the world, which I mentioned above, not only provides him with a literary model for many of his views but also motivates him to create what we may well call a literary product. Nietzsche's positive thinking consists not so much in the specific ideas with which the individual chapters that follow are concerned (though it does certainly include such views) as, even more important, in the presentation, or exemplification, of a specific character, recognizably literary, who makes of these philosophical ideas a way of life that is uniquely his. The fact that this character is unique, that it is not described in a traditional sense, and that it is produced in a way that prevents it from ever being a model for direct imitation allows Nietzsche, as we shall see, to persist in his perspectivism without being obliged to construct positions that are merely negative. In fact his remarkable approach to these problems undermines any easy distinction between what constitutes a positive and what a negative view. It therefore helps to account for Nietzsche's essentially ambiguous relation to the philosophical tradition.

Nietzsche's irresolubly equivocal relation to philosophy is the subject of Chapter 1, which also touches on some questions that appear later in the book. The ambiguity of this relation is reflected perfectly in Nietzsche's attitude toward Socrates, which is neither purely positive nor purely negative but irreducibly ambivalent. Nietzsche realizes that his project is very similar to the project of Socrates and therefore, in his own eyes at least, to the various projects that have characterized philosophy. He therefore also realizes that it runs the risk of appearing, and indeed of being, one more philosophical project of the traditional sort. This problem is created for Nietzsche by what he considers Socrates' dogmatism, his effort to present his views and values not simply as his own, suitable for himself and for those who may be like him, but as views and values that should be accepted by everyone on account of their rational, objective, and unconditional authority. Nietzsche's perspectivism, however, prevents him from presenting any of his views, even perspectivism itself, in this manner. Yet it is not clear how one can argue for a position, as Nietzsche often clearly wants to do, and yet not suggest that this position is, to use the only possible term in this context, true.

Is Nietzsche, then, trapped in an impasse of his own creation? I suggest that Nietzsche's effort to resolve this problem involves partly his adoption of a vast, and so far largely unnoticed variety of literary genres and styles: his purpose is in this way to make his presence as an individual author unforgettable to his readers. I do not argue that this is the only reason why style is so important to Nietzsche's writing, nor do I claim that my view can even try to account for the important question why Nietzsche adopts particular styles for particular works. I do not even examine his style in any detail. What I claim is simply that his stylistic variations play a crucial philosophical (or, from his point of view, antiphilosophical) role in his writing.

Generally, Part I, entitled "The World," discusses Nietzsche's literary model, his conception of the world as a text, and the methodological problems of interpretation. Chapter 2 deals explicitly with perspectivism and introduces its artistic and literary basis. It examines some of the self-referential difficulties that confront the view that all views are interpretations, and it tries to show to what extent such difficulties can be avoided. The chapter argues that perspectivism does not imply that any interpretation is as good as any other. In the process it also offers a characterization of those whom Nietzsche calls "free spirits" and who realize that all is in fact interpretation, and yet find in this realization not an obstacle to producing new ideas and values but a spur toward it.

In Chapter 3 I discuss that aspect of Nietzsche's view of the will to power that identifies each object in the world with the sum of its effects on every other thing and construes everything else in turn as the sum of further such effects. In order to account for the difficulty that this view faces when it asserts that there are effects without things, properties without substances, and activities without agents, I appeal once again to Nietzsche's literary model and argue that literary objects, and in particular literary characters, are constituted simply as sets of features or effects that belong to no independent subjects. In addition (and this is true of the general as well as the literary case), features are grouped together as aspects of a particular subject always from some specific point of view. Different points of view, proceeding from and manifesting different interests and values, result in different groupings and therefore in different objects. There is no absolute answer to the question which grouping is the best (or which grouping accurately reflects the nature of things themselves), because there is no background set of values that must be unconditionally accepted by all. Nietzsche believes that interpretation reveals the value dependence of various points of view and that therefore it also shows that what we often take as facts are the products of earlier, and forgotten, values and interpretations. At the same time, our own interpretations of these earlier values embody and carry forth the interests and values through which we are most likely to thrive.

But if this is true, can Nietzsche's own interpretation, or genealogy, of morality, which reveals the specific needs and values presupposed and intentionally obscured by Christianity, possibly be correct? Does not this genealogy simply manifest one further partial and arbitrary point of view? What then entitles Nietzsche to claim, as he seems to do, that Christianity is to be rejected? Genealogy generates this paradox even as it reveals the paradox which Nietzsche believes Christianity itself constitutes. This problem is the subject of Chapter 4, which discusses Nietzsche's view that the radical asceticism praised by Christianity directs the faithful to aim at nothing short of their own annihilation. Yet, Nietzsche argues, to the extent that Christianity has succeeded in persuading its followers to pursue this self-destructive end, it has also succeeded in preserving them; for horrible and self-defeating as this aim may be, it is still an aim. And an aim is precisely what the people for whom Christianity was originally designed have needed as much as they have lacked: "a will to nothingness, an aversion to life, a rebellion against the most fundamental presuppositions of life . . . is and remains a *will*" (*GM*, III, 28).

Can Nietzsche claim that he has revealed the most basic and objectionable features of Christianity and not also imply at the same time that both his revelations and his accusations are correct? And if he does so, does he not then violate his own perspectivism and fall back into the dogmatic tradition from which he wants to escape?

These are the questions that Part II, entitled "The Self," examines. In particular, it asks how Nietzsche proposes to present views of his own if the picture of the world, of knowledge, of interpretation, and of philosophy which Part I attributes to him is at all correct. At this point the second aspect of his aestheticism—the fact that his product as well as his model is literary—takes on central importance.

Chapter 5 discusses the eternal recurrence, which, in my opinion, has little if anything to do with the nature of the universe, as many believe. Nietzsche, I argue, does not claim that the history of the world repeats itself in an eternal cycle, or even that it is possible that it might do so. Rather, he believes that the world and everything in it are such that if anything in the world ever occurred again (though this is in fact impossible) then everything else would also have to occur again. This is so because Nietzsche accepts the view that the connections that constitute everything in the world, and in particular the connections that constitute each person out of its experiences and actions are absolutely essential to that person. Everything one does is equally crucial to who one is. If, then, we ever were to be given a second life, it would necessarily have to be identical to the life we have had so far; otherwise there would be no reason to consider it *our* life in the first place. The eternal recurrence is therefore not a theory of the world but a view of the ideal life. It holds that a life is justified only if one would want to have again the same life one had already had, since, as the will to power shows, no other life can ever be possible. The eternal recurrence therefore holds that our life is justified only if we fashion it in such a way that we would want it to be exactly as it had been already.

This view, which once again depends on Nietzsche's literary model, introduces two further dimensions of his thought. The first is Nietzsche's immoralism. For all that I have said, I could be perfectly willing to live my life over again, to have it changed in no respect whatsoever, and thus satisfy his conception of the ideal life, and yet I could be deeply repulsive from a moral point of view. Nothing Nietzsche writes precludes this from being a consequence of his view. The second dimension, which is connected with the idea that a life is something to be fashioned, is Nietzsche's emphasis on the process of becoming who one is. This is the topic of Chapter 6.

The self, according to Nietzsche, is not a constant, stable entity. On the contrary, it is something one becomes, something, he would even say, one constructs. A person consists of absolutely everything one thinks, wants, and does. But a person worthy of admiration, a person who has (or is) a self, is one whose thoughts, desires, and actions are not haphazard but are instead connected to one another in the intimate way that indicates in all cases the presence of style. A self is just a set of coherently connected episodes, and an admirable self, as Nietzsche insists again and again, consists of a large number of powerful and conflicting tendencies that are controlled and harmonized. Coherence, of course, can also be produced by weakness, mediocrity, and one-dimensionality. But style, which is what Nietzsche requires and admires, involves controlled multiplicity and resolved conflict. It still, however, does not seem to require what we generally consider moral character.

What are Nietzsche's ideal people like? How can we become like them? These questions, and their connections to Nietzsche's immoralism, are discussed in Chapter 7. I offer an account of Nietzsche's slogan, "Beyond good and evil," which takes it to claim that the qualities we consider moral and immoral are, like everything else in the world, essentially connected to one another. Their character and value are, therefore, once again a matter of perspective. And I argue that any effort to attribute to Nietzsche a positive view of human conduct, consisting perhaps of a description of the right kind of life or of a set of principles for becoming the sort of person he admires, is bound to fail.

The reason for this is that Nietzsche does not believe that such a kind of life or person exists. That is, he does not believe that there exists a single proper kind of life or person. He thinks, as we shall see, that admirable people are one and all what he calls "individuals." But the very notion of an individual is one that essentially refuses to be spelled out in informative terms. To give general directions for becoming an individual is surely as self-defeating as is offering general views when one believes that general views are all simply interpretations. And this, of course, provides another reason why Nietzsche does not have anything like a traditional positive moral view. Nietzsche solves this double problem by refusing to offer any descriptions of what an ideal person or an ideal life would be like. We must not suppose that the eternal recurrence is such a description: many types of life are perfectly compatible with satisfying its general conditions.

Instead, Nietzsche exemplifies through his own writings one way in which one individual may have succeeded in fashioning itself—an individual, moreover, who, though beyond morality, is not morally objectionable. This individual is none other than Nietzsche himself, who is a creature of his own texts. This character does not provide a model for imitation, since he consists essentially of the specific actions—that is, of the specific writings—that make him up, and which only he could write. To imitate him directly would produce a caricature, or at best a copy—something which in either case is not an individual. To imitate him properly would produce a creation which, making use of everything that properly belongs to oneself, would also be perfectly one's own—something which is no longer an imitation.

Nietzsche's effort to create an artwork out of himself, a literary character who is a philosopher, is then also his effort to offer a positive view without falling back into the dogmatic tradition he so distrusted and from which he may never have been sure he escaped. His aestheticism is, therefore, the other side of his perspectivism. This is the central claim of the interpretation of which this book consists.

This interpretation concerns primarily the texts Nietzsche composed in the 1880s, beginning with *Thus Spoke Zarathustra* (1883–1885), through *Beyond Good and Evil* (1886), the fifth book of *The Gay Science* (1887), *On the Genealogy of Morals* (1887), *The Case of Wagner* (1888), *The Twilight of the Idols* (1888), and *The Antichrist* (1888), to *Ecce Homo* (1888) and the notes collected posthumously under the title *The Will to Power* (1883–1888).

I cite and discuss passages from Nietzsche's earlier works, all of which are naturally important in their own right. But these works are not my central concern. I realize that my practice leaves many questions about Nietzsche's development unanswered, for whole books could be written not only about these questions but also about the views Nietzsche expressed in these works. In reply I can only claim that whole books, different from mine, could also be written about the very same texts on which I have chosen to concentrate.

Some justification for my relying on *The Will to Power* may be considered necessary. I am aware that these notes do not constitute a "work" in any traditional sense: the idea to publish them and even their very arrangement, which has necessarily imposed some initial (but in my view ultimately defeasible) interpretations of their sense, came not from Nietzsche himself but from Elizabeth Förster-Nietzsche after her brother's death. But this collection has become, for better or worse, an integral part of Nietzsche's literary and philosophical work, and it has been instrumental in forming our reactions to him over the past eighty years. It has often been claimed that its influence has been for the worse and that many views would never have been attributed to Nietzsche had his published work been given the priority that by rights belongs to it. I am not sure that in fact the situation is quite so simple. To be sure, some views were attributed to Nietzsche only on the strength of his notes. But sometimes, as in the case of the cosmological version of the will to power, this depended on unsatisfactory readings of a number of notes and not on the "nature" of these notes themselves. But such misreadings show little about the status and priority of Nietzsche's notes. Nietzsche's anti-Semitism, for example, was for years attributed to him on the basis of his published texts—equally misinterpreted. Other scholars find in the notes views that are inconsistent with some of Nietzsche's published positions. This is sometimes true. But once again, this has no implications about priority. In any case, the notes that constitute *The*

Will to Power, along with the rest of the material from Nietzsche's unpublished *Nachlass*, bear roughly the same relationship to his published works as a whole that these works bear to one another: there are as many inconsistencies within the latter group as there are within the former; and these are as many, or as few, as one might reasonably expect from an author who wrote as much as Nietzsche did over such a short span of time.

The point is that there can be no single answer to the question of priority. Nietzsche is an author, a public figure, and all his writings are relevant to his interpretation. The importance we attach to any part of his work cannot depend on general principles about which is essentially primary and which necessarily follows. The importance of each text depends on the specific contribution that text makes to our construction of a coherent and understandable whole. It must be determined separately in each individual case. This principle (if the term is at all appropriate) would have been quite acceptable to the author whom this book constructs. And to the apparently natural objection that such a principle depends on conceptions of coherence and on values regarding understanding that cannot be objectively justified, this author would reply that, really, this is not an objection at all.

I | THE WORLD

1 | *The Most Multifarious Art of Style*

The nineteenth century dislike of Realism is the rage of Caliban seeing his own face in a glass. The nineteenth century dislike of Romanticism is the rage of Caliban not seeing his own face in a glass.

Oscar Wilde, *The Picture of Dorian Gray*

Works on Nietzsche, the present one included, conventionally begin with some commonplaces about his style. Among these the most elementary is that Nietzsche's thinking is inseparable from his writing and that coming to terms with his style is essential to understanding him at all. But this commonplace has been interpreted in a vast number of ways, and each of these has given rise to strikingly different readings of his thinking as well as of his writing.

In the coarsest sense, to say that Nietzsche's style is important is to say that his writing is unusual and idiosyncratic. This in turn is just to say that his works do not exhibit the features we have been accustomed to expect of philosophical treatises. And, forgetting that philosophical treatises themselves have been written in the most various styles imaginable, this has often been taken to show that Nietzsche's works are not, in some sense, philosophical.[1] So the view that Nietzsche was really a poet and not a philosopher, perhaps originated and certainly encapsulated in Stefan George's verse "It should have sung, not spoken, this 'new soul,' " came to be popular, and havoc was wreaked both upon poetry and upon philosophy.[2]

T. S. Eliot's youthfully patronizing view was only slightly more sophisticated. Eliot realized that the "literary" quality of Nietzsche's writing could not be separated from the "philosophical" content of his thought, but he thought that by mixing elegance and precision, Nietzsche hurt both:

> Nietzsche is one of those writers whose philosophy evaporates when detached from its literary qualities, and whose literature owes its charm not alone to the personality and wisdom of the man, but to a claim to scientific truth. Such authors have always a peculiar influence over the large semi-philosophical public, who are spared the austere effort of criticism required by either metaphysics or literature, by either Spinoza or Stendhal; who enjoy the luxury of confounding, and avoid the task of combining, different interests.[3]

The serious discussion of Nietzsche's style begins with attention to his use of the aphorism, a genre that Nietzsche employed at least partly because of his admiration for the pre-Socratic philosophers and for the French moralists, and of which he remains one of the great masters.[4] Aphorisms, of course, are not systematic, not discursive, and not argumentative; also, for the most part they are much more difficult to interpret than they at first appear.[5] And for most of Nietzsche's earlier English-speaking readers (those at least who tried to read him "philosophically"), the aphorism constituted the essence, as well as the essential weakness, of his project. "Nietzsche's work," Crane Brinton wrote in a passage that is characteristic of many, "contains a great variety of ideas, sometimes mutually contradictory, difficult if not impossible to reduce to a 'system,' made still more bewilderingly varied by the aphoristic form in which they are cast."[6]

In stark contrast to Brinton, and as part of his effort to vindicate Nietzsche's reputation among the English-speaking public, Walter Kaufmann treated the aphorism much more positively. Kaufmann also located the aphorism at the heart of Nietzsche's writing, and he too was disturbed by its fragmentary nature. In fact he thought that Nietzsche's "sketch of the style of decadence" in section 7 of *The Case of Wagner* may have been, perhaps inadvertently, "the best critique" of his own style: "What is the mark of every *literary* decadence?" Nietzsche writes. "That life no longer resides in the whole. The word becomes sovereign and leaps out of the sentence, the sentence reaches out and obscures the meaning of the page, and the page comes to life at the expense of the whole—the whole is no longer a whole. This, however, is the simile of every style of decadence: every time there is an anarchy of atoms."[7] Kaufmann was nevertheless determined to show that Nietzsche's aphorisms are ultimately unified, that behind them "there is a whole philosophy" (p. 74). In order to accomplish this, he interprets the aphoristic style as an expression of Nietzsche's philosophically grounded objections to system building and of his preference for posing questions rather than for giving answers: "Nietzsche," Kaufmann writes, "is, like Plato, not a system-thinker, but a problem-thinker" (p. 82). He then argues that Nietzsche transcended the limitations of the style of decadence by putting it into the service of what Kaufmann calls his "experimentalism": this is an attitude which essentially involves "the good will to accept new evidence and to abandon previous positions, if necessary" (p. 86). Each aphorism is therefore, for Kaufmann, an "experiment." And even if not all of Nietzsche's experiments confirm the same theory, they are still unified by his "intellectual integrity," which "makes each investigation a possible corrective for any inadvertent previous mistakes. No break, discontinuity, or inconsistency occurs unless there has been a previous error or there is an error now . . . His 'existentialism' prevents his aphorisms from being no more than a glittering mosaic of independent monads" (p. 91).

Kaufmann's is an effort to find an underlying unity, at least of method and attitude if not of doctrine, behind Nietzsche's aphorisms. Directly opposed to any such effort is the more recent reading of Sarah Kofman, who also complicates our picture of Nietzsche's style by paying serious attention to his use of metaphor as well as to the aphorism. Kofman attributes to both these features of Nietzsche's writing a single, apotropaic function. "Metaphoric style," she writes, "is 'aristocratic'; it allows people of the same kind [*race*] to recognize each other; it excludes the member of the herd as inappropriate, foul smelling: to speak commonly is to become vulgar."[8] And like metaphor, aphoristic writing too "wants to be understood only by those who are related by a common set of refined impressions; it wants to repel the *profanum vulgus* and to attract the free spirits" (p. 166). But what is even more important, according to her view, is that both metaphor and aphorism constantly resist all attempts at a final, definitive interpretation. Each stretch of Nietzsche's text provides us with an indefinite number of possible and conflicting interpretations. Kofman emphasizes just those features of the aphorism that Kaufmann, in his attempt to find the unity underlying Nietzsche's fragmented style, tends to underplay. She even offers, as a compliment, what can only be considered another version of Brinton's earlier criticism: "The aphorism, because of its discontinuous character, disseminates meaning; it is an appeal to a pluralism of interpretations and to their renewal: nothing is immortal except movement" (p. 168).

By the nineteen-thirties Heidegger had already initiated an interpretive task that bears some similarity to Kaufmann's project. Instead of emphasizing the published works, however, Heidegger insisted that Nietzsche's central thoughts are all to be found in *The Will to Power*, a posthumously published selection from his notes. "What Nietzsche himself published during his creative life was always foreground . . . His philosophy proper was left behind as posthumous unpublished work."[9] According to Heidegger, Nietzsche's thought in *The Will to Power* constitutes the final stage in the development and "overcoming" of Western philosophy, or metaphysics. And doubtless in order to underscore the symmetry between the beginning and the end of what he took to be a single enterprise, in order to underline the irony that binds the readers of the pre-Socratics and of Nietzsche together, Heidegger introduced a new notion into the reading of Nietzsche—the notion of the fragment: "What lies before us today as a book with the title *The Will to Power* contains preliminary drafts and fragmentary elaborations of that work. The outlined plan according to which these fragments are ordered, the division into four books, and the titles of these books also stem from Nietzsche himself."[10] For Heidegger the task in reading Nietzsche is to reconstruct his real thought, in which Western philosophy culminates and through which it ends, from these surviving fragments.

In *Spurs: Nietzsche's Styles*, Jacques Derrida radicalizes the notion of the fragment in order to undermine the Heideggerian, hermeneutical project of capturing Nietzsche's real thought. "The very concept of fragment," Derrida writes, "since its fracturedness is itself an appeal to some totalizing complement, is no longer sufficient here."[11] To construe anything as a fragment, Derrida argues, is at the same time to envisage the whole of which it is a part. But Nietzsche's textual fragments are for him sentences that essentially lack a context, a whole to which they belong, and to which an appeal is necessary if we are to interpret them. In his well-known discussion of the sentence "I have forgotten my umbrella," which was found among Nietzsche's papers, Derrida claims that the sense of fragments, as he construes them, is in principle undecidable. Joining Kofman, he refuses even to attempt to attribute a definite interpretation to this sentence. He denies that there is a determinate thought lurking within or behind it, and he tentatively suggests that this may also hold true of "the totality of Nietzsche's text."[12] In fact Derrida claims that precisely because they lack a context, fragments also lack style, for style depends on the existence of interconnections among pieces of language that, insofar as they are interconnected, are no longer fragments in his sense. This is why, despite his emphasis on Nietzsche's writing, Derrida concludes that even if one knows the meaning of the terms constituting a fragment, one still lacks the ability to offer an interpretation of it.[13]

A strikingly similar view of Nietzsche's style (or rather of its absence, since, as I have said, style involves organization, interconnections, and dependences) is held by Arthur Danto, who writes: "Nietzsche's books give the impression of having been assembled rather than composed. They are made up, in the main, of short, pointed aphorisms, and of essays seldom more than a few pages long . . . And any given aphorism or essay might as easily have been placed in one volume as in another without much affecting the unity or structure of either."[14] The very same point, Danto believes, holds true of Nietzsche's books themselves. Ultimately, according to his view, Nietzsche's works can be read in almost any order without making a great difference to what one learns from them. As a matter of fact, Danto does not allow this theoretical view of Nietzsche's writing to prevent him from offering a systematic and, to a serious extent, chronological interpretation of Nietzsche's thought. Nevertheless, his attitude toward Nietzsche's style aligns him with Derrida, even if the two approaches are at a slight angle to one another.

Toward the end of *Spurs* Derrida writes, "If there is going to be style, there can only be more than one" (p. 139). This statement recalls the fact that in order to identify an author's style, we must distinguish it from the style of at least one other, and this may suggest that there is no such thing as style but only, so to speak, a difference between various texts.

Derrida's important comment raises a further issue which is absolutely crucial to the reading of Nietzsche presented in this book, for it brings to mind a point that has not emerged at all in my overview of discussions of Nietzsche's writing. This is the fact that, during his very short productive life Nietzsche depended, beyond the aphorism, the metaphor, and the fragment, on a truly astounding variety of styles and genres. It is remarkable that, in a secondary literature essentially concerned with questions about the pluralism of interpretation, Nietzsche's *stylistic* pluralism has been almost completely overlooked. Once this pluralism has been noticed, however, the issue of its function can no longer be avoided. It becomes necessary to ask a number of new questions about Nietzsche's style—questions that are different from others that have already been asked—and to offer new answers concerning its importance.

The aphorism may be at least superficially the most striking of Nietzsche's styles, but it is only one style among many. Primarily it characterizes, not always adequately, the works of Nietzsche's middle period: *Daybreak, Human, All-Too-Human,* and *The Gay Science,* books 1–4. Parts of *Beyond Good and Evil* and *The Twilight of the Idols* consist of aphorisms, and Zarathustra is undeniably fond of them. But the notion of the aphorism cannot begin to capture the style of the notes (which is not to say the "fragments") that constitute *The Will to Power* and a large part of the rest of Nietzsche's unpublished work. *The Birth of Tragedy* depends on the form of the scholarly treatise, even though part of its aim is to demonstrate the limitations of scholarly or scientific (*wissenschaftlich*) discourse, and despite its obvious departures from some of the central requirements of that genre.[15] *Untimely Meditations,* and a number of other works from Nietzsche's early period, are essays in a most classical sense. *Thus Spoke Zarathustra* is notoriously difficult to classify; it has been variously called "epic," "dithyrambic," and "evangelical." But whatever it is, it certainly is not aphoristic. Though, like all of Nietzsche's books, it contains many aphorisms, it embodies a complex narrative structure in the course of which the character of Zarathustra develops radically.[16] *Beyond Good and Evil* is neither a failed philosophical treatise nor a collection of short, unrelated essays. The structure of this deeply unified text cannot even begin to become apparent until it is read as a sustained monologue through which a definite and striking personality is exhibited or perhaps constructed. The connections between its 296 sections, its nine parts, and the concluding "Aftersong" (a poem) will remain obscure unless they are construed conversationally and, in a classical sense, dialectically. The same is true of the magnificent fifth book of *The Gay Science* and, to a lesser extent, *The Twilight of the Idols. On the Genealogy of Morals* returns to the form of the scholarly philological treatise, though Nietzsche again exploits the genre for his own purposes. Nevertheless, the work is deeply and carefully organized, rivaled only by *Beyond Good and Evil* in the control it manifests.[17] *The Case of Wagner, Nietzsche Contra Wagner,* and *The Antichrist* depend on at least some of the features of the polemical pamphlet, while *Ecce Homo* plays with the form of the autobiography. Finally, we must not leave out Nietzsche's lyric, epigrammatic, and dithyrambic poems or the vast number of letters, all of which belong to his writing as surely as every one of his aphorisms.

In this form my remarks cannot possibly illuminate the style or structure of any of these works, nor are they meant to do so. Their point is simply to recall the vast variety of Nietzsche's styles and to suggest that any treatment of his writing that concerns only the aphorism, even if this is supplemented by the figure of the metaphor and by the notion of the fragment, is bound to be incomplete. Nietzsche himself was always aware of this feature of his writing and wrote about it using a crucial trope to which we shall have to return: "I have many stylistic possibilities—the most multifarious art of style that has ever been at the disposal of one man" (*EH*, III, 4).

The question with which I am concerned is not the question why Nietzsche uses this rather than that particular style on each particular occasion, though this question is, of course, important in its own right. No specific discussion of any individual work of his can proceed, in my opinion, without confronting that issue directly. It is no accident, for example, that *On the Genealogy of Morals* combines the form of the scholarly treatise, to which dispassionate argument and reasoned comparison of alternative viewpoints has always been essential, with some of the most vehement and outrageously partisan language. The reason for this, crudely put, is that Nietzsche wants to show that interpretation, which is what genealogy also is, is essentially value laden and polemical, and that even dispassionate argument is a special case of such polemics. In particular, he wants to suggest that some particular instances of dispassionate argument are simply efforts to mask their own partial and partisan nature.

Nevertheless, such important questions are not the ones with which I am directly concerned here. My interest in Nietzsche's style is much more general and abstract. My question addresses not the style of individual works or passages but the fact that he shifts styles and genres as often as he does. It addresses not so much his style but, as he puts it himself, his "stylistic possibilities." My answer, as I shall try to show in detail, is that Nietzsche's stylistic pluralism is another facet of his perspectivism: it is one of his essential weapons in his effort to distinguish himself from the philosophical tradition as he conceives it, while at the same time he tries to criticize it and to offer alternatives to it.

As a matter of fact, Nietzsche's stylistic pluralism was noticed by Kaufmann, who discusses it briefly. But Kaufmann's account replicates his view of the aphorism in particular, since he insists on taking this genre as the essence of Nietzsche's style. Just as aphorisms are for him "experiments" aiming "to get to the objects themselves" beyond "concepts and opinions" (p. 85), so Nietzsche's various styles are themselves part of the same effort to try, in various ways, to get things right once and for all: "Involuntarily almost, Nietzsche is driven from style to style in his ceaseless striving for an adequate means of expression. Each style is characteristically his own, but soon found inadequate, and then drives him to another newer one. Yet all the experiments cohere because they are not capricious. Their unity one might call existential" (p. 93).

We must thoroughly reject the view that Nietzsche's many styles reflect his effort to find a single "adequate means of expression," since he himself writes, almost as if he had anticipated this interpretation, that "the demand for an adequate mode of expression is senseless" (WP, 625). Far from being directed toward getting to "the things themselves," the very idea of which Nietzsche radically repudiates, his many modes of writing are directly connected to his view that "facts are precisely what there is not, only interpretations" (WP, 481). We must not, however, simply assume that Nietzsche's stylistic variety is just another expression of the pluralism and indeterminacy which, according to the readings of Kofman and Derrida, characterize each single individual aphorism or fragment. Though Nietzsche's writing as a whole supports his perspectivism, it does not do so by being itself beyond interpretation, by failing to have a determinate structure, form, or meaning.

The connection between Nietzsche's stylistic pluralism and his perspectivism is more subtle and oblique. His many styles are part of his effort to present views without presenting them as more than views of his own and are therefore part of his effort to distinguish his practice from what he considers the practice of philosophers so far.

In order to make clear the relationship between Nietzsche's styles, his perspectivism, and his distrust of traditional philosophy as he conceives of it, we must ask the two questions that inevitably face a serious examination of Nietzsche's style, but that have been obscured by the almost exclusive attention the aphorism has received so far. Instead of turning directly to this genre and to the other few figures that have occupied previous writers, let us take a step back and ask, first, why it is that the aphorism has in fact loomed so large in earlier discussions, and second, why it is that Nietzsche depends on such an unusually large variety of styles and genres in his philosophical writing.

The second question, as we just saw, may suggest that the relationship between Nietzsche's various works replicates the relationship between his individual aphorisms. One may take this either as a sign that Nietzsche is striving for the methodological monism that Kaufmann attributes to him or as an indication that the radical pluralist reading of Kofman and Derrida is after all correct. Either alternative may in turn provoke the suspicion that Nietzsche's sketch of "literary decadence" does after all apply to his own writing, though not everyone would agree that what Nietzsche describes there *is* decadence or that decadence is necessarily something that must be avoided. But it also raises the possibility that only self-deception or, as Jaspers thought,[18] his inevitable involvement with self-contradiction allowed Nietzsche to write, thinking obviously of himself, that "this alone is fitting for a philosopher. We have no right to *isolated* acts of any kind: we may not make isolated errors or hit upon isolated truths. Rather do our ideas, our values, our yeas and nays, our ifs and buts, grow out of us with the necessity with which a tree bears fruit—related and each with an affinity to each, and evidence of *one* will, *one* health, *one* soil, *one* sun" (*GM*, Pref., 4). Should we simply overlook statements like this? Should we accept them as evidence that Nietzsche's thinking cannot be coherently described? Should we try to account for them by subordinating Nietzsche's changing masks to his search for his one true face? Or can we interpret them in a new way, distinct from these more or less traditional approaches?

To provide such an interpretation we must return to the first of our two questions. One obvious reason for the central place of the aphorism in previous discussions of Nietzsche's style is the fact that his aphorisms are so very good. But this fact, though it may account for the prominence of the aphorism, cannot by itself account for the almost universal blindness to his many other styles, modes, and manners. To offer an explanation of this more complicated phenomenon we must turn to yet another feature of Nietzsche's writing, a feature that remains remarkably constant from the time of *The Birth of Tragedy* to that of *Ecce Homo* and that itself constitutes a traditional rhetorical trope: the figure of exaggeration or hyperbole. This single most pervasive feature of his writing, which attracts a certain kind of reader to him, repels another, and causes still a third to alternate between comprehension and blankness, between exhilaration and despair, and so ultimately to pass him by, may also explain why the aphorism has dominated all discussions of Nietzsche's writing so far.

Nietzsche's writing is irreducibly hyperbolic. It is, for example, one thing to claim that Greek tragedy came to its end through the dramas of Euripides, that the genre was exhausted by them, that tragedy had nowhere to go after Euripides wrote.[19] It is quite another to write, and to mean, as Nietzsche does, that "Greek tragedy . . . died by suicide . . . tragically" (*BT*, 11), that Euripides actually killed it, and that he used and was used by "aesthetic Socratism as the murderous principle" (*BT*, 12). It is one thing to be suspicious of the notion of truth and to question whether a general theory of truth and knowledge is possible or even desirable. It is quite another to ask, "*What* in us really wants truth? . . . Suppose we want truth: *why not rather* untruth? and uncertainty? even ignorance?" (*BGE*, 1). We accept, often as a necessary evil, the fact of human cruelty. But how can we come to terms with the view that "to see others suffer does one good, to make others suffer even more: this is a hard saying but an ancient, mighty, human, all-too-human principle . . . Without cruelty there is no festival: thus the longest and most ancient part of human history teaches" (*GM*, II, 6)? Voltaire, for one, was certainly not a friend of Christianity. But how much in Voltaire compares to Nietzsche's statement, chosen almost at random, "I call Christianity the one great curse, the one great innermost corruption, the one great instinct of revenge, for which no means is poisonous, stealthy, subterranean, *small* enough—I call it the one immortal blemish of humanity" (*A*, 62)? Humility has never been a central character trait of the great figures in the history of philosophy, art, or science. But even among them, the tone of the Preface to *The Antichrist* or of the whole of *Ecce Homo* is remarkable for its stridency.

These few instances are not even the beginning of an elementary listing of the hyperbolic in Nietzsche. I am merely using them to call to mind how often passages like these confront his readers and how difficult it is to know quite how to react to them. I want them to bring out what may well be the most consistent and the most conspicuous feature of his writing, the fact that Nietzsche, as he very well knew, shouts: "The spell that fights on our behalf, the eye of Venus that charms and blinds even our opponents, is *the magic of the extreme*, the seduction that everything extreme exercises: we immoralists—we are the most extreme" (*WP*, 749).

Nietzsche's aphorisms, like most of the rest of his writing, are often hyperbolic. Hyperbole is in fact particularly well suited to the aphoristic style because it helps the aphorism attract attention and, in its startlingness, reveals quite unexpected connections. But the aphorism is an essentially isolated sentence or short text, and precisely because of its isolation it disarms the hyperbole as, at the very same time, it highlights it. This, for example, is just what happens in section 260 of *The Gay Science: "Multiplication table.*—One is always wrong, but with two truth begins.—One cannot prove the case, but two are irrefutable." The aphorism has bracketed the hyperbole; it prevents it from functioning as part of a continuous narrative or, more important, as a premise in an argument. The spaces that separate aphorisms from one another also act as frames that magnify the power of exaggeration within them but don't allow it to penetrate beyond their confines. It is just this simultaneous foregrounding and neutralizing of hyperbole in the aphorism that has tempted Nietzsche's readers so far to concentrate almost exclusively on that genre: doing so has enabled us to avoid having to come to terms with hyperbole in its own right. But since this figure of speech is much more common in Nietzsche than the aphorism, we can no longer refuse to face it directly. We must therefore ask why Nietzsche relies so heavily—sometimes to the point of buffoonery—on this most unscholarly of tropes.

Precisely because hyperbole is unscholarly, it may be tempting to think, as many have, that Nietzsche has nothing serious to say. One can therefore react to his writing with indifference and simply let it pass by. A second reaction to Nietzsche, based on an awareness that he is concerned with serious and important problems, is indignation. Such questions, one might think, should never be asked in Nietzsche's manner; his way of putting them can make them appear to be irresponsible efforts to undermine just what cannot, and should not, be undermined. And finally there is the complicated reaction involved in critical or uncritical discipleship, which is produced by Nietzsche's uncanny ability to captivate totally at least part of his audience.

It is remarkable how these obvious reactions to hyperbole bring to mind the one figure in the history of philosophy with whom Nietzsche never ceased to be involved in a highly complicated, deeply equivocal relationship, a figure who prompted, by very different means and with catastrophic results for his person though not for his character, exactly the same range of reactions—the figure of Socrates. It is, I now want to suggest, within the context of the confrontation between Nietzsche and Socrates, along with everything else which Nietzsche took Socrates to represent, that we shall find the answers to the questions we have asked.

In Plato's *Euthyphro*, for example, Socrates has a conversation with a man who unself-consciously declares himself to be an expert on religious matters, and who is willing and eager to discourse at length on the question of the nature of piety. Euthyphro is a religious seer who is engaged in a highly controversial and apparently impious legal action against his father, having accused him of murder. It is crucial in reading the dialogue to note that Euthyphro explicitly agrees with Socrates that unless he knows very well what piety is, he cannot be justified in pressing such an unusual suit. And it is also important to remember that, as Plato is very careful to make clear, it is not Socrates but Euthyphro himself who begins the conversation, Euthyphro who volunteers his expertise, Euthyphro who offers to instruct Socrates on the nature of piety, and Euthyphro, of course, who fails time after time to answer Socrates' seemingly elementary questions concerning the topic on which he has presented himself as expert. Despite all this, it is also Euthyphro himself who, after a number of unsuccessful attempts to say what constitutes piety, is still blithely confident that he has the necessary knowledge and shrugs Socrates off with a transparent excuse that shows how little he cares for Socrates' concerns, how totally untouched this conversation has left him. Having acted up to that point as if he had all the time in the world, he now suddenly responds to Socrates' repeated question by abruptly cutting the conversation off: "Some other time, Socrates," he says; "right now I am in a hurry to go somewhere, and I really must be going" (15e3-4).

By contrast, Plato's *Meno* shows how Socrates' questions can be perceived as a threat. The wealthy, respectable Anytus, who was eventually to be one of the plaintiffs in the trial that cost Socrates his life, also wants to stop talking with him. But he does so with a threat of his own that shows he does not at all think Socrates is to be shrugged off. On the contrary, Anytus takes Socrates very seriously indeed and is unsettled by what he takes as Socrates' attack on the virtue of the great Athenians and on the ability of the democratic city to impart virtue to the children of its citizens. For Anytus, Socrates puts into question everything that he, a staunch democrat, has always stood for without second thought. "Socrates," he says as he leaves, "I think you are too eager to speak ill of people. My advice to you, if you would take it, is to be careful. It is everywhere easier to come to a bad rather than to a good end, and this is even more true here in Athens. But I expect you already know all this yourself" (94e3–95a1).

Before we turn to discipleship, which introduces a further complication of its own, we must note that the similarity in the reactions Socrates and Nietzsche often produce in their audience is not accidental. The exasperation Socrates produced in his contemporaries was doubtless due in part to his radically new philosophical interests, his new and still unclear way of doing philosophy; and the same is true, to some extent, of Nietzsche. But this is only a small part of the reason for the parallel; the important factor lies elsewhere.

Consider, for example, Plato's *Laches*, in which Socrates is about to discuss whether it is good for young men to learn how to fence. Before the conversation on this rather trivial topic begins in earnest, Nicias, a famous general and Socrates' friend, warns the company:

> I don't think you know what it is like to get involved in a discussion with Socrates. Whatever the subject you begin with, he will continue to press the argument and he will not stop until he has made you give a general account of yourself. You will have to account not only for your present mode of life, but also for everything that you have done in the past. And even when he has made you do all this, Socrates will not let you go until he has examined each question deeply and thoroughly. (187e6–188a3)

Nietzsche's project is essentially similar to and overlaps the project of Socrates, so described. Both Nietzsche and Socrates are intensely personal thinkers, actively engaged in changing, in one way or another, the moral quality of the life of the people around them, though they pursue their goals in radically different ways. Socrates constantly employs everyday situations in order to show that they all involve deep and serious issues of the sort that today we consider philosophical. Nietzsche always raises just such abstract philosophical issues only to drop them suddenly in his readers' laps as questions that immediately affect their everyday lives. While the *Laches* transforms a discussion of fencing into a consideration of courage, virtue, and the good life, *Beyond Good and Evil* begins with questions concerning the notion of truth, the possibility of certainty, the issue of freedom and necessity, and other traditional philosophical problems, and develops all of them into questions about the moral character of the person who, like most of us today, is more or less convinced by the traditional answers to them. More accurately perhaps, Nietzsche tries to show how often and how unsuspectingly his readers have given answers to such questions, sometimes not even aware that these are questions at all and that these answers shape their everyday life. But what he centrally objects to is not the specific answers these questions have been given but the very assumption that they are to be answered, and perhaps even asked, at all.

Socrates of course always pursues his goal personally and in conversation, while Nietzsche is the most writerly of philosophers. Socrates believes that not enough questions have been asked, while Nietzsche is afraid that too many answers have been given. Socrates considers self-knowledge at least the beginning if not the very content of the good life, while Nietzsche denies that in Socrates' sense there is either a self that can be known or a knowledge that can capture it. Socrates thinks that action must be grounded in objective value, while Nietzsche urges that values are created through actions. Socrates considers explicit and articulate rational understanding the greatest and most distinguishing human achievement, while Nietzsche laments that "the task of *incorporating* knowledge and making it instinctive is only beginning to dawn on the human eye and is not yet clearly discernible" (*GS*, 211; cf. *TI*, VI, 3). Finally, irony, which in Socrates' case consists of saying "too little," functions for him just as hyperbole, which is saying "too much," functions for Nietzsche.

Despite Nietzsche's claims to have found his antipode in Ernest Renan ("It is so neat, so distinguished to have one's own antipodes!" *BGE*, 48) and Paul Rée (*GM*, Pref., 4), his real antipodes are constituted by none other than Socrates. Nietzsche disagrees with Socrates, issue for issue, on every question about the content and the method of philosophy, yet he is engaged in exactly the same effort of affecting people's lives: the two are constantly and directly competing with one another. Socrates and Nietzsche are inextricably joined by their common efforts, but each is inevitably repelled by the direction the other wants life to take as a result of his influence.

It is, then, just this personal, Socratic element in Nietzsche's project that accounts for his exaggerated, swaggering, polemical, self-conscious and self-aggrandizing, un-Socratic style. Both desperately need their audience's attention. Socrates tried to secure it in conversation, through his ironic humility, his arrogant self-effacement, which draws people either unsuspectingly or angrily into argument—but which in either case draws them in. Nietzsche attempts to attract attention through his thick style, which is often insulting and in bad taste, but which never lets his readers forget that the argument they are getting involved in is always in more than one sense personal. Both Socrates and Nietzsche often fail in their efforts and have no effect at all; but as long as they even manage to upset their audience, they have already partly won the contest: in such situations, any attention is better than no attention at all. Hence, for Nietzsche the supreme irony of Socrates' death: "Socrates *wanted* to die: not Athens, but he himself chose the hemlock; he forced Athens to sentence him" (*TI*, III, 12).

In one instance Nietzsche argues that it is extremely difficult to translate Aristophanes, Petronius, and Machiavelli into German, and in the course of his argument discusses at least ten different authors (*BGE*, 28). What he says about these authors and about the inherent limitations of the tempo of German is often wrong-headed and even silly, especially since he writes that German is "almost incapable of presto" in a passage that itself is a wonderful instance of that very tempo. How are we to react to a passage like this? Should we argue with Nietzsche about these authors, even if only to show how wrong and silly he is? But to do so it is necessary to read them; and if we have read them already, it is necessary to read, or at least to think about them again. These, however, are some of Nietzsche's favorite authors, and to have them read is exactly what he wants to accomplish in the first place; thus he establishes common ground with his audience, even if this proceeds from and results in disagreement. Perhaps we might even come to agree with him on some point; but even if we don't, we end up reading what Nietzsche has read, and we now have that reading in common with him. The one reaction Nietzsche cannot tolerate is indifference, and this is what his use of hyperbole is designed to eliminate. Like Socratic irony, it often fails to accomplish its end, and some people are particularly unsusceptible to it. But the aim is the same in both cases, and the effect the two tropes are intended to have is identical.

We can now return to discipleship, the third reaction both Socrates and Nietzsche often provoke. The greatest manifestations of the will to power, to use Nietzsche's term, are to be found in the greatest intellectual achievements, in the arts and religion, in science, morality, and philosophy. Artworks, scientific theories, religious views, moral, political, and philosophical systems embody and carry forth a particular individual's picture or interpretation of the world, the values, and the preferences through which that individual can best live and flourish. The greatest among such individuals succeed in establishing their pictures and preferences as *the* world within which, and *the* values by means of which other people come to live their lives, often unaware that these are not given facts but the products or interpretations of someone else. Great intellectual achievements, especially those that are embodied in texts or in other enduring works that require reinterpretation, are immense because, as Nietzsche sees it, their influence is constantly renewed. It is true that, so to speak, every time we look at the map of Europe we see the will to power that was manifested in Napoleon, who remained throughout one of Nietzsche's greatest heroes, and who will continue to affect history indefinitely. But for Nietzsche, someone like Socrates is even more important: in addition to inserting himself into history once, he keeps reentering it and constantly renewing and modifying his previous effects every time he is, as he has been so far, read again by a new generation.

Nietzsche may have had a naive view of the importance of writing, an exaggerated sense of the effects of the activity for which he himself was best suited. But the fact remains that of the roughly 120 proper names that appear in *Beyond Good and Evil*, well over a hundred are the names of authors, artists, scientists, and fictional characters. In order to depict the bloody vengefulness of Christianity in *On the Genealogy of Morals* Nietzsche, instead of even alluding to the Inquisition or the Crusades, prefers instead to quote St. Thomas' description of heaven and hell and Tertullian's anticipation of the Second Coming of Christ (*GM*, I, 15). His physical imagery is directly connected with what, in Blake's words, we might appropriately call "the mental fight," the only fight Nietzsche ever seriously envisages and in which he engages; in fact we might say that the more violent his imagery becomes, the more abstract is the fight in which he is involved (cf., for example *BGE*, 29–30). His writerliness is nowhere more evident than in his advice on how to come to understand the "common" people (*BGE*, 26). He believes, of course, that "choice human beings" must isolate themselves from the vulgar; but he also believes that if they are "destined for knowledge," they must come to see what such people are like and that they must "go down, and above all . . . 'inside.' " But instead of recommending any of the obvious ways of doing so, Nietzsche writes that what is necessary for coming to know what most people are like is *reading*. He mentions two kinds of authors who must be read in this connection: first, cynics, who recognize what is vulgar in themselves, detest it, but still need to make their feelings plain; second, authors like Galiani, who also know how common they are but love their vulgarity, wallow in it, and write in order to celebrate it. Both kinds of authors, Nietzsche claims, are describing the same set of features, one to praise it and one to put it down. From their different attitudes we are to derive a stereoscopic image of commonness and vulgarity and thus complete "the long and serious study of *average* people" (cf. *CW,* Pref.). Writing, the chapters that follow will try to show, always remains both the main model and the main object of Nietzsche's thinking.

In discussing Nietzsche's attitude toward Socrates' importance, I claimed that Socrates is read by every new generation of Western readers. But this is inaccurate, since Socrates never wrote anything himself and consequently cannot be read. It is rather Plato, or Plato's Socrates, who is continuously read and reread. For Nietzsche, Socrates was enabled to exercise his will to power on the course of our thought simply (if this is at all the appropriate word) by virtue of creating a single disciple who in turn created the Socrates with whom we have all become more or less familiar (cf. *BGE*, 190). This is one more irony that Nietzsche, who devoted his life to writing, cannot possibly have missed. Nor could we have missed the final irony involved in the fact that so many of Plato's dialogues show Socrates failing to convince the people with whom he is talking of the correctness of his approach and failing to have any effect on their lives. Time after time Socrates fails to reach the knowledge he seeks and to persuade his listeners that this knowledge, or at least the knowledge that this knowledge is lacking, is essential for the good life. Yet it is just in being shown to fail to change the mind and life of those who talk to him that Socrates has succeeded in changing the mind and life of all those who have read the Platonic dialogues, and of many others besides.

This double irony, in addition to the combination of attraction and repulsion we have already discussed, may perhaps account for what I take to be the irreducibly ambivalent attitude of Nietzsche toward Socrates. Without being able to give this very complicated subject the necessary attention, I want to resist the two most common current views of their relationship. Walter Kaufmann argues that "Nietzsche, for whom Socrates was allegedly a 'villain,' modelled his conception of his own task largely after Socrates' apology" (p. 391). Werner Dannhauser, by contrast, has replied that for Nietzsche "the quarrel with Socrates is part of a vast historical drama which he recounts and which features Socrates as the first villain and Nietzsche himself as the final hero."[20] Both views are too unequivocal. They take sides too easily on an issue about which it is not clear that there are sides to be taken at all.

Socrates' task, as I have described it, is in fact the same as Nietzsche's; this, as Kaufmann claims, ties them to one another. But their method of pursuing it, and the direction in which they pursue it, as well as a further, more important feature of their approach which I shall presently discuss, are fundamentally opposed; this makes Socrates, if such a straightforward term is at all appropriate here, a "villain" in Nietzsche's eyes. Socrates, however, is a villain not for the independent reasons Kaufmann discusses but precisely because his task and Nietzsche's are one and the same. Nietzsche, as I have said, is always in direct competition with Socrates, and their relationship, like the relationship between many great opponents, is inescapably ambiguous. It is best captured in the lines from Wilde with which this chapter begins. What is ambivalent in Nietzsche's attitude toward Socrates is not his rage or his enmity: these are always there. What is necessarily ambivalent is his reaction to the gnawing question whether the protruding eyes that stare back at him when he squints at Socrates' portrait may not be his own, whether in looking at Socrates he may not after all be looking into a mirror.

Zarathustra at one point tells his disciples: "You may have only enemies whom you can hate, not enemies you despise. You must be proud of your enemy: then the successes of your enemy are your successes too" (*Z*, I, 9; cf. *GM*, III, 15). In *Beyond Good and Evil* (p. 210) Nietzsche discusses Socrates in a manner that shows that at least sometimes he thinks of him as an enemy in just that way. Yet it is very difficult to find the pride that Zarathustra commands us to take in our enemy in Nietzsche's writing that Socrates was "plebs," "ugly," hardly a Greek, a "criminal" and "decadent," a wanton of the instincts, a "buffoon who got himself taken seriously," that he was vengeful and repellent (though also a great "erotic"), a "misunderstanding," and a true disease (*TI*, III). What is it then about Socrates and the tradition which he represents that forces Nietzsche to despise him as well as to hate him, to disdain him as well as to admire him? Why is Nietzsche so *suspicious* of Socrates? The answer to this question returns us to our discussion of Nietzsche's style, which we have left aside, and provides an answer to the second of our two questions about Nietzsche's writing.

We have seen that the answer to the question concerning the importance of the aphorism in previous discussions of Nietzsche's style is that the aphorism makes it much easier to come to terms with hyperbole, on which Nietzsche relies studiously and consistently. Nietzsche's hyperboles, as I have said, call attention to his writing and engage his readers in a personal argument. This, it should be clear, is not to say that hyperbole is merely a dispensable means of accomplishing an independently accessible goal: Nietzsche's writing, and his thinking, is *essentially* hyperbolic. We might vaguely define hyperbole as a figure by means of which one says more than is strictly speaking appropriate. But the standard by which how much is said is to be judged is not given by a perfectly literal, perfectly accurate mode of expression that represents things just as they are. This standard is, rather, given by what is usually expected in writings concerning the sorts of philosophical problems with which Nietzsche is commonly concerned. It is true that Nietzsche's texts, compared to many other philosophical works, often say too much; but this comparison leaves open the possibility that the excess may after all be even more accurate than the literal standard, which may itself come to be seen as a trope in its own right, as a litotes or understatement. To this we might add that Nietzsche's self-aggrandizing, aristocratic, esoteric manner also provides one further contrast with Socrates' constant self-effacement, which, even when it is perfectly ironic, succeeds in making his personality appear to take second place to the general issues involved in his discussions. And this brings us back to the question of why Nietzsche makes use of so many genres and styles in his various writings.

I have already mentioned Nietzsche's view that (as we shall see in more detail in later chapters) the will to power is manifested in the ability to make one's own view of the world and one's own values the very world and values in which and by which others live. This is exactly what he thinks Plato and Socrates, whom we can here consider a single character, have accomplished. But if this is so, then Nietzsche, for whom "the objective measure of value" is "solely the quantum of enhanced and organized power" (*WP*, 674), should not find Socrates objectionable in the way and to the extent that he does. He may well disagree quite strongly with the content of Socrates' views and with the specific values he has imposed upon the world. But this does not account either for his vitriolic attitude or for his constant effort not only to disagree with Socrates but also, somehow, to *expose* him.

Nietzsche is so suspicious of Plato and Socrates because he believes that their approach is essentially dogmatic. He attributes to them the view that their view is not simply a view but an accurate description of the real world which forces its own acceptance and makes an unconditional claim on everyone's assent. This, we shall see, is one of Nietzsche's most central criticisms of philosophers, of whom he takes Plato and Socrates to be emblematic. Apart from objecting to their specific ideas, he objects even more to the fact that philosophers "are not honest enough in their work," that they write as if they had reached their ideas in an objective and disinterested manner, motivated only by the search for truth. But according to him these same philosophers "are all advocates who resent that name, and for the most part even wily spokesmen for their prejudices which they baptize 'truths'—and *very* far from having the courage of the conscience that admits this, precisely this, to itself; very far from having the good taste or the courage which also lets this be known, whether to warn an enemy or friend, or, from exuberance, to mock itself" (*BGE*, 5).

It is in the interest of dogmatic approaches to hide their specific origins; in this way they are enabled to make universal claims. This is one of the reasons, as we shall see, why Nietzsche engages in the practice he calls "genealogy," for genealogy reveals the very particular, very interested origins from which actually emerge the views that we have forgotten are views and take instead as facts. Genealogy reveals both these origins and the mechanisms by which the views in question try to conceal them. This is notoriously true of morality: "A morality, a mode of living tried and *proved* by long experience and testing, at length enters consciousness as a law, as *dominating.*—And therewith the entire group of related values and states enters into it: it becomes venerable, unassailable, holy, true; it is part of its development that its origin should be forgotten—That is a sign that it has become master" (*WP*, 514; cf. *BGE*, 202). Having an origin is being part of history, and this implies that it is at least possible also to have an end. It is just this possibility that, according to Nietzsche, dogmatism must render invisible, since it aims to be accepted necessarily and unconditionally—not as the product of a particular person or idiosyncracy but as the result of a discovery about the unalterable features of the world.

Nietzsche's opposition to dogmatism does not consist in the paradoxical idea that it is wrong to think that one's beliefs are true, but only in the view that one's beliefs are not, and need not be, true for everyone. His own "new philosophers" have just that attitude regarding their beliefs:

> Are these coming philosophers new friends of truth? That is probable enough, for all philosophers so far have loved their truths. But they will certainly not be dogmatists. It must offend their pride, also their taste, if their truth is supposed to be a truth for everyone— which has so far been the secret wish and hidden meaning of all dogmatic aspirations. "My judgment is *my* judgment": no one else is easily entitled to it—that is what such philosophers of the future may perhaps say of themselves. (*BGE*, 43)

Like every other writer Nietzsche too wants his audience to accept his views. Though he launches a sustained and complicated attack on the notions of truth and knowledge, it would be absurd to claim that he writes so as not to be believed. The point of his attack, as we shall see in later chapters, is different and is directed at the conditions under which views are accepted as true. He wants to be believed, but not unconditionally; even more, he does not want to *appear* to want to be believed unconditionally. That is, he wants to avoid engaging, and to be perceived as engaging, in what he often calls "metaphysics." Both dogmatism and metaphysics are, like everything else according to his view, manifestations of the will to power. But what distinguishes them from other similar manifestations and allows him to attack them is that they are, as he thinks, self-deceptive. They are attempts to project one's own views on the world, and they are just as much attempts to hide precisely this projection from themselves as well as from their audience. They lack "the courage of the conscience" that either in warning or in mockery admits that the view being projected is nothing more than a reading onto the world of the conditions under which its own author can thrive, and which need not be the right conditions for anyone else: "We seek a picture of the world in that philosophy in which we feel freest; i.e., in which our most powerful drive feels free to function. This will also be the case with me!" (*WP*, 418). Accepting a view is therefore not simply a question of assenting to a set of propositions, as the matter is sometimes put. It also involves accepting the values that are the preconditions of that view and the mode of life that is implied and made possible by those values. And since Nietzsche believes that there is no mode of life that is proper, desirable, or indeed possible for everyone, he also holds, very consistently, that there is no set of views that commands universal assent by virtue of depending merely on the features of the world in itself or of human beings as such.

At this point, however, Nietzsche is faced with an urgent problem. He wants, on the one hand, to distinguish himself from Socrates and from the philosophical tradition. One way in which he might have achieved this goal would have been to refrain from writing anything that might in any conceivable manner be construed as philosophical—the only certain method for accomplishing this purpose being to refrain from writing altogether. But this is not, and cannot be, Nietzsche's way. Refraining from writing, assuming that this was something he had any choice about, would not simply have distinguished him from the tradition; it would have prevented him from being related to it in any way. But Nietzsche also wants, on the other hand, to criticize that tradition and to offer views of his own which, in their undogmatic manner, will compete with other views. Yet this procedure always involves the risk of falling back into the philosophical tradition after all. We can think of philosophy as a mirror in which those who belong to it are reflected, while those who are not reflected are totally irrelevant to it. Wilde's image of the rage of Caliban applies to Nietzsche, then, in one more way. Can Nietzsche maintain the ambiguous relationship to philosophy he clearly wants to have? Or are his only choices either to be part of it or else to pass it by totally?

What are those authors to do who want to produce views about the world but who also want to warn their readers that what they are reading is no more than one author's approach? And what, even more urgent, is an author to do who wants to make the point that all writing is of this nature? An obvious solution to the problem, of course, is simply to admit that the view one is presenting is just that—that it is simply one's own interpretation. Nietzsche does precisely this when, having attacked the mechanistic interpretation of physics, he presents his own hypothesis of the will to power and concludes, "Supposing that this is also only interpretation—and you will be eager enough to make this objection?—Well, so much the better" (*BGE*, 22).

This strategy, however, faces two serious difficulties. The first, which I shall discuss in the next chapter, is that it may prove to be self-refuting. If the view that everything is an interpretation is itself an interpretation, and therefore possibly false, it may follow that all is not after all interpretation. The second difficulty is that this strategy may be self-defeating in a less formal sense. Constantly to repeat the phrase "This is only my interpretation" as one's sole concession to this anti-dogmatic orientation would soon rob it of all credibility. The qualification would simply make no difference to what was being asserted: it would become an empty gesture. Had Nietzsche made this admission more frequently than he did, he would have defeated his purpose as surely as Socrates, who made his admission only once (*Apol.* 20c–23c), would have defeated his own goal had he pointed out as a matter of course that his interlocutors lacked just that knowledge of which they were, wrongly, so confident and proud.

Nietzsche's central problem as an author, therefore, is that he wants his readers to accept his views, his judgments and his values as much as he wants them to know that these are essentially *his* views, *his* judgments, and *his* values. At least some of his preoccupation with the problem of his proper audience (cf. *GM*, Pref., 8; *A*, Pref.) springs from his desire to have as readers only those who will always be aware of the nature of his views, and of all views in general. He is constantly resisting the dogmatic self-effacement that is directed at convincing an audience that the views with which they are presented are not their authors' creations but simply reflections of the way things are. Though Nietzsche wants to avoid the opposite extreme, which takes views as simply the creations of their authors, he also wants his readers to know that accepting a particular view is not so much a result of obligation as a product of choice. And though this choice is not dictated by considerations that are absolutely binding, it is still difficult, complex, and in no obvious sense arbitrary.

The will to power which Nietzsche sometimes calls "affirmative" is a will to power that affirms itself as such, that sees itself as a view of the world by which its author and perhaps some other people can live their lives (cf. Z, II, 13). But how is such an acknowledgment to be made? Making it explicitly, as we have seen, soon prevents it from being believable; not making it at all immediately collapses the approach into dogmatism and masks its will to power. Is it then impossible to present a view as true, by which one can live, without also presenting it as a view that is true necessarily, by which all must live? Nietzsche, I think, is afraid that he may not have finally resolved this difficult problem. This is why he suspects that his task may not after all be so very different from the task of Socrates. And since these are attitudes he has toward himself, they account not only for his irreparably divided feelings toward Socrates but also for his own equivocal relation to philosophy, and for the irreducible ambiguity of his own position within it.

The problem of absolutism has another side. Is it possible to present a view as true and admit that other views are true as well without undermining one's own position? Or must one who makes this admission fall into a vicious relativism that concedes that every view is as true as every other? Nietzsche's discussion of these issues in regard to morality shows that he does not take these two as the only alternatives. Many historians of morality, "mostly Englishmen," he writes, "affirm some consensus of the nations, at least of tame nations, concerning certain principles of morals, and then they infer from this that these principles must be unconditionally binding also for you and me; or, conversely, they see the truth that among different nations moral valuations are *necessarily* different and then infer from this that no morality is at all binding. Both procedures are equally childish" (GS, 345).

With this we can finally return to the question of style, for we now have what we need in order to account both for what I earlier called the thickness, the self-consciousness, of Nietzsche's writing and for his constant shifting of genres. The dilemma I have been discussing applies to the effort to state explicitly that one has adopted a perspectivist position. Nietzsche's highly original solution is to try to avoid this dilemma by turning his attention to the manner in which he presents the views he considers his own interpretations and which he wants his readers to recognize as such. Nietzsche uses his changing genres and styles in order to make his presence as an author literally unforgettable and in order to prevent his readers from overlooking the fact that his views necessarily originate with him. He depends on many styles in order to suggest that there is no single, neutral language in which his views, or any others, can ever be presented. His constant stylistic presence shows that theories are as various and idiosyncratic as the writing in which they are embodied. If the very same style is used consistently over time, it becomes easy to think that some views at least are independent of style, since it may appear that they are presented in no style at all. Nietzsche's shifting genres serve to prevent this.[21] They also suggest that the very distinction between the content of a view and the manner in which that view is presented is to be seriously questioned. As Arthur Danto has written in *The Transfiguration of the Commonplace*, it is through the presence of style that "in addition to representing whatever it does in fact represent, the instrument of representation imparts and impresses something of its own character in the act of representing it, so that in addition to knowing what it is of, the practiced eye will know how it was done." I don't think that we need to be disturbed by Danto's distinction between what is represented and how the representation is accomplished because, as he goes on to write, "the structure of a style is like the structure of a personality."[22] The distinction between "what is said" and "how it is said" is not a useful one in this context. When I claim that we must pay attention to Nietzsche's style, I am claiming only that his changing styles convey significant information to his readers. The point is not that we must pay attention to the (ill-characterized) "literary" aspects of his work but that in addition to presenting his views, Nietzsche's varying, self-conscious writing enables the practiced reader always to be aware of who it is whose views are being presented, what personality these views express and constitute.

Nietzsche's many styles are therefore to be explained through his relation to Socrates and to philosophy: they are an essential part of his constant war against them. They are the means and products of his effort always to insinuate himself between his readers and the world. His manner of writing is not an invitation to interpret him in an unending number of ways but an ever-present reminder that if we are convinced by it, we are convinced by *his* writing, which is a product of his own values, idiosyncrasies, and goals, a product of himself. If therefore we agree with his views, we must also be willing and able to live with his values, his idiosyncrasies, and his goals. This is why, though agreeing with a view may be a matter of choice, that choice is neither easy nor arbitrary; it involves not only assenting to propositions but also fashioning a mode of life. If we cannot make that choice, then we must accept the views of someone else, again with the same understanding, or else we must make up our own views and our own life. These tasks are all of exactly the same order of difficulty, and Nietzsche wants to make that difficulty inescapably obvious. He accomplishes this by making, through his many styles, his own presence as an author impossible to overlook.

But Nietzsche's views, whatever they are, are not simply there, available for inspection. In order to know what they are we must first, as I have already begun to do here, interpret his texts. And interpretation itself, according to Nietzsche, is a highly personal and creative affair: "Ultimately, the individual derives the values of its acts from itself; because it has to interpret in a quite individual way even the words it has inherited. Its interpretation of a formula at least is personal, even if it does not create a formula; as an interpreter, the individual is still creative" (*WP,* 767).

The creativity of interpretation has implications in two directions. First, it is reflected inward, into the very content of Nietzsche's writing. Nietzsche's style, as we have seen, makes a point of his perspectivism, of his view that his texts present only one among many possible views. But this view urges on his readers a sort of person and a mode of life in which that very view is itself manifested: " 'This is *my* way; where is yours?'—thus I answered those who asked me 'the way.' For *the* way—that does not exist," says Zarathustra (Z, III, 11). One of Nietzsche's most central concerns, as we shall see in detail, is to outline a character type, a structure that can be embodied in a large number of particular characters. The main feature of this character type is that each of the specific characters in which it is manifested is aware of the fact that it too is only one among many possible characters. Apart from being constantly asserted, and once again defeating its own purpose, this fact can be expressed only through a distinctive style. The actions and beliefs, the passions and desires, the preferences and values of each character must be organized in the idiosyncratic, recognizable manner that reminds oneself as well as others that these are not discrete, independent objects that can be chosen, discarded, or exchanged at will.

A central theme of this book is Nietzsche's aestheticism, his essential reliance on artistic models for understanding the world and life and for evaluating people and actions. This aestheticism results from his effort to bring style into the center of his own thought and to repeat once more what he took to be the great achievement of the Greeks and the Romans: to make of "the grand style no longer mere art but . . . reality, truth, *life*" (*A*, 59). We shall also see that Nietzsche presents the character type I have mentioned not so much by describing it as by exemplifying it. He develops and commends a specific character, which emerges from the interaction of what he writes with how he writes it and which therefore essentially undermines the distinction between the form and the content of his work.

As I have already said, the distinction between style and content on which this interpretation depends does not involve the problematic distinction between the "what" and the "how." It is only related, though it is not identical, to the distinction between description and exemplification, which I just mentioned, and which will become increasingly important as the argument of the book progresses. Exclusive attention to the "mere" content of Nietzsche's writing has produced the caricatures of the *Übermensch*, the master morality, and the eternal recurrence, of which the secondary literature about him is full. Exclusive attention to its "pure" form has naturally given rise to the idea that Nietzsche has nothing of substance to say (except, perhaps, that to look for substance is itself the greatest error). But the character who is the product of his work, and of both its elements together, is both commendable and undogmatic, both someone we can admire and someone we need not want to be. Nietzsche's aestheticism, therefore, his use of and emphasis on style, is itself part of his effort to undermine the distinction between form and content in life as well as in writing: "One is an artist at the cost of regarding that which all non-artists call 'form' as content, as 'the matter itself.' To be sure, then one belongs in a topsy-turvy world: for henceforth content becomes something merely formal—our life included" (*WP*, 818).

But the creativity of interpretation is also projected outward, toward the very different treatments that Nietzsche's writing has received and among which the present reading is only one. Brigid

Brophy has described a characteristic look that animates the face of some of Mozart's admirers after the performance of one of his operas as "a look which asserts '*my* Mozart.' "[23] This book cannot claim such total possession; if it did, it probably could not have been written, and it certainly could not have begun with this chapter. Nor again is it written in the belief that the interpretation it offers is only one among many equally true ones. But in view of what this introductory discussion has claimed in regard to style and to discipleship, it may be better to let the rest of the book speak for itself—though it can do so only in a manner of speaking, and only to those who may find it engaging enough to want to try to give it an interpretation of their own.

Nietzsche's stylistic pluralism, then, is his solution to the problem involved in presenting positive views that do not, simply by virtue of being positive, fall back into dogmatism. It is his means of reminding his readers that what they are reading is always Nietzsche's own interpretation of life and the world. His many styles make it impossible to get used to his presence and, as we do with many of the things we take for granted, to forget it. They therefore show that his positions are expressions of one particular point of view besides which there may be many others. They show his perspectivism without saying anything about it, and to that extent they prevent his view that there are only interpretations from undermining itself.

If this is so, then perhaps it was neither self-deceptive nor self-contradictory of Nietzsche to have written that everything a philosopher does must be evidence of "*one* will, *one* health, *one* soil, *one* sun." His many styles are all part of his single project to present an interpretation that demands to be believed even as it says that it is only an interpretation. This interpretation may not be one we like, but as the passage just quoted goes on to ask, "Whether *you* like them, these fruits of ours?—but what is that to the trees! What is that to *us*, to us philosophers!" (*GM*, Pref., 2). What matters is not whether or not we like an interpretation but whether the interpretation masquerades as something that it is not. Nietzsche's interpretations announce themselves as such. They transmit that information through the very forms, the very styles, in which they are presented. Nietzsche's styles are therefore essential to our own interpretations of his interpretations, and they are, once again, in a strict sense indistinguishable from the content of his views. What for Nietzsche was a necessary but consistently overlooked feature in all philosophy became in his own case, through a lifetime of effort, a self-conscious achievement: he showed that writing is perhaps the most important part of thinking. And since he also believed that thinking "*is* an action" (*WP*, 458), we might with some appropriateness attribute to him the hyperbolic view, which this book aims to investigate, that writing is also the most important part of living.

2 | Untruth as a Condition of Life

> Belief in absolute values, illusory as it is, seems to me a condition of life. But my friend's gifts measured themselves against values the relative character of which seemed to lie open to him, without any visible possibility of any other relation which could have detracted from them as values.
>
> Thomas Mann, *Doctor Faustus*

Two startling views form the basis of Nietzsche's perspectivism: the first emerges through his vitriolic questioning of the value of truth and knowledge, and the second is expressed in his notorious statement that "facts are precisely what there is not, only interpretations" (*WP*, 481). Both come into prominence in Nietzsche's later writings, though he had expressed doubts about the optimism of science and the adequacy of language as early as *The Birth of Tragedy* (14–15) and *On Truth and Lies in a Nonmoral Sense*. At that time, mainly under the influence of Schopenhauer and of his reading of Kant, Nietzsche seems to have believed that there are some ultimate facts, some noninterpretive truths, concerning the real nature of the world. But he denied that these facts could ever be correctly stated through reason, language, and science. Yet he also believed (and here the influence of Schopenhauer became dominant) that tragedy, primarily through the musically inspired, "Dionysian" chorus, can intimate the final truth that the ultimate nature of the world is to have no orderly structure: in itself the world is chaos, with no laws, no reason, and no purpose. Tragedy gives a nondiscursive glimpse of the contrast between "the real truth of nature and the lie of culture that poses as if it were the only reality," a contrast that "is similar to that between the eternal core of things, the thing-in-itself, and the whole world of appearances" (*BT*, 8). It shows that the orderly, apparently purposeful world within which we live is a creation we have placed between ourselves and the real world, which pursues its course without any regard for our views, our values, and our desires. But what makes tragedy even more remarkable in Nietzsche's eyes is that in the very process of revealing this painful truth, it offers a consolation for the negative and desperate reaction this is bound to generate. It shows that ultimately we are not different from the rest of nature, that we are part and parcel of it, and belong totally to it. It leaves its audience, which at least for a moment ceases to regard itself as separate from the rest of the world, with the "metaphysical comfort . . . that life is at the bottom of things, despite all the changes of appearance, indestructibly powerful and pleasurable" (*BT*, 7), and that its blind, purposeless, constant ebb and flow is to be admired and celebrated.

In the later writings Nietzsche comes to deny the very contrast between things-in-themselves and appearance which was presupposed by his discussion of tragedy. "The antithesis between the apparent and the true world is reduced to the antithesis between 'world' and 'nothing'—," he now writes in a representative passage (*WP*, 567; cf. *TI*, IV). Nietzsche bases his attack on this distinction on the two views with which this chapter began, and which I must now discuss.

The idea that the value of truth and knowledge must be put into question provides a particularly stark opening to *Beyond Good and Evil*. Nietzsche begins this work by writing that "the will to truth"— the drive, need, tendency, and desire to know things for what they are and not to be deceived about them—has prompted us to ask innumerable questions, to which no end is yet in sight. Among them, there have arisen questions about this will to truth itself: "*Who* is it that really puts questions to us here? *What* in us really wants 'truth'? Indeed we came to a long halt at the question about the cause of this will—until we came to a complete stop before a still more basic question. We asked about the *value* of this will. Suppose we want truth: *why not rather* untruth? and uncertainty? even ignorance?" (*BGE*, 1). Yet to ask even these questions is inevitably an effort to get matters right concerning them, and they are therefore themselves motivated by the very will to truth they call into question. The search for truth, as Nietzsche is aware, cannot therefore just be given up, even by those who question its value and its ultimate legitimacy (cf. *GS*, 344; *GM*, III, 25). The question of the value of truth necessarily originates in the will to truth, which, in the paradoxical manner in which Nietzsche so delights, assures, in the very process of casting suspicion upon itself, its own perpetuation.[1]

Even so, the questions the will to truth poses about itself require an answer, and an early section of the second part of *Beyond Good and Evil* hints at Nietzsche's own reply: "From the beginning we have contrived to retain our ignorance in order to enjoy an almost inconceivable freedom, lack of scruple and caution, heartiness and gaiety of life—in order to enjoy life! And only on this solid, granite foundation of ignorance could knowledge rise so far—the will to knowledge on the foundation of a far more powerful will: the will to ignorance, to the uncertain, to the untrue! Not as its opposite, but—as its refinement!" (*BGE*, 24). Nietzsche, who also writes that "the will to logical truth can be carried through only after a fundamental *falsification* of all events is assumed," and that "a drive rules here that is capable of employing both means, firstly falsification, then the implementation of its own point of view" (*WP*, 512), knows that this is, at the very least, a deeply peculiar view. And early on in *Beyond Good and Evil* he has an imaginary interlocutor object, "How *could* anything originate out of its opposite? for example, truth out of error? or the will to truth out of the will to deception?" (*BGE*, 2). But the central purpose of this book, as its very title suggests, is to reject the "fundamental faith of the metaphysicians . . . the faith in the opposition of values." The origin and the value of "the true, the truthful, the selfless," Nietzsche suggests, may lie precisely in "deception, selfishness and lust . . . It might even be possible that what constitutes the value of these good and revered things is precisely that they are insidiously related, tied to, and involved with these wicked, seemingly opposite things—maybe even one with them in essence" (*BGE*, 2).

Nietzsche wants to claim that truth and error, knowledge and ignorance, good and evil are not to be opposed to one another; on the contrary, he imagines them as points along a single continuum. This sweeping monism, the view that not only opposites but all things in general are essentially interrelated and derive their character from their interrelations, is already foreshadowed in book 3 of *The Gay Science*, where Nietzsche had written that in regard to cause and effect we have today "uncovered a manifold one-after-another where naive people and inquirers of older cultures saw only two separate things" (*GS*, 112). The next chapter examines in detail this general view.

But what is Nietzsche's specific view in regard to truth and falsehood? What is the point of his claim that "only degrees and subtleties of gradation" separate truth from falsehood? Why does Nietzsche want to "laugh at the way in which science precisely at its best seeks most to keep us in this *simplified*, thoroughly artificial world, suitably constructed and suitably falsified world—at the way in which, willy-nilly, it loves error, because, being alive, it loves life?" (*BGE*, 24). What exactly is the error that science, being alive, loves?

There is a simple answer to these questions. We could say that Nietzsche believes that the world is not what our most sweeping, most fundamental, or best supported views and theories hold it to be and that he takes it to be something else instead. We would then attribute to him the view that, in itself, the world is characterized by features that all our sciences and disciplines, even at their ideal best, necessarily cannot capture, and that the world, therefore, is falsified by every one of our descriptions. But his perspectivism, which I shall discuss in detail, seems to be precisely an effort to move away from the idea that the world possesses any features that are in principle prior to and independent of interpretation. In itself, the world has no features, and these can therefore be neither correctly nor wrongly represented. The idea that we are necessarily incapable of representing the world accurately presupposes the view that the world's appearance is radically different from its reality. Nietzsche denies this presupposition itself: "We do not 'know' nearly enough to be entitled to any such distinction. We simply lack any organ for knowledge, for 'truth' " (*GS*, 354). Or, as he puts it in his notes: "Science has today resigned itself to the apparent world; a real world—whatever it may be like—we certainly have no organ for knowing it. At this point we may ask: by means of what organ of knowledge can we posit even this antithesis?" (*WP*, 583). The apparent world, Nietzsche believes, is not a world that appears to be and is distinct from reality but simply the world *as* it appears to any being that needs to survive in it and that therefore must arrange it selectively for its own purposes. Reality is not something behind appearance but simply the totality of these various arrangements. The very notion, therefore, of a "merely" apparent world is a fiction: "No shadow of a right remains to speak here of appearance" (*WP*, 567).

A gentler view would provide a more sophisticated interpretation of Nietzsche's claim that science falsifies the world and that the will to knowledge is a refinement of the will to ignorance. At one point, for example, Nietzsche writes that synthetic a priori judgments "must be *believed* to be true, for the sake of the preservation of creatures like ourselves; though they might of course be *false* judgments for all that! Or to speak more clearly and coarsely: synthetic judgments *a priori* should not 'be possible' at all; we have no right to them, in our mouth they are nothing but false judgments. Only, of course, the belief in them is necessary" (*BGE*, 11). Such a statement, which is echoed elsewhere in Nietzsche's writings (for example *GS*, 110, 265; *WP*, 493), could be taken to show that Nietzsche claims only that we have no grounds for *knowing* whether our most basic beliefs correspond to the way the world is, however necessary it is for us to continue to rely upon them for our survival. After all, a careful reader might remark, Nietzsche writes only that synthetic a priori judgments "might" be false (*sie natürlich noch falsche Urtheile sein konnten*) and that they are false "in our mouth" (*in unserm Munde*). He may therefore be free to think that these judgments may after all be true and that they may reflect the structure of the world: we simply will never know.

I would insist, however, that though this interpretation may well be possible, it is not correct. For one thing, it conflicts with a number of passages in which Nietzsche asserts categorically that such judgments are false (*BGE*, 21; *WP*, 551).[2] But more important, this construction is too weak to capture Nietzsche's view that the will to knowledge is only a refinement and not the opposite of the will to ignorance. It cannot even explain why Nietzsche thinks that there is such a thing as a "will to ignorance" in the first place. If it is even possible that synthetic a priori judgments are true, then the term "will to ignorance" would actually be inept as well as inappropriate, for in that case it would have to apply to our tendency to go beyond the available evidence in the hope that some day we might hit upon the truth—a hope that might well be realized. But there can be no will to ignorance unless the judgments it disposes us to believe are false and we are, moreover, in some sense aware of their falsehood. We need a different approach to our problem, and a different answer to our question altogether.

By itself, of course, the claim that this interpretation fails to make Nietzsche's view sensible is not a reason for rejecting it, since Nietzsche's view may not in fact be sensible. But it may become part of such a reason if we present an alternative interpretation that actually motivates, and ideally gives some plausibility to, Nietzsche's attitude. In order to offer this interpretation we shall have to take a longer and more elaborate route; as we shall see repeatedly in this book, Nietzsche's writing often makes such oblique approaches to his views necessary—which is simply another way of saying that his views are not haphazard but systematically connected with one another. We shall have to read a number of apparently unrelated passages and interpret them carefully (that is to say, creatively) in order to show that they are relevant to our concerns.

In one such passage Nietzsche argues that every morality necessarily imposes extremely strict constraints upon those who practice it. The assumption that human nature is best expressed in perfect freedom, he very correctly insists, is unjustified. There is nothing unnatural in being subjected to rules; on the contrary, he writes, "all that there is or has been on earth of freedom, subtlety, boldness, dance and masterly sureness, whether in thought itself or in government, or in rhetoric and persuasion, in the arts just as in ethics, has developed only owing to 'the tyranny of such capricious laws'; and in all seriousness, the probability is by no means small that precisely this is 'nature' and 'natural' " (*BGE*, 188). Nietzsche goes on to appeal to his favorite model—that of the artist who finds the greatest freedom and the most natural state to be the result of strict and subtle obedience to a "thousandfold" laws that are internalized and finally become instinctive. And he generalizes this to the view that "what is essential . . . seems to be . . . that there should be *obedience* over a long period of time and in a *single* direction: given that, something always develops, and has developed, for whose sake it is worthwhile to live on earth, for example, virtue, art, music, dance, reason, spirituality" (*BGE*, 188).[3]

Nietzsche's view, captured perfectly in Yeats's verse "Where but in custom and in ceremony are innocence and beauty born?" depends on another idea, to which we shall have to turn in detail later on. This is the idea that an organized and organizing system of behavior can exist before a new interpretation, by means of which people's lives are guided in a new and different direction, is put upon it. Christianity, for example, took a form of life that was already well established and, through a long and sustained effort, gave it a completely new significance (*GS*, 353). And since changes in meaning eventually bring along changes in form as well (*GM*, II, 12–13), Christianity developed its own system of rules, its own distinctive "tyranny." This system may now itself be ready to be appropriated for a new purpose; it may itself now constitute the custom out of which a new innocence is to be born (cf. *GM*, III, 27). Nietzsche never attacks Christianity because it has "tyrannized" its followers or because it has imposed an overarching direction upon people's lives. He himself is not (as is sometimes thought) an enemy of single, distinct, clear ends and purposes: "The formula of my happiness: a Yes, a No, a straight line, a *goal*" (*TI*, I, 44; cf. *A*, 1). What he cannot accept is the particular direction Christianity has chosen. And even more, he cannot tolerate the fact that Christianity has always been dogmatic, and has always tried to conceal the fact that its direction is only one direction among many others. He is quite aware, however, that to pursue any of these other directions would have entailed no less a subjection to similar "capricious laws." In itself, therefore, this is not an objection to Christianity. On the contrary,

> this tyranny, this caprice, this rigorous and grandiose stupidity has educated the spirit. Slavery is, as it seems, both in the crude and in the more subtle sense, the indispensable means of spiritual discipline and cultivation, too. Consider any morality with this in mind: what there is in it of "nature" teaches hatred of the *laisser aller*, of any all-too-great freedom, and implants the need for limited horizons and the nearest tasks—teaching the *narrowing of our perspective*, and thus in a certain sense stupidity, as a condition of life and growth. (*BGE*, 188)[4]

We must now return to the discussion of synthetic a priori judgments in light of these texts. In particular I want to exploit them in reading the final sentence of section 11 of *Beyond Good and Evil*, which I omitted in my earlier quotation: "In our mouth they are nothing but false judgments. Only, of course, the belief in them is necessary as a foreground belief and visual evidence belonging to the perspective optics of life." Consider now the following as a first approximation of Nietzsche's view that the will to knowledge is essentially related to the will to ignorance and that falsification is necessary for life. To engage in any activity, and in particular in any inquiry, we must inevitably be selective. We must bring some things into the foreground and distance others into the background. We must assign a greater relative importance to some things than we do to others, and still others we must completely ignore. We do not, and cannot, begin (or end) with "all the data." This is an incoherent desire and an impossible goal. "To grasp everything" would be to do away with all perspective relations, it would mean to grasp nothing, to misapprehend the nature of knowledge. If we are ever to begin a practice or an inquiry we must, and must want to, leave unasked indefinitely many questions about the world.

The whole family of visual metaphors to which perspective belongs fits well in this familiar context.[5] Since every inquiry presupposes a particular point of view, it therefore excludes an indefinitely large number of others. We must be clear that this does not imply that we can never reach correct results or that we can never be "objective," since it is impossible to be correct about anything if one tries to be correct about everything. The fact that other points of view are possible does not by itself make them equally legitimate: whether an alternative is worth taking, as we shall see, must be shown independently in each particular case. Perspectivism, as we are in the process of construing it, is not equivalent to relativism. But perspectivism does imply that no particular point of view is privileged in the sense that it affords those who occupy it a better picture of the world as it really is than all others. Some perspectives are, and can be shown to be, better than others. But a perspective that is best of all is not a perspective at all. Perspectivism also implies that our many points of view cannot be smoothly combined into a unified synoptic picture of their common object. In effect it denies that our perspectives are all directed in more than a trivial sense upon a single object.[6] In this trivial sense, all our perspectives are directed upon "the world." But in order to say what that is, beyond saying that it is what our perspectives are perspectives of, we must use terms that every point of view must acknowledge; and this is either to dispense with points of view altogether or to claim that one of them is inherently superior to the rest and represents the world as it really is, "as if a world would still remain over after one deducted the perspective!" (*WP*, 567).

Yet the traditional ideal of knowledge, according to Nietzsche, assumes that at least in principle everything that there is can be known, that the very idea of "everything that there is" is sensible. It assumes that ultimately all points of view are dispensable or that they all can be combined into a single all-embracing perspective which, emanating from no specific location, can represent things as they really are. It is just for this reason that, though he often relies on cognitive terms, Nietzsche is also eager to deny that we can have what has traditionally been considered knowledge: "Our apparatus for acquiring knowledge is not *designed* for 'knowledge' " (*WP*, 496).[7]

Knowledge, in contrast to "knowledge," involves for Nietzsche an inherently conditional relation to its object, a relation that presupposes or manifests specific values, interests, and goals. There is no reason to suppose that these can ever be eliminated or that they are ultimately commensurable. Objectivity, he insists, is not "contemplation without interest . . . There is *only* a perspective seeing, only a perspective 'knowing'; and the *more* affects we allow to speak about one thing, the *more* eyes, different eyes, we can use to observe one thing, the more complete will our 'concept' of this thing, our 'objectivity' be" (*GM*, III, 12). These different eyes need not ever yield a single unified picture. Though Nietzsche writes, "They say: the world is only thought, or will, or war, or love, or hate . . . separately, all this is false: added up it is *true*," the addition need not produce a unique stereoscopic image.

We must therefore try to connect the falsification of which Nietzsche so often writes with the simplification which almost as often accompanies it in his texts (*BGE*, 24, 229). Perspectivism implies that in order to engage in any activity we must necessarily occupy ourselves with a selection of material and exclude much from our consideration. It does not imply that we see or know an appearance of the world *instead of* that world itself. The perspective is not the object seen, a self-contained thing which is independent of and incomparable to every other. What is seen is simply the world itself (in the trivial sense mentioned above) from that perspective.[8]

To pursue this visual metaphor (though we could make the same point through literature), let's consider the case of painting. There is no sense in which painters, even if we limit our examples to realistic depictions of one's visual field, can ever paint "everything" that they see. What they "leave out" is in itself quite indeterminate, and can be specified, if at all, only through other paintings, each one of which will be similarly "partial." Analogously, Nietzsche believes, there can be no total or final theory or understanding of the world. On his artistic model, the understanding of everything would be like a painting that incorporates all styles or that is painted in no style at all—a true chimera, both impossible and monstrous.

Perspectival approaches to the world are therefore not, as Nietzsche himself may have sometimes believed, disjoint from one another.[9] Each approach is capable of correcting itself, and many can incorporate new material and even combine with others to form broader systems of practices and inquiries. What is not possible is that at some point we can incorporate "all" the material there is into a single approach or that we can occupy "every" possible point of view.

This idea is well illustrated in the final sequence of Alain Resnais' *Mon Oncle d'Amérique*, a film that deals with the different, not always mutually consistent levels on which human behavior can be described and explained. This sequence opens with what seems a sparkling country landscape filling the screen. We are then made to realize, and to puzzle over, the fact that this landscape is in the middle of a city. We now see that what we took as a landscape is actually a superrealist fresco covering an entire side of an abandoned building. Its details are as minute as its lines are crisp and clean: every branch and every leaf stands out; there are no rough edges. But this effect is lost as soon as the camera moves in closer. At this distance we see that the wall is not smooth but that it consists of quite unevenly spaced bricks; the lines are now coarse, the colors rough; the landscape is still there, but it is more like the work of an impressionist than that of a superrealist. When the camera moves in closer still, when it is focused on a few individual bricks in all their roughness, the landscape is completely lost from sight. All we can see now are splashes of paint overlapping with other splashes of paint and separated from still others by the grooves between the bricks. The sequence asks: Which are the real lines and colors of the painting? Which is the real painting? The film's answer is that, whatever we know about the facts of the case, we cannot see one group of lines and colors, one "version" of the painting, if we are seeing another. The painting is all of these added together, but this is a peculiar addition that does not produce a single thing that is the reality of which all these versions are appearances. The painting just is these appearances, each seen from a particular distance, from a particular point of view. And if these are not the appearances of a single thing which is to be found in all of them (except in the trivial sense in which there is, of course, only one wall or painting, one "object" there), then indeed "no shadow of a right remains to speak here of appearance."

When Nietzsche therefore opens *Beyond Good and Evil* with the question of why we value truth over untruth, uncertainty, and ignorance, we must be very careful. We must take what he says seriously, but we must also be guided by the intuition that governs this work as well as the rest of his late writings. He is not arguing for the absurd idea that we should abandon truth and search for what we take to be error instead. He is not even saying, as is sometimes thought, that we could change our mind about what is the case if only we wanted to, if only "we adopted a different perspective." Perspectives cannot be adopted at will; new interpretations, which necessarily involve new forms of life, are reached only through great effort and only for what at least seems like good reason at the time (*BGE*, 55, 188). Nietzsche is making a different point. He suggests that just as the same character trait may have a very different value in different contexts, just as "the virtues of the common people might perhaps signify vices and weaknesses in a philosopher" (*BGE*, 30), so it may be wrong to think that the same things are true or false from every point of view or that truth is always useful and falsehood always harmful: "Something might be true while being harmful and dangerous in the highest degree. Indeed, it may be a basic characteristic of existence that those who would know it completely would perish, in which case the strength of a spirit should be measured according to how much of the 'truth' one could still barely endure—or to put it more clearly, to what degree one would *require* it to be thinned down, shrouded, sweetened, falsified" (*BGE*, 39).

This is a view that occurs often in Nietzsche's writings (for example *BT*, 7; *D*, 507; *GS*, 344, 347). But this, in my opinion, makes it very difficult to accept the popular and influential approach that attributes to him a version of what has come to be known as the "pragmatist" theory of truth.[10] According to this approach, Nietzsche's attack on truth is directed only at the most traditional conception of truth—that is, at truth as correspondence to the facts. By contrast he himself accepts and praises truth construed as what is useful and valuable to the human species.[11] As Danto has succinctly put it, Nietzsche's own positive theory of truth holds that "p is true and q is false if p works and q does not" (p. 72).

According to this interpretation Nietzsche believes that if we accept the correspondence theory of truth, all our beliefs are bound to be false, since there are no facts and therefore nothing to which these beliefs can correspond. Nevertheless, as the following passage is taken to show, he still claims that if we accept the pragmatist theory, at least some of our beliefs will be true after all: "*Life no argument.*—We have arranged for ourselves a world in which we can live—by positing bodies, lines, planes, causes and effects, motion and rest, form and content; without these articles of faith nobody could now endure life. But that does not prove them. Life is no argument. The conditions of life might include error" (*GS*, 121; cf. *BGE*, 4).[12] But it seems to me that if Nietzsche accepts any theory of truth at all here, this is the correspondence theory itself. He claims that our basic beliefs, whatever their value to life, are false; this is far from rejecting that theory. On the contrary, it seems to presuppose that very theory and to express his pessimism about our prospect of living both well and in truth. Nietzsche makes a similar point in *The Will to Power*: "A belief, however necessary it may be for the preservation of a species, has nothing to do with truth" (487). This passage argues strongly against attributing to him the pragmatist theory, since it does not in any way propose to *replace* correspondence to the world with indispensability to life as a criterion of truth. Truth, conceived traditionally, involves the idea that it is independent of background, interests, or values. Nietzsche often seems to deny that this idea is sensible, but he does not propose his own positive theory instead.

Nietzsche is seriously concerned with the question whether what is true is always valuable. But since he clearly does not think that it is, I find it difficult to attribute to him an analysis of truth as usefulness, which is what the pragmatist interpretation proposes. He often writes that error, however we construe it, is more valuable and useful than truth. But he does not write, as according to that interpretation he should, that therefore what the correspondence theory considers to be error is, from a pragmatist point of view, the truth: "Error is the most expensive luxury that human beings can permit themselves; and if the error happens to be a physiological error, then it is perilous to life. What consequently, have human beings hitherto paid for most dearly? For their 'truths': for they have all been errors *in physiologicis*" (*WP*, 544; cf. 453).

As John Wilcox has convincingly shown, Nietzsche relies extensively on "cognitivist" vocabulary. But it is not necessary, in order to be able to characterize particular beliefs, attitudes, or views as true or false, to have a *general* theory of what constitutes truth and falsehood. That Nietzsche is not concerned with such a theory, especially with a pragmatist one, is shown by the following text: "We 'know' (or believe or imagine) just as much as may be useful in the interests of the human herd, the species: and even what is here called 'utility' is ultimately also a mere belief, something imaginary, and perhaps precisely that most calamitous stupidity of which we shall perish some day" (*GS*, 354). Even here, in a passage that is always cited in support of the pragmatist interpretation of Nietzsche's theory of truth, Nietzsche is mixing together the notions of knowledge, belief, and imagination. And he does not claim that utility constitutes, or even that it explains, truth. He writes instead that our *belief* that a view is useful, a belief which may well itself be false, is what makes us consider that particular view as true, whether this is or is not in fact the case. This claim is not, in any recognizable sense, a theory of truth that aims to explicate that concept, to give a general characterization of it, and to account for the reason why all those views of ours that happen to be true do in fact have that relation to the world.

In addition, Nietzsche does not ever analyze truth as utility or power, as is sometimes argued.[13] He does write that truth is related to the feeling of power: "The criterion of truth resides in the enhancement of the feeling of power" (*WP*, 534; cf. 455). But far from being his own account of the nature of truth, this is only his explanation of the fact that people accept certain views as true even if, as it turns out, they are not. He rejects everything that is associated with the Christian interpretation of life and the world, but devotes most of *On the Genealogy of Morals* to an effort to show that this false view has enabled "the weak" to have, and to feel that they have, power over "the strong": "The will of the weak to represent *some* kind of superiority, their instinct for devious paths to tyranny over the healthy—where can it not be discovered, this will to power of the weakest!" (*GM*, III, 14). Power and the feeling of power do not therefore secure truth any more than utility does. Nietzsche, I think, does not offer these ideas as analyses, as positive proposals for what constitutes truth. He claims instead that what we customarily take to be true is what we *think* is useful and what makes us feel, or actually makes us, powerful. But we may be wrong about what is useful. And in any case, what is useful in one context may be harmful in another; what benefits and strengthens the herd harms and weakens the individual; what is important for today may be deadly for the future (cf. *GM,* Pref., 6; *WP,* 647). Nietzsche, as the following famous passage shows, is not interested in providing a theory of truth: "The falseness of a judgment is not for us necessarily an objection to a judgment . . . The question is to what extent it is life-promoting, life-preserving, species-preserving, perhaps even species-cultivating . . . To recognize untruth as a condition of life— that certainly means resisting accustomed value feelings in a dangerous way: and a philosophy that risks this would by that token alone place itself beyond good and evil" (*BGE,* 4).

Nietzsche writes that "the falsest judgments (which include the synthetic judgments *a priori*) are the most indispensable for us." But he does not propose that indispensability or the promotion and cultivation of life replace "correspondence with the facts" as our conception of the nature of truth. He simply cautions against assuming that truth and knowledge, whatever they are, are always beneficial and that ignorance and falsehood always cause harm. We should not, if at all possible, take a philosophy that wants to "recognize untruth as a condition of life" to offer a different analysis of truth according to which our most fundamental beliefs *are* after all true. Nietzsche claims that many of our most central beliefs are false, and that, far from hurting us, these beliefs have so far produced some of the greatest benefits. But he never argues that their being beneficial makes them true.

In explicating Nietzsche's view, I have appealed to an artistic model from which he is eager to generalize to other domains. In one sense a novelist narrates everything that there is to be narrated in a novel, just as a painter represents everything that there is to be represented in a painting. But in another sense all narration and representation leaves out an indefinitely large amount of information. Painters may paint "exactly what they see," but what they see is necessarily a highly idiosyncratic, mediated "part" of the landscape, and often not a part of any landscape or other part of the world at all. Even the most faithful representation of the most elementary subject matter, as Ernst Gombrich has shown in *Art and Illusion,* is not simple representation.[14] All painters necessarily employ a style, and this forces certain choices, decisions, and exclusions upon them; further, within that style each must make a large number of more specific decisions. Every decision, no matter how general or specific, foregrounds some of the elements of one's subject matter at the expense of others and is therefore responsible for the very creation of that subject matter. There is an important ambiguity in this context, which will occupy us again in the course of this book: should we say that painters describe an antecedently existing subject matter, or are they creating it as they go along? Impressionism cannot represent or even countenance the clear outlines of objects that characterize neoclassical works; but the interaction of colored shadows is, by the same token, beyond both the means and the imagination of neoclassical painters.

All of this, I think, is part of what is involved in Nietzsche's exclamation, "In what strange simplification and falsification do human beings live!" (*BGE*, 24). But it is only part, and this is why I earlier characterized what I have said so far as no more than a first approximation to his view. The reason is simple. Choosing, selecting, and simplifying do not amount to falsifying what is before us, unless we believe that there can be a representation of the world that depends on no selection at all, and that this representation constitutes the standard of accuracy. But Nietzsche's perspectivism is a direct denial of this possibility. He is therefore not entitled to claim that we falsify the world just because we simplify it in order to deal with it.

Consider again the analogy with painting. Paintings may be said to falsify their subject matter if they flout, without reason, the dictates of the style in which they are done. A superrealist portrait, for example, would be a falsification if the face of its sitter were without reason done in royal purple or if part of the work involved the vocabulary of analytical cubism. If we find a reason for the feature in question, it will no longer be obvious that the work belongs to the style to which we originally assigned it: successful flouting of convention is innovation, and the question of falsification does not come up in that case. Falsification that arises out of the groundless flouting of established rules is a phenomenon with which Nietzsche was certainly familiar. But it is totally unclear how simple errors of this sort can account for his desire, in stark and uncompromising terms, to "recognize untruth as a condition of life."

Simplification and falsification differ greatly from one another. Why then does Nietzsche write of them so often together? To answer this question we must again take a longer route. We must first turn to another apparently unrelated text: "Morality in Europe today is herd animal morality—in other words, as we understand it, merely *one* human morality besides which, before which, and after which many other types, above all *higher* moralities, are, or ought to be, possible. But this morality resists such a 'possibility,' such an 'ought,' with all its power: it says stubbornly and inexorably, 'I am morality itself, and nothing besides is morality' " (*BGE*, 202; cf. *A*, 57). What is important for us here is the idea that a particular system of thought and action includes within itself the premise that it is the only possible such system. Its claim to objective truth and correctness, to its being binding, consists precisely in that premise and stands or falls with it. Nietzsche's point is general and not specific to morality (*WP*, 514). He believes that all human practices—moral, religious, artistic, or cognitive—involve the sort of selection and simplification that I have been discussing. There can therefore always be alternatives to any given system. But he also believes that though we necessarily simplify whatever we are to deal with, it is also true that at least in many cases we think that we don't. And it is just here that falsification enters the picture: it is produced by the belief that the particular enterprise in which one is involved or which one values the most is exempt from simplification, that it is the only possible or correct mode of proceeding.

But does even this interpretation account for Nietzsche's strong view that untruth is a condition of life? Suppose we come to understand that realism in painting is only one among many possible genres: can't we then simply give up the belief that realistic paintings alone represent the visual world as it really is? And can't we develop the same tolerant attitude in regard to whatever enterprise occupies us? What we need to do, one might urge at this point, is to become more self-conscious and less arrogant about our practices and modes of life, to become aware of their contingent bases, and perhaps to abandon the goal of ever representing the world as it really is. This new modesty might well do away with falsification. In that case Nietzsche's view that we must inevitably falsify the world in which we live would appear to be little more than another dispensable hyperbole.

Nietzsche, however, is thinking of something much more complicated:

> With the strength of their spiritual eye and insight grows distance and, as it were, the space around human beings: their world becomes more profound; ever new stars, ever new riddles and images

become visible to them. Perhaps everything on which the spirit's eye has exercised its acuteness and truthfulness was nothing but an occasion for this exercise, something for children and those who are childish. Perhaps the day will come when the most solemn concepts which have caused the most fights and suffering, the concepts "God" and "sin," will seem no more important to us than a child's toy and a child's pain seem to the old—and perhaps "the old" will then be in need of another toy and another pain—still children enough, eternal children! (*BGE*, 57; cf. Z, I, 1)

Our most fundamental beliefs and values, this passage suggests, may someday be discarded along with other outmoded and useless ideas. No matter how inevitable and inescapable they have seemed so far, our greatest values will one day appear nothing more than a child's toy to an adult: of little consequence and, like all outgrown toys, destined to be cast aside.

This text carefully avoids saying that the religious attitude was never of any value. In any case Nietzsche does not believe this, and the third essay of *On the Genealogy of Morals* is his effort to show why Christianity, despite what he saw as its horrors, was still essential to the life it appeared to condemn. But Nietzsche does believe that the Christian interpretation of the fact of human misery has now lost its power and cannot serve the purpose it has served so far—at least for some people. Christianity must therefore at some point be thrown away like an old toy; the serious misery it previously satisfied so deeply may someday appear little more than a childhood pain.

This would have been the perfect place for Nietzsche to pursue further his metaphor of aging and maturing. He could have written that we must now give up childish pains and childish toys altogether, that we must look at the world without props, as it really is, with unclouded eyes and without the wishes and fears of childhood. But instead of elaborating the metaphor in this direction, he replicates its first stage and suggests that the old may still need "another toy and another pain," in relation to which they can be, of course, no more than children once again. And when Nietzsche characterizes them as "eternal children," he implies that this new toy and this new pain will only be given up in turn and replaced by still others.

"One's maturity—consists in having found again the seriousness one had as a child, at play" (*BGE*, 94). Wisdom and age do not replace youth and naiveté once and for all (cf. *BGE*, 31). What to the old now seems only a toy was not merely representation but reality to the child.[15] But the present toys of the old must also, from within their own point of view, appear to be reality themselves. Applied to our topic, the metaphor suggests that in our efforts to come to terms with the world not only do we simplify it but, in addition, we cannot think that we do. In order to be motivated to produce a new view, interpretation, painting, theory, novel, or morality, one must not think that it is simply one among many equally good alternatives; one must believe that it is a very good, perhaps the best, view, interpretation, painting, theory, novel, or morality. Nietzsche writes that truth is created and not discovered (*BGE*, 211; *WP*, 552); but he still believes that we must think of it as something we discover in order to go on to create it (*Z*, I, 8; II, 13; *WP*, 597).

Consider for example a radical innovation in painting or in literature: single-point perspective or cubism, naturalism or stream of consciousness. We often speak of these as "styles," and accordingly think of them as means for depicting in novel ways what was there all along to be depicted. Yet such innovations do not allow us simply to represent a preexisting world in new ways. At least as much, they produce new things to paint or write about; they create new aspects of reality to which we can now, for the first time, be true.

According to one view of analytical cubism, Picasso made it possible to represent many sides of an object at the same time. In doing this he made more than the facing surfaces of the world part of the subject matter of painting. He himself said that if his *Nude with Draperies* (1907) was successful, then it should be possible to "cut up" the canvas and, having put it together again, "according to color indications . . . find oneself confronted by a sculpture."[16] His achievement was not simply a formal innovation; in a serious sense, Picasso created something in the very act of depicting it—not simply a new way of looking at the world but, equivalently, a new aspect of the world to look at. The equivocal manner in which this and other similar achievements have to be described matches perfectly the ambiguities in Nietzsche's own attitude toward truth and reality. He believes, based once again on a generalization from the arts, that great movements in science as well as in morality produce something new to be described or evaluated in the very process of devising new methods of description and evaluation. And to the natural question whether the laws of motion did not exist before Galileo and Newton formulated and quantified them, Nietzsche's answer would be that of course they did—just in the way that all the surfaces of material objects were there to be painted before Picasso showed us for the first time how it could be done.

Beyond Good and Evil opens with a discussion of traditional philosophical ideas. Many of them, like the absolute value of truth and the possibility of objective knowledge, Nietzsche writes, have been too easily and unthinkingly taken for granted. In what is often a cursory manner at best, he questions these views; sometimes, even more briefly, he hints at his own novel answers. The work then proceeds gradually to sketch a type of character, the "free spirit" or the "new philosopher," who accepts these answers, or who at least knows that the traditional questions need to be questioned themselves. In this process the work also generates the figure of its own author, who is as aware of the problems that confront traditional philosophy as is the character he describes, but who is in addition aware of the problems this awareness, as we shall see, in turn generates.

Sometimes Nietzsche writes as if his free spirits were perfectly free of the illusions that are so necessary to the rest of the world. His new philosophers appear to believe that all they can ever hope to do is continually to proliferate, simply for their own sake, new interpretations. According to Sarah Kofman, they are strong enough "to want the truth, that is, to become conscious of the absence of the truth of being, of the enigma that life is, and to offer, accordingly, an indefinite multiplicity of possible interpretations."[17] Nietzsche does sometimes seem to suggest that total freedom from illusion is indeed possible:

> How much one needs a *faith* in order to flourish, how much that is "firm" and that one does not wish to be shaken because one *clings* to it, that is the measure of the degree of one's strength (or, to put the point more clearly, of one's weakness) ... Conversely, one could conceive of such a pleasure and power of self-determination, such a *freedom* of the will that the spirit would take leave of all faith and every wish for certainty, being practiced on maintaining itself on insubstantial ropes and possibilities and dancing even near abysses. Such a spirit would be the *free spirit* par excellence. (*GS*, 347; cf. *A*, 54; *GM*, III, 24)

But a careful reading of this passage shows that there are no clear end points to this continuum of strength and weakness: even for the strongest there are still ropes, though they are "insubstantial"; even their dancing occurs "near," and not over, abysses. We have already seen that freedom does not consist in leaving rules and principles behind but in their appropriate internalization (*BGE*, 188, 213). The free and the unfree will, conceived as perfect autonomy and as total determination respectively, are for Nietzsche both creatures of "mythology"; "in real life it is only a matter of *strong* and *weak* wills" (*BGE*, 21). And by the same token, total independence and absolute subservience are equally impossible: we have already seen Nietzsche write that even in interpreting a formula the individual is still creative; even when guided only by faith and convention, we must still interpret their dictates ourselves (*WP*, 767).

Both his view that untruth is a condition of life and his metaphor of the eternal child imply that Nietzsche denies the possibility of a millennial elimination of illusion and falsification. To recognize, as the free spirits do, the necessity of illusion is not to realize that everything is false and that the only thing one can do is to produce more and more "mere" illusions and interpretations for their own sake. Illusions are difficult to construct, to accept, and to abandon. To recognize that illusion is inevitable is to recognize that the views and values we accept wholeheartedly and without which our life may not even be possible depend on simplifications, on needs and desires which we may not at the moment be able to locate specifically. It is also to realize that though these simplifications are necessary for us and for those like us, they are *not* necessary for everyone. In order to become aware of the specific points where our own mode of life depends on simplifying the world, on overlooking some of its features or some alternative mode of life, it is necessary to have already begun to develop another interpretation, another illusion, for only in the light of such a new framework can the old one be seen as the particular simplification it is; and this is already to have begun to change one's views, values, mode of life, and, in a strict sense, oneself. Such a new interpretation, the toy of the old, will itself include assumptions and simplifications that cannot be made explicit unless still more alternatives, which will generate the very same situation, are developed. Nietzsche's free spirits are always looking for new interpretations, but not simply for their own sake; they are always looking for that mode of life which is best for them, though not necessarily (Nietzsche would say necessarily not) for everyone else. They are "curious to a vice, investigators to the point of cruelty, with uninhibited fingers for

the unfathomable, with teeth and stomachs for the most indigestible
... arrangers and collectors from morning till late, misers of our
riches and our crammed drawers, economical in learning and forgetting, inventive in schemas, occasionally proud of our tables of categories, occasionally pedants, occasionally night owls of work even in
broad daylight" (*BGE*, 44; cf. *GS*, 351). The ironic distance, which
seems to me essential to those who proliferate new interpretations
simply for the joy of multiplying illusion, is perfectly absent from
Nietzsche's description of his free spirits. Their interpretations are
nothing short of their tables of values, by which their very lives are
guided and even constituted.

Nietzsche often construes the world as a text of which our various
practices and modes of life are interpretations (see for example *BGE*,
22, 230). His metaphor has been taken to do away with truth altogether; for since no text seems to be meaningful independently of all interpretation, no interpretation, it seems, can discover a meaning that exists antecedently; instead, every interpretation actually creates the
meaning it attributes to its text. There is therefore no question of ever
being accurate or true to a text, since without an interpretation already in place, there is nothing for it to be true *to*. Furthermore, once
an interpretation has been offered, to discuss the possibility that it is
true is simply to produce a further interpretation of the text in question, which will itself create its own meaning for it. Interpretation,
therefore, can only give rise to further interpretation; it thus creates
more texts that need to be interpreted instead of bringing us closer to
the end of the interpretation of the original text. By adding to this series of texts, each interpretation changes the object that its successors
will have to concern themselves with. And within this series there are
bound to be interpretations between which, despite the fact that they
are incompatible with one another, it will be impossible to choose
and that will therefore be equally acceptable. Just in this manner, it
can be claimed, the actual world can be transformed and dealt with in
ways we cannot possibly now envisage, ways that will be as valid and
justified as the best we have developed so far, even if they are quite incompatible with them. Like textual interpretations, all our modes of
interacting with the world are additions that make an already indeterminate object even more multifarious and complex.

We should not want to deny that in regard to every text there are
many interpretations that can in principle be produced but that have

not yet been developed. Many of these are inaccessible to us today and will be reached only after all sorts of unpredictable developments have occurred. But this is not in itself a reason for thinking that texts are indeterminate and that they can be interpreted in many conflicting but equally legitimate ways. It is therefore not a reason for thinking that the very notion of an interpretation that is adequate to a text is illegitimate. The claim that there can always be two or more equally correct though conflicting readings of a given text, and that therefore truth or correctness is not a significant feature of interpretation, can be substantiated only by comparing two or more *complete* interpretations of that text. If two *partial* interpretations conflict, then they may well be incorporated in a further reading that resolves their conflicts. But it is in principle as impossible to produce a complete interpretation of a text as it is impossible to develop a complete view or theory of anything. Therefore the claim that every text has as many meanings as there are interpretations of it cannot possibly be substantiated, for, not knowing what would constitute a text's complete interpretation, we cannot know when we are faced with two or more distinct readings of it. In addition, new interpretations that we are not now capable of producing can come into being only through the production of other interpretations which we are in fact capable of producing. But the reason for looking for new interpretations is always that they will be better than the readings (or some of the readings) we have produced so far, and not simply the fact that they are new.[18]

The argument is sometimes made that a reading is "only" or "merely" an interpretation because an alternative *could*, in principle, always be devised. But this challenge is serious only if a better alternative is *in fact* devised, and in most cases this is not at all a simple task. The new alternative must be, according to some set of criteria, at least as satisfactory as the view it challenges. If it shows that the previous reading was "merely" an interpretation, the new reading cannot be characterized as a "mere" interpretation in turn until yet another, still better interpretation is produced. It has been claimed, for example, that M. H. Abrams' *Natural Supernaturalism* cannot be taken at face value, that it is only an interpretation, because a different history of romanticism, emphasizing different poems, different poets, and different events of the movement, could always be written. I cannot possibly take sides on the historical issues themselves, but it seems to me that Wayne Booth's reply to this general charge is serious and to the point:

> It . . . seems likely that we *could* have other legitimate histories of Abrams' subject . . . But whether or not one could be written that would falsify any of his central theses will be settled not by propositional argument but by the argument peculiar to writing a history: can the history be written and, once written, can it be read? . . . If someone can write a debunking history of Wordsworth and Romanticism, one that will make its connections and establish its values as thoroughly and with as little stylistic forcing as Abrams' manages, then of course we must take his view into account. Go try.[19]

In order to avoid the view that the world has a determinate structure in itself, many of Nietzsche's contemporary readers have repeated his occasional claims to the effect that the world, like every text, "has no meaning behind it, but countless meanings" (*WP*, 481). But I think Nietzsche was wrong to think that this ontological pluralism could support his perspectivism. An object is not indeterminate because it has many characters instead of having only one; for since each of these characters is itself determinate, this claim is not an alternative to but a particular instance of the idea that the object in question has a determinate character. Nietzsche's perspectivism denies precisely this last idea, but this denial is not, as he himself occasionally thought, equivalent to the view that the world is "infinite" in that "it may contain infinite interpretations" (*GS*, 374). What must be denied instead is the more fundamental claim that there could ever be a complete theory or interpretation of anything, a view that accounts for "all" the facts; we must deny the claim that the notion of "all the facts" is sensible in the first place. The pluralistic view I am discussing assumes that this notion is sensible and argues that there can be many (complete) interpretations of the world. But this is not to deny that the world *has* a character, which is what perspectivism denies; it is to deny that it has *one*, which amounts to relativism. Perspectivism requires only a world that is perfectly finite and dense: it must be always possible to reinterpret and reevaluate even what already seems to have found its ultimate position within it.

Nietzsche calls our views, practices, and modes of life "interpretations" because of the constant possibility of such readjustment, and also because he believes that every view of the world makes possible and promotes a particular kind of life and therefore presupposes and manifests specific interests and values. He calls them "interpretations" in order to call to our attention the fact that they are never detached or disinterested, that they are not objective in a traditional sense. If there are different interpretations of the world, it is not because the world has an indeterminate number of characters but because there are many kinds of people, not all of whom can live by the same views and values. When Nietzsche writes that science is an interpretation, he does not seem to me to be claiming that no particular theory can ever be true. Science, he argues, provides neither an *ultimate* description of the world nor a description of the world as it is *in itself*. It is therefore not a practice to which all the others are secondary and inferior. He does not object to science itself (see for example "Long live physics!" *GS*, 335) but rather to an interpretation which refuses to acknowledge that science is itself an interpretation in the sense that it provides a revisable description of a part of the world which is no more real than any other. The problem has been that the methods of science have been assumed to be better than any others, and its objects have been considered to be more real or ultimate than anything else. Nietzsche attacks only this privileging of the methods and objects of science and not its methods or objects themselves. This is obvious in the following passage, which denies only the view that science makes an *exclusive* claim to truth and correctness: "That the only justifiable interpretation of the world should be one in which *you* are justified because one can continue to work and do research scientifically in *your* sense (you really mean, mechanistically?)—an interpretation that permits counting, calculating, weighing, seeing, and touching, and nothing more—that is a crudity and naiveté, asuming that it is not a mental illness, an idiocy" (*GS*, 373). This is what the free spirits and the new philosophers of *Beyond Good and Evil* realize, and this is why they are not dogmatists. This too seems to be just what the "old philologist" himself has in mind when, implicitly commending Don Quixote rather than Odysseus, he writes, "Whoever has attained intellectual freedom even to a small extent cannot feel but as a wanderer upon the face of the earth—and not as a traveler *toward* some final destination; for that does not exist" (*HH*, I, 638).

Another group of Nietzsche's readers has been disturbed by the fact that his view that there are no facts but only interpretations seems to generate a self-referential paradox. Suppose that we characterize

Nietzsche's perspectivism as the thesis (P) that every view is an interpretation. Now it appears that if (P) is true, and if every view is in fact an interpretation, this would apply to (P) itself. In that case (P) also turns out to be an interpretation. But if this is so, then not every view need be an interpretation, and (P) seems to have refuted itself.

This argument is supposed to be a version of the paradox of the liar, which does in fact create serious logical and semantical problems; but the supposition is wrong. If (P) is an interpretation, it may indeed be false. But from the possibility that (P), the thesis that every view is an interpretation, may be false, all that follows is the conclusion I have already stated—that is, that not every view need be an interpretation. But (P) does not assert that every view necessarily is an interpretation; it cannot therefore be refuted by showing (which is all I have done so far) that it is *possible* that some views are not interpretations. To show that (P) is false, we must show that some views are actually not interpretations. But this involves showing not that (P) may be false (which is again what has been shown up to this point) but that it is *actually* false.

Yet our argument can show that (P) is actually false only if we assume that, being an interpretation, (P) may be false and that therefore it is in fact false. This last conclusion would truly refute (P), for if the thesis that every view is an interpretation is in fact false, then indeed some views are actually not interpretations. But the conclusion that (P) is in fact false does not follow from the fact that (P) is itself an interpretation. It is reached only by means of an invalid inference, by means of equating, as above, the fact that (P) is an interpretation and therefore possibly false with the fact that it is actually false.

In a curious and suggestive way, this equation repeats the very same error which I discussed in my examination of the notion of a "mere" interpretation. That error consists in thinking that because there always may be alternatives to a given view, that view is "merely" an interpretation. But all that follows from the possibility of alternatives to a view is just that that view is an interpretation. To say that it is "merely" an interpretation is to take a further and unjustified step and to claim that there are in fact alternatives (of which we are aware) that rob it of its claim to being correct.

Both these approaches rely on the same wrong conception of interpretation: they presuppose that to consider a view an interpretation is to concede that it is false. They both assume that interpretation is a second-best mode of understanding and thus misunderstood perspectivism, which denies that there can be even in principle a mode of understanding that is better, more secure, or more accurate than interpretation. The view that all views are interpretations *may* be false; of what view does this not hold? But this is not in itself an objection to perspectivism. To say that it might be false (which is all this claim amounts to) is not to say that it *is* false; this is the very same error once again. Perhaps not all views are interpretations. But we shall know this to be true only when one is actually produced. Perspectivism cannot be shown to refute itself as easily as we have often supposed.

What can be shown is that, in admitting its own status as interpretation, perspectivism does not require that it be accepted. It concedes that no one is obliged to believe it. This is where it differs from dogmatism, which, according to Nietzsche, makes just this claim. Perspectivism grants that some people may always refuse to accept it. But in itself this fact makes neither perspectivism wrong nor those people right. It merely shows that questions of truth and falsehood can be answered only in relation to specific cases and not by means of the abstract considerations I have provided so far.

The general problem with both positive and negative approaches to perspectivism so far is that they have been too quick to equate possible with actual falsehood, interpretation with mere interpretation. The claim, however, that a view is mere interpretation can be made only in light of a further interpretation, which is of course not a mere interpretation itself in that context. Nietzsche's perspectivism claims that there is no view of the world that is binding on everyone. He believes that every view depends on and manifests specific values and attitudes toward life, that it is to be accepted only by those who want to make those values their own. Even a serious alternative to (P), a view to the effect that at least one view, perhaps that very view in question, is not an interpretation, may still be shown to be just that if it is shown to depend on and promote its own specific values. This is just what Nietzsche tries to show in connection with Christianity and with all dogmatic views: though motivated and directed by particular desires and values, they always try to conceal that fact. This too is the object of genealogy, which is an effort to reveal that behind their disinterested appearance and their claim to be binding on everyone, all such views are attempts to promote their own special interests without admitting their partiality: "*What, then, is regressive in philos-*

ophers?—That they teach that *their* qualities are the necessary and sole qualities for the attainment of the 'highest good' (e.g., dialectic, as with Plato). That they order people of all kinds *gradatim* up to *their* type as the highest" (*WP*, 446).

Nietzsche's perspectivism, then, is a refusal to grade people and views along a single scale. It cannot be refuted simply because it applies to itself, and it need not be defended against attempts to refute it just on those grounds.[20] In order to refute it, we must develop a view that does not depend on antecedent commitments and that does not promote a particular kind of person and a particular kind of life—a view that applies equally to everyone at all times and in all contexts. The task may well be possible, but simply saying that it can be done is not the same as doing it. Alternatively, we must show, in the same detail in which Nietzsche revealed the presuppositions of the views he attacked, that his efforts were a failure, that he was wrong to claim that these views made such commitments. And in doing so we might even find ourselves doing exactly what Nietzsche saw himself doing when he took up Paul Rée's views on the development of morality. He discusses Rée's ideas, he writes, "not in order to refute them—what have I to do with refutations!—but, as becomes a positive spirit, to replace the improbable with the more probable, possibly one error with another" (*GM*, Pref., 4). Until this is done, and perhaps even afterward, perspectivism, freed from the notion of mere interpretation, can stand as a serious view in its own right. Just as it cannot support all the claims of its more enthusiastic admirers, so it cannot crumble at the first logical touch of its more bitter opponents.

When, therefore, Nietzsche's free spirits pursue the truth in the knowledge that they are not free from illusion, they are constructing or describing a world in which their own values—particularly their desire to be aware that this is the sort of world they are constructing or describing—are manifested. Anything but disinterested, they no longer see the will to truth as the effort to discover, once and for all, the real nature of the world.[21] They now see it, in suitably ambiguous terms, as an effort to establish its character. The will to truth now appears very different: "A curiosity of my type remains after all the most agreeable of all vices—sorry, I meant to say: the love of truth has its rewards on heaven and even on earth" (*BGE*, 45). The will to truth turns out to be an effort to establish a world in which one's best impulses and strongest needs can find expression, and in which perhaps, at least for a time, they can be satisfied. In other words, it turns out to be the will to power: " 'Will to truth,' you who are wisest call that which impels you and fills you with lust? A will to the thinkability of all beings; this *I* call your will. You want to *make* all being thinkable, for you doubt with well-founded suspicion that it is already thinkable . . . That is your whole will, you who are wisest: a will to power" (Z, II, 12). But the will to power is not the arbitrary imposition of order on a world that is in principle chaotic or unstructured. Even the notion of chaos is relative to a particular interpretation: "This is what the will to truth should mean to you: that everything be transformed in what can be thought by human beings, seen by human beings, and felt by human beings . . . And what you have called world, that shall be created only by you: your image, your reason, your will, your love shall thus be realized. And, verily, for your own bliss, you lovers of knowledge . . . You could not have been born either into the incomprehensible or into the irrational" (Z, II, 2).

In the context of investigation we can look at the will to truth, construed as the will to power, from an external as well as from an internal point of view. From within a particular practice, one is related to that practice, to truth, and to the world much as a child is related to its toy. We do not engage in such practices in the specific awareness that they are illusions, though we can know in general terms that illusions are necessarily present within them. Painters do not work in the specific knowledge of which among the indefinitely many features of their subject matter they are leaving out of account, though they are often aware that they employ only one among many possible styles; nor of course can they change styles at will. Such thoughts don't seem to function in the context: a painter simply tries to get matters right. A more detached attitude, Nietzsche suggests, might even be crippling: "It is not enough that you understand in what ignorance humans as well as animals live; you must also have and acquire the *will* to ignorance. You need to grasp that without this kind of ignorance life itself would be impossible, that it is a condition under which alone the living thing can preserve itself and prosper: a great, firm dome of ignorance must encompass you" (*WP*, 609). The will to ignorance, therefore, is not simply the tendency or desire not to know some things. It must also turn upon itself and become the will not to know that one is failing to know many things in the process of coming to know one. The will to knowledge, Nietzsche claims, can function only on this foundation, or, as he would doubtless prefer to put it, only in this way can the will to ignorance be refined into the will to knowledge itself: the effort to ignore is itself an effort to know.

Such tentative absolutism, however, can easily cease being tentative and become merely absolutism; as we have seen, for example, it is part of the development of a morality "that its origin should be forgotten" (*WP*, 514). At any particular moment Nietzsche's free spirits, apart from their generalized awareness that their views are interpretations, can have every faith in the practices in which they are engaged: they know that, at that time at least, they cannot live without them. But in addition they also know that others could not live with them. And this realization distinguishes them from those whose absolutism is not tentative. The free spirits know that their mode of life is their own creation and that it is not the only mode that is necessary or even possible. They therefore do not want to impose it upon others, and they do not try to cling to it once it has outlived its usefulness: "The view that *truth is found* and that ignorance and error are at an end is one of the most potent seductions there is. Supposing it is believed, then the will to examination, investigation, caution, experiment is paralyzed: it can even count as criminal, namely as *doubt* concerning truth" (*WP*, 542). The free spirits do not believe in "the" truth (cf. *WP*, 540), and they therefore do not believe that it can be found once and for all. They will therefore refuse to privilege the practices in which they are engaged. Aware that nothing about them need remain the same over time, and that nothing about the world will, the free spirits are "at home, or at least . . . guests, in many countries of the spirit; having escaped again and again from the musty agreeable nooks into which preference and prejudice, youth, origin, the accidents of people and books or even exhaustion from wandering seemed to have banished us" (*BGE*, 44).

The generalized awareness that all practices are interpretive and value laden can make us realize that, even in the most elementary matters, we may well change our mind and thus our life. Others may come to see things, with at least equal justice, in a manner totally different from ours. We ourselves may, and probably will, develop entirely different views over time: "Whoever reaches one's ideal transcends it *eo ipso*" (*BGE*, 73). It does not follow from this that any interpretation is as good as any other ("We must reject the Christian interpretation and condemn its 'meaning' as counterfeit," *GS*, 357) or that it is undesirable and even impossible to try to devise better interpretations. Both inferences are themselves instances of what Nietzsche calls "nihilism," and they embody its fundamental assumption that if some single standard is not good for everyone and for all time, then no standard is good for anyone at any time. By appearing to provide such a universal standard, according to Nietzsche, Christianity repressed the symptoms of this "European disease" while it strengthened its causes. But "the death of God" (*GS*, 108, 125, 343) has now brought the disease out into the open: "The 'meaninglessness of events': belief in this is the consequence of an insight into the falsity of previous interpretations, a generalization of discouragement and weakness—not a *necessary* belief" (*WP*, 599).

Uncommitted to the basic nihilist assumption, Nietzsche's free spirits are always willing, and sometimes able, to create new and better interpretations—better for particular people, at particular times, for particular reasons. The world is neither totally beyond their ken nor perfectly within their grasp: "Thus the world offered itself to me today; not riddle enough to frighten away human love, not solution enough to put to sleep human wisdom; a humanly good thing the world was to me today, though one speaks so much evil of it" (*Z*, III, 10). The free spirits see their creations as views that are best for them and for those like them, if there are any. This contrast with the efforts to mask one's interpretation and to present it as a view that is binding on all is what distinguishes the free spirits from dogmatists and "metaphysicians" (*BGE*, 43; *WP*, 446). But they are also aware of two further points. First, they know that even the most familiar facts are themselves products of interpretation, as we shall see in more detail in the next chapter. They are therefore constantly trying to find where they have unwittingly accepted without question such interpretations. This effort does not consist in first isolating these facts and then trying to determine what interpretation produced them. On the contrary, these most familiar facts are what we take most for granted and what we are the least aware of: "What is familar is what we are used to; and what we are used to is most difficult to 'know'—that is, to see as a problem; that is, to see as strange and distant, as 'outside us' " (*GS*, 355). The difficulty is not so much in reconstructing the interpretation as in becoming explicitly aware of what we have taken for granted in the first place. Once we have done this, we have seen it as the product of an interpretation; and we can see it as such only on the basis of a further interpretation on our own part. Second, the free spirits know that in producing new views they inevitably change their own situation and thus make further interpretations necessary; these interpretations will in turn create still other new situations. They can thus accept the contingency of their views when that becomes apparent, and they can part with them when that becomes necessary. A "noble will" is one, as Sarah Kofman writes, "which, though capable of affirming one perspective over a long time is still distant enough from it to be able to change it and to see the world with 'other eyes' " (p. 150).

This is what Zarathustra tells his disciples: "Indeed, there must be much bitter dying in your life, you creators. Thus are you advocates and justifiers of all impermanence. To be the child who is newly born, the creator must also want to be the mother who gives birth and the pangs of the birth-giver" (Z, II, 2). Nietzsche's ever-recurring metaphors of child and childbirth prevent us, I think, from construing the continual process of revision he describes as a linear progression toward a single goal. The members of a single genealogical sequence, as we shall soon see, need share no single feature with one another. Our practices need not all have the same goal, and even the goal of the same practice need not remain the same over time.

The realization that all our activity is partial and perspectival does not therefore, except in the generalized way I have discussed, enter into our specific projects. Nietzsche's apparently extreme view that untruth is a condition of life ultimately refers to our ignorance of the exact ways in which our views, at every time, are simplifications of the world and are dependent on particular values; it calls to our attention the fact that we may have to remain ignorant of these simplifications and values if we are to engage in a practice for some time. Even the constant search for unjustified assumptions must proceed on some unquestioned assumptions of its own. Perspectivism does not result in the relativism that holds that any view is as good as any other; it holds that one's own views are the best for oneself without implying that they need be good for anyone else. It also generates the expectation that new views and values are bound to become necessary as it produces the willingness to develop and to accept such new schemes: "What is the greatest experience you can have? It is the hour of the great contempt. The hour in which your happiness, too, arouses your disgust, and even your reason and your virtue" (Z, Pref., 3). New alternatives may appear on their own—that is, as the result of the creations of others. But the greatest achievement is to devise them one-self, to see of one's own accord one's previous views as (here the word is perfectly appropriate) *mere* interpretations: "Some should find; others—*we* others!—should import!" (*WP*, 606).

I began this chapter with the opening of *Beyond Good and Evil*, and it may be appropriate to finish with its end, for this work closes by expressing toward itself the very attitude that I have been discuss-ing: "Alas, what are you after all, my written and painted thoughts! It was not long ago that you were still so colorful, young, and malicious, full of thorns and secret spices—you made me sneeze and laugh—and now? You have already taken off your novelty, and some of you are ready, I fear, to become truths" (*BGE*, 296). *Beyond Good and Evil* be-gins with the demand of the will to truth that it be put itself into ques-tion. Motivated by this will, and following it relentlessly, and to that extent incapable of putting it completely into question, the text con-strues the will to ignorance and the will to knowledge as one, as the will to power. In particular, it construes them as a will that finds its greatest moments in questioning the pursuit of truth and knowledge and that regards itself as creating rather than discovering new truths. At the book's end, the case now apparently made, this questioning of truth appears itself true to its author. True to himself, he warns against accepting it complacently. He does not disown it; he does not call it a mere interpretation, since to do so he must engage in a new question-ing, and for this he must produce a new text and a new truth, all of which, as he has shown, will generate the very same problem. By the strange artifice of calling his views true, Nietzsche underscores their deeply personal and idiosyncratic nature, the fact that they are his own interpretations. Having presented his perspectivism not so much as a traditional theory of knowledge but as the view that all efforts to know are also efforts of particular people to live particular kinds of lives for particular reasons, he now applies that view to itself. And in the interval between presupposing what cannot be presupposed and questioning what cannot be questioned, he shows that even his ques-tioning of the will to truth and knowledge can proceed only in their name. Untruth can be recognized as a condition of life only if it truly is such a condition.

3 | *A Thing Is The Sum of Its Effects*

> What was Unity? Why was one to be forced to affirm it?
>
> Here everybody flatly refused to help . . . He got out his Descartes again; dipped into his Hume and Berkeley; wrestled anew with his Kant; pondered solemnly over his Hegel and Schopenhauer and Hartmann; strayed gaily away with his Greeks,—all merely to ask what Unity meant, and what happened when one denied it.
>
> Apparently one never denied it. Every Philosopher, whether sane or insane, naturally affirmed it.
>
> Henry Adams, *The Education of Henry Adams*

It often seems as if the aim of Nietzsche's writing is to construct ideas that grip the imagination without giving it anything to grasp in return. "Hitherto," he writes, "one has generally trusted one's concepts as if they were a wonderful dowry from some sort of wonderland; but they are, after all, the inheritance from our most remote, our most foolish as well as our most intelligent ancestors . . . What is needed above all is an absolute skepticism toward all inherited concepts" (*WP*, 409). The kind of skepticism he advocates, when practiced slowly, carefully, and for a long time, sometimes produces remarkable new ideas, concepts that may one day become part of a later age's inheritance from its most intelligent ancestors. But even his best readers, those who read him "*well,* that is to say . . . slowly, deeply, looking cautiously before and aft, with reservations, with doors open, with delicate eyes and fingers" (*D*, Pref., 3), may come to a complete stop when they are faced with what Nietzsche emphatically calls "*my* proposition" (*BGE*, 36): the will to power.

It is difficult to say what the appropriate reaction is to at least some of Nietzsche's statements of this "proposition." Indeed, it is difficult to say whether one should react at all, or pass over in silence, a passage like the following:

> The will to accumulate force is special to the phenomena of life, to nourishment, procreation, inheritance—to society, state, custom, authority. Should we not be permitted to assume this will as a motive cause in chemistry, too?—and in the cosmic order? Not merely conservation of energy, but maximal economy of use, so the only reality is the will to grow stronger of every center of force—not self-preservation, but the will to appropriate, dominate, increase, grow stronger. (*WP*, 689)

At best this seems like a barely plausible and quite horrible theory of behavior according to which ruthless individuals, or worse, races and even species constantly overpower equally ruthless but weaker opponents. At worst it appears a no less horrible but now wildly implausible picture of a voluntaristic universe in which everything, human and inhuman, animate and inanimate, organic and inorganic, is engaged in an unending struggle, trying to increase its power and to suppress everything else by any conceivable means.[1]

"All Being is for Nietzsche," Heidegger wrote, "a Becoming. Such Becoming, however, has the character of action and the activity of willing."[2] This view is actually traditional in German philosophy and can be traced back to Kant and Leibniz.[3] We can find an early expression of it in Nietzsche in his essay *Philosophy in the Tragic Age of the Greeks*, where he associates it with Heraclitus and Schopenhauer: "Everything which coexists in time and space has but a relative existence . . . Each thing exists through and for another one like it, which is to say through and for an equally relative one . . . The whole nature of reality lies wholly in its *acts* and . . . for it there is no other sort of being" (*PTG*, 5). At that time Nietzsche did not develop this idea. And though his middle works contain many passages on power, the feeling of power, and the place of both in the general economy of life, it is only in the late writings, particularly in his notes, that the will to power as such becomes absolutely central to his thought: "And do you know what 'the world' is to me? Shall I show it to you in my mirror? . . . *This world is the will to power—and nothing besides!* And you yourselves are also this will to power—and nothing besides!" (*WP*, 1067).

Nietzsche strains language by writing that things *are*, and not that they *have*, the will to power. But before we turn to this question, we must make clear that though the view sometimes seems to apply only to living things (*BGE*, 13; *WP*, 254, 681, 688), its scope is not always restricted. Nietzsche gives a characterization of things in general when, in discussing mechanism in physics, he writes, "A quantum of force is designated by the effect it produces and that which it resists" (*WP*, 634; cf. 552). His view is nothing short of the hypothesis that we may "have gained the right to determine *all* efficient causation univocally as—*will to power*" (*BGE*, 36).

The problem is that this hypothesis also strains the notion of the will, tied as it is to psychology, beyond sense and recognition. That has been enough for many of Nietzsche's readers to stop being his readers just at this, and just on this, point. Yet, and in very typical fashion, Nietzsche denies the legitimacy of the common psychological notion of the will altogether: "The will of psychology hitherto . . . does not exist at all" (*WP*, 692); "there is no such thing as will" (*TI*, VI, 3; *A*, 14; *WP*, 488, 671, 715). And if Nietzsche does not believe that the psychological notion of the will applies even to human behavior, then it may be that the will to power does not after all attribute, as it so paradoxically appears to do, consciousness and intention to the whole universe.

But why does Nietzsche deny that the will exists? "Willing," he writes, "seems to me above all something complicated, something that is a unit only as a word"; it includes, he continues, at least sensation, thought, and "command" or modality (*BGE*, 19). Elsewhere he also adds its aim or purpose, which is essentially dependent on evaluation (*WP*, 260). And he insists that all these elements are inextricably connected with one another: "Let us not imagine it possible to sever the thought from the 'willing,' as if any will would then remain over! " (*BGE*, 19); "one has eliminated the character of the will by subtracting from it its content, its 'whither' " (*WP*, 692). Nietzsche denies that there exists a distinct sort of mental acts consisting of the causes, accompaniments, or necessary conditions of other acts. He denies that any of these acts can be separated from their many features, and that they thus can be made to appear uniform and qualitatively identical to one another. There is therefore no need for a distinct faculty in which they all reside and which makes them possible: "There is no such thing as 'willing,' but only a willing *something*: one must not remove the aim from the total condition—as epistemologists do. 'Willing' as they understand it is as little a reality as 'thinking' is: it is pure fiction" (*WP*, 668; cf. *BGE*, 11).

Nietzsche often looks at psychological events in this way, and this attitude is central to his thought. He believes that behavior consists of long, complicated events with neither obvious beginnings nor clear ends (cf. *WP*, 672). The parts of these events are essentially connected with one another, and where one part ends and another begins is as undecidable an issue as the question of the nature of the whole event of which they are parts. All these events are immensely more complex than we can ever discover by purely psychological means. But because we so often rely on introspection for self-knowledge, we have come to believe that our behavior consists of the simple and discrete events that are the only aspects of our life available to consciousness. We take the surface of our behavior for its reality and essence:

> In regard to bodily motions and changes . . . one has long since abandoned the belief in the explanation by means of a consciousness that determines purposes. By far the greater number of motions have nothing to do with consciousness; nor with sensations. Sensations and thoughts are something extremely insignificant and rare in relation to the countless number of events that occur every moment . . . We are in the phase of the modesty of consciousness. (*WP*, 676; cf. *Z*, I, 4; *GS*, 354)

Only a few of these events, or better only small parts of each one of them, ever rise to consciousness. These are actually, Nietzsche believes, points along a single continuum which we cannot see in its totality. Instead, however, we assume that each of them is an object in its own right: a thought, a desire, a wish, a belief. We separate them from one another, subordinate some to others, consider some causes and others effects. We therefore think that each has a character of its own, independent of its interrelations with other such events as well as with the events of which we are not aware in the first place. Nietzsche claims that this is a special case of our overwhelming tendency to separate all subjects from their features and from one another. This is one of his most crucial views, and we shall have to return to it not only in this but in later chapters as well:

> We separate ourselves, the doers, from the deed, and we make use of this pattern everywhere—we seek a doer for every event. What is it

we have done? We have misunderstood the feeling of strength, tension, resistance, a muscular feeling that is already the beginning of the act, as the cause . . . A necessary sequence of states does not imply a causal relationship between them . . . If I think of the muscle apart from its "effects," I negate it . . . A "thing" is the sum of its effects. (*WP*, 551)

According to Nietzsche, we arrive at the idea of "the will of psychology hitherto" by projecting a small and insignificant part of a longer process into an event in its own right, possessing a causal character in itself. But Nietzsche thinks that there are no such events and no faculty that makes them possible. The parts of events do not possess a character in themselves any more than do the very events to which, from certain points of view, they may be said to belong. Both these parts and the events themselves are so closely interconnected with one another that they actually determine what each one is through their interconnections (cf. *WS*, 11). These interconnections, as we shall see, are in constant flux and are always in the process of being reinterpreted in the light of subsequent "events" to which earlier ones are seen to be connected. The nature and character, and indeed the number, of these events do not remain constant. Removing or altering even one element from the whole to which it has been construed to belong destroys both whole and part: it alters what needs to be explained and changes that which might provide the explanation. As with all wholes that depend on interpretive connections of this sort, no individual connection is accidental. This is why Nietzsche writes that we eliminate the character of the will once we subtract from it its content.

In denying that "there is such a thing as will," Nietzsche is trying to sever the connections of that idea to our ordinary notions of wanting and desiring. By considering those events which we have so far construed as acts of will to be simply parts of an ongoing, continuing activity to which they are essentially and not merely causally related, he wants to bring that activity itself to the fore. He wants to show that willing is, as Heidegger saw, not a desire but a complicated activity, not a causally privileged part of human behavior but that behavior itself considered provisionally, without regard for its outcome. Willing so construed is independent of intention, of the ability to entertain the idea of an aim distinct from the act that leads to it. It is therefore independent of its traditional association with living, and perhaps only conscious, organisms.

Willing as an activity does not have an aim that is distinct from it; if it can be said to aim at anything at all, that can only be its own continuation. Willing is an activity that tends to perpetuate itself, and this tendency to the perpetuation of activity, which, as we shall see, may sometimes result in the actual destruction of the subject that manifests it, is what Nietzsche tries to describe by the obscure and often misleading term "the will to power." This is the tendency to produce more and more effects upon the world; it is a tendency in connection with which there is no question of choice. It is the manifestation of what Nietzsche often calls a "drive" *(Trieb)* which is common to animate and inanimate objects, and to which the idea of freedom, so often associated with the will, is not naturally suited: "The drive to approach—and the drive to thrust something back are the bond, in both the organic and the inorganic world. The whole distinction is a prejudice" (*WP*, 655).

This is an aspect of Nietzsche's thought which, central though it is to so many of his views, remains unflinchingly obscure. It is not my purpose to offer a general explication but only to ask the following question about it: let us suppose that Nietzsche, along with a great part of the philosophical tradition to which he belongs, believes that the character of things is to engage in constant activity; what general picture of the world does this view presuppose, and is this picture yet another metaphysical theory aiming to reveal the ultimate nature of reality?

The drive that is manifested in the will to power, an activity which, even when it is directed at its own destruction, remains an activity and therefore perpetuates itself, is common to everything in the world: "The connection between the inorganic and the organic must be in the repelling force exercised by every atom of force" (*WP*, 642). But if the will to power involves such a force, then it necessarily requires resistance, something upon which it is to be exercised. And since this incessant activity characterizes everything, everything in the world is at least in principle connected to everything else: "Every atom affects the whole of being—it is thought away if one thinks away this radiation of power-will. This is why I call it a quantum of 'will to power': it expresses the characteristic that cannot be thought out of the mechanistic order without thinking away this order itself" (*WP*, 634). The will to power, then, depends on the fact that for Nietzsche all things in the world are interconnected and that their interconnections are crucial to their very character. But from these ideas a more radical conclusion seems to follow: "No things remain but only dynamic quanta, in a relation of tension to all other dynamic quanta: their essence lies in their relation to all other quanta, in their 'effect' upon the same" (*WP*, 635). The will to power is then an activity that affects and in fact constitutes the character of everything in the world and that is itself the result of such effects. Since these effects embody, establish, and carry forth the character of whatever effects them, Nietzsche characterizes them generally as "power." The will to power is an activity that consists in expanding a particular sphere of influence, physical or mental, as far as it can possibly go. As such, it ranges from the crudest to the most sophisticated, from mere physical resistance and brute subjugation to rational persuasion.

Nietzsche's continual stress on the interconnectedness of everything in the world constitutes his attack on the "thing-in-itself," by which he understands the concept of an object that is distinct from, more than, beyond, or behind the totality of its effects on every other thing. A thing, he insists, cannot be distinguished (except provisionally, as we shall see) from its various interrelations. Objects are conditioned by other objects through and through: " 'Things that have a constitution in themselves'—a dogmatic idea with which one must break absolutely" (*WP*, 559). Construed in this manner, the will to power is not a general metaphysical or cosmological theory. On the contrary, it provides a reason why no general theory of the character of the world and the things that constitute it can ever be given.

To speak of a thing-in-itself is to speak of a thing that can be conceived to exist independently of all other things and that is to that extent unconditioned. But this implies either that at least some of its features, through which it is to be conceived, apply to it quite independently of the existence of any other thing or that it can be conceived to exist without any features at all. Nietzsche cannot agree with either of these two alternatives, and this is why he claims that the notion of the thing-in-itself is unacceptable.

If we assume, as we should, that the idea of a thing without qualities is incoherent, this leaves us only with the first possibility. But Nietzsche does not believe that things can have properties on their own, properties that attach to them independently of the existence of other things, because he believes that properties are nothing but a thing's effects on other things, including ourselves as perceivers: "That things possess a constitution in themselves quite apart from interpretation and subjectivity, is a quite idle hypothesis; it presupposes that interpretation and subjectivity are not essential, that a thing freed from all relationships would still be a thing" (*WP*, 560). But if such interrelations are necessary, this alternative carries with it the radical implication that if any object has any features at all, then at least one other object, which conditions and is in turn conditioned by it, must exist as well: "The properties of a thing are effects on other 'things': if one removes other 'things,' then a thing has no properties, i.e., there is no thing without other things, i.e., there is no 'thing-in-itself' " (*WP*, 557). Even such logical features as unity and identity seem to depend on the existence of numerous things that can be unified with, and distinguished from, one another. But we cannot assume that these things have such relations with one another in themselves, independently of interpretation, for what there is is always determined from a specific point of view that embodies its particular interests, needs, and values, its own will to power. " 'Essence,' 'the essential nature,' is something perspectival and already presupposes a multiplicity. At the bottom of it there always lies 'what is it for *me*?' (for us, for all that lives, etc.)" (*WP*, 556). Since Nietzsche believes that this question can never have a single answer that holds good for everyone, we can begin to see why his view of the essential interconnectedness of everything is part of his effort to show that there is no ready-made world to which our views and theories can be true once and for all.

But it is one thing to say that the properties of a thing are its effects on other things and quite another to claim, as Nietzsche does, that a thing is nothing but the sum of these effects. Since it does not allow that an independent subject, of which these are the effects, exists, Nietzsche's radical view immediately generates a serious problem: how can we determine that some effects belong together and form a unity? How do we know that we are using the pronoun correctly when we say, "A thing is the sum of *its* effects"? And even before we can face this question, we must come to terms with Nietzsche's view that no event or object has a character in its own right, independently of its interrelations with everything else. How can there even be interrelations if there are not already things that are capable of having them?

Remarkably, this is the very question Ferdinand de Saussure tried to answer when he construed the linguistic sign as a "differential unit," and by means of which he revolutionized linguistics at the beginning of this century. "In a language," Saussure wrote, "there are only differences. Even more important, a difference generally implies positive terms between which the difference is set up; but in language there are only differences *without positive terms*."[4] Though linguistic signs generate a set of "positive values" through which language actually functions, Saussure claims that in themselves these signs have no linguistically relevant features. Nothing inherently suits the phoneme *b* for its role in the language apart from its systematic contribution to those compounds, like *bed, bang,* or *bat,* of which it is a proper part. But this is also to say that nothing inherently suits it for its role apart from its systematic differences from other equally arbitrary sounds, like *r,* which is in turn defined through its contribution to compounds like *red, rang,* or *rat*—that is, through its differences from all other phonemes. What matters is not the phoneme's intrinsic character but only its difference from other phonemes. The same principle, according to Saussure, applies to all linguistic signs without exception: "A linguistic system is a series of differences of sounds combined with a series of differences of ideas" (p. 120).

These views have become almost commonplace by now. But I want to suggest that twenty years before Saussure was to apply this intuition to language, Nietzsche had already taken the more radical step, from which Saussure explicitly refrained, and had looked at the whole world in its terms. Prefiguring one of the great intellectual events of the next century, Nietzsche in effect claimed that nothing in the world has any intrinsic features of its own and that each thing is constituted solely through its interrelations with, and differences from, everything else. We can say that Nietzsche looks at the world as if it were a vast collection of what can only, at least in retrospect, be construed as signs; and once again, it appears to be no accident that he likes to think of the world as a text. Of course there is an enormous contrast between Saussure's orderly structuralist approach to the system underlying everyday communication and Nietzsche's effort to dispel the notion that the world possesses an underlying structure that is subject to laws and regularities. But the point remains that the world for Nietzsche, like language for Saussure, is a whole without which no part can exist, and not a conglomerate of independent units: "The 'thing-in-itself' is nonsensical. If I remove all the relationships, all the 'properties,' all the 'activities' of a thing, the thing does not remain over" (*WP,* 558). Conversely, every unit, conceived now as a position within that whole, is absolutely essential to it and cannot be removed or affected without altering the whole to which it belongs: "In the actual world, in which everything is bound to and conditioned by everything else, to condemn and to think away anything means to condemn and to think away everything" (*WP*, 584).[5]

This parallel may place Nietzsche's view in a more reasonable context, but it does not by itself account for our being able to use the phrase "a thing is the sum of its effects." In Chapter 6 we shall see that in the case of the human subject the answer to this question is provided by our occasional ability to take certain activities to be coherently connected with one another, to have compatible purposes—that, at least anthropocentrically, we can interpret them by appealing to their common ends and functions. The human body is simply the unification of these low-level activities. The body in turn gives us an elementary unity upon which we can base more complicated organizations of activities, sometimes even activities that are in conflict with one another. In more general terms Nietzsche writes, "A multiplicity of forces, connected by a common mode of nutrition, we call 'life' " (*WP*, 641). An object, according to this view, is just the unity or organization of certain activities which, when interpreted from some particular point of view, can be taken to be directed toward a coherent end. The identity of each object consists in its differences from all other similar organizations.

Nietzsche's view, we should note, is not skeptical. It does not deny the reality of things any more than Saussure's approach denies the reality of linguistic signs. Both Nietzsche and Saussure offer a radical reinterpretation of the nature of the objects with which they are concerned; they deny that any object can possess the features that make it what it is in isolation from other objects. Nietzsche, in addition, and in contrast to Saussure, grants a crucially active role to people and to our interests: different conditions, different ends and values can result in different groupings and so, literally, in different things.

Nietzsche therefore allows for a serious fluidity in our interpretations of the world and so also for a serious fluidity in what there is. His view implies that ontological categories are subject to change, and this in turn suggests that there are no such things as ontological categories. But this is not to doubt that the world exists. It is only to doubt that the existence of the world requires the existence of a description that is true of it from every possible point of view, a description that would depict it in itself, as it really is. Nietzsche's view is simply an attack on all such realist conceptions, which, as he writes, "always demand that we should think of an eye that is completely unthinkable, an eye that is turned in no particular direction, in which the active and interpretive forces, through which alone seeing becomes seeing *something*, are supposed to be lacking; these always demand from the eye an absurdity and nonsense" (*GM*, III, 12).

We have seen that this view does not imply that all perspectives are equally good. The first essay of *On the Genealogy of Morals*, for example, argues that, despite their radical differences, the opposite points of view involved in the noble and slave modes of valuation are different reactions to the very same facts, different interpretations of the very same text, and that one of them is definitely preferable to the other (*GM*, I, 11). Nietzsche, as I have argued in the preceding chapter, is not an enemy of objectivity, though what he takes as objectivity is "not . . . 'contemplation without interest' (which is a nonsensical absurdity), but . . . the ability to *control* one's Pro and Con and to dispose of them so that one knows how to employ a *variety* of perspectives and affective interpretations in the service of knowledge" (*GM*, III, 12). Objectivity so construed is precisely the feature that distinguishes the free spirits of *Beyond Good and Evil*. Attempts to show that objectivity is more than this sort of detachment are for Nietzsche self-deceptive efforts to conceal the partial and interested nature of one's position from oneself.

But if Nietzsche's view is not skeptical, what are we to make of his notorious insistence that the concept of the object is a "fiction"? Doesn't this show that in some way the world as we think of it is for him not real? In order to begin answering this complicated question, we must consider in some detail the following passage:

> Suppose all unity were unity only as organization? But the "thing" in which we believe was only invented as a foundation for the various attributes. If the thing "effects," that means: we conceive all the other properties which are present and momentarily latent as the cause of the emergence of one single property; i.e., we take the sum of its properties—"x"—as cause of the property "x"—which is utterly stupid and mad! (*WP*, 561)[6]

If unity is simply the organization of features, Nietzsche argues, it is superfluous to posit the object, which is simply that organization itself, as its cause and ground. An object is not for him an enduring substance that underlies its features. It is simply a complex of events with which other events may be compatible or harmonious, which still others may harm, and which yet further ones may assist or enhance. The object is generated by an interpretive hypothesis that links certain events to one another and distinguishes them from other groups. The object emerges through such events; it is in a serious sense their product and not their ground.

But Nietzsche does not think that the hypothesis that there are objects that endure over and above their features is simply superfluous. He also considers it, in much stronger terms, incoherent, misleading, and harmful. He supports his view by two central considerations. His first reason is, characteristically, psychological. He believes that we begin from the unjustified conviction that the soul is a substance in its own right and that we project "this faith in the ego-substance upon all things" (*TI*, III, 5).[7] This is one of his most famous views: "The concept of substance is a consequence of the notion of the subject: not the reverse! If we relinquish the soul, 'the subject,' the precondition for 'substance' in general disappears" (*WP*, 485). Famous as this view is, however, I still find it deeply unsatisfactory. First, Nietzsche correctly believes that consciousness has a social origin and a social function: it is inherently connected with the need to communicate with others (*GS*, 354). He should therefore also hold that at the very least the concepts of ego and object, subject and substance, develop in parallel to one another.[8] Second, at one point he writes that our naive belief in the body as an entity in its own right lies at the origin of our separation between doer and deed, thing and property. And he claims that we eventually reach the idea of the soul as the immaterial subject behind all possible deeds by constantly refining that separation: "Psychological history of the concept 'subject.' The body, the thing, the 'whole' constructed by the eye, awaken the distinction between a deed and a doer; the doer, the cause of the deed, conceived even more subtly, finally left behind the 'subject'" (*WP*, 547). In this context the body seems to be an external, public object, a part of the social world. The order of dependence on which Nietzsche so often insists is here reversed, and the enduring object precedes the substantial subject. Third, and perhaps more important, it is central to Nietzsche's late writings that the idea that the human subject is something over and above the totality of its deeds is a specific invention: it was designed in order to convince people that, whatever their deeds have been, they could have acted quite differently and that they are therefore totally responsible for them and subject to punishment on their account (*GM*, I, 13; II, 21–22). The postulation of the substantial subject, to which no particular action is essential, according to Nietzsche, created the space that made possible the insertion of the fiction of freedom of choice. But Nietzsche also believes that this invention is the accomplishment of the slave revolt in morality and of Christian metaphysics, which, just in this context and just for this reason, he calls "the metaphysics of the hangman" (*TI*, VI, 7). Yet, on his own version of the history of philosophy, the hypothesis of enduring objects was already well established by the Greek philosophers long before Christianity ever emerged (*WP*, 539; *PTG*, 11).

Nietzsche also gives a second reason for our "faith" in enduring objects. In a manner that anticipates a central tenet of twentieth-century analytical philosophy, he argues that our metaphysical views are products of the grammatical structure of our language, which forces us to speak as we have been doing all along in this discussion, not only of effects but also, necessarily, of things that effect, of subjects of properties as well as of those properties themselves. He writes that we are dominated by "our grammatical custom that adds a doer to every deed" (*WP*, 484). And indeed, since from a grammatical point of view subject and predicate are correlative notions, there has to be a doer as soon as there is a deed or doing (*Thun*). But by itself this linguistic feature does not dictate any specific philosophical view: it could also be interpreted, for example, as a way of saying that a particular event is part of a broader set of events, that it is involved in a process of mutual interaction, of "interpenetration" (*WP*, 631), with them. Yet, Nietzsche argues, here as elsewhere we forget the existence of interpretation and try to read the structure of the world directly from the features of our language. Thus he writes that we have "faith in grammar," faith that "the metaphysics of language" mirrors without distortion the nature of the world (*TI*, VI, 5). And he claims that the inference from the grammatical distinction between subject and predicate to the ontological separation between doer and deed, substance and attribute, is illegitimate and must not be made.

According to section 561 of *The Will to Power*, objects are generated in the following way. In our effort to find an independent entity in which a particular feature with which we happen to be concerned might inhere, we take for granted all the other features with which (on our own interpretation) it belongs and which are not at issue at that time. We then identify these features, though they are only a subset of the total collection, with the very object that provides the ground for the existence of the feature in which we are interested. But these latent features, Nietzsche believes, have no more of a claim to being that object than has the particular feature that is in question—that is, none at all. Both are simply parts of the same collection, and though one is much larger than the other, this does not give it a privileged position in the constitution of the object.

So far this is simply the claim that we have mistaken a part for the whole. But the most intriguing part of Nietzsche's discussion comes at the very end of this note, when he writes that when we generate an object by identifying it with only some of its features, "we take the sum of its properties—'x'—as cause of the property 'x'—which is utterly stupid and mad!" Nietzsche makes this extravagant charge because he seems to believe that when we appeal to some of an object's features in order to account for others, we actually take the totality of these features twice, first as its own ground and then as its own effect. This is a view to which Nietzsche is deeply committed and for presenting which he often appeals to the image of lightning: "The popular mind in fact doubles the deed; when it sees the lightning flash, it is the deed of a deed: it posits the same thing first as cause and then a second time as its effect" (*GM*, I, 13; cf. *WP*, 531). And since he also thinks that "the *causa sui* is the best contradiction that has been conceived so far; it is a sort of rape and perversion of logic" (*BGE*, 21), we are brought back immediately to his charge that the concept of the object is sheer madness.

But why does Nietzsche think that the concept of the object constitutes this sort of madness? Why should he hold that when we try to account for *some* feature by appealing to the *other* features with which it is associated we are in fact trying to account twice for the very same thing? Why does he think that this reference to two obviously distinct sets of features is merely apparent and succeeds in picking out only one thing?

Nietzsche's charge is motivated by the view, which I have already begun discussing and which we must now face squarely, that all the effects of what we construe as a single thing are essentially interconnected and derive their character from their interconnections. What something is or does is not independent of anything else that it does or is. And whatever a thing is or does is itself not given: it is constantly in motion, being changed, revised, reconstrued, and reinterpreted in the light of new events, which are in their own turn fluid and indeterminate (*WP*, 672). The character and nature of every event is inseparable from the character and nature of every other occurrence with which it is associated. This relationship is holistic and hermeneutical. Nietzsche expresses a similar view in regard to judgments in a note of almost Hegelian character: "There are no isolated judgments! An isolated judgment is never 'true,' never knowledge; only in the connection and relation of many judgments is there any surety" (*WP*, 530).

Nietzsche's view must therefore be that when we single out a particular effect and attribute to it a particular character, a particular relation to other effects, we in fact implicitly attribute a character to the whole set of which we construe it as a part. Effects are related to one another just as things, their collections, are: each one is what it is through its relations to the others, and these in turn derive their character, their very nature, in the same manner. A feature and the whole to which it belongs are not conceptually independent from one another as causes, in particular, are said to be independent of their effects. For Nietzsche, the whole is somehow to be found implicitly in every one of its features. This is Zarathustra's point when he exhorts his disciples to see to it "that your self be in your deed as the mother is in her child" (Z, II, 5). When therefore we separate the object from its property, we in effect claim that the whole set of features, which is implicit in the one feature we have singled out and without which that feature would not have been the feature it is, is distinct from and responsible for the feature in which it is implicit and without which it would have been an altogether different whole. In both cases we succeed only in referring to the single whole which both sets of features, though apparently distinct, essentially constitute.

This account may explicate the ending of the note under discussion. But this explication only raises the further question of why Nietzsche thinks that wholes and parts are so indissolubly connected with one another. Earlier we saw that a linguistic parallel may motivate Nietzsche's view, and I have said that the relationship between whole and part is hermeneutical. These considerations may suggest that a literary model can again shed some light on Nietzsche's approach.

Consider, then, the true and noncontroversial point that a literary character is nothing over and above the totality of its features and actions, just as it is nothing less: absolutely everything characters do makes them what they are. Provided that, for the moment, we concentrate on individual texts, we can say that characters who are inconsistently depicted are not really single characters at all. They are artificial unities held together by a single name, a "mere word" (cf. *WP*, 482). And it is also true, though perhaps slightly more controversial, that when we specify a character's action on a particular occasion, we implicitly commit ourselves to a general interpretation of that character as a whole. In fact it seems that the preposition *of* in the expression "the action of a character" is problematic in just the way that the view of the world presupposed by the will to power finds the relation between substance and attribute, thing and effect, to be problematic.

We can make this clear by means of a very elementary example. We cannot possibly suppose that in reading *Moby-Dick* we can understand what Ahab means when he yells, "I would strike the sun if it insulted me," without having already made at least a tentative commitment as to who Ahab is—without, that is, a tentative interpretation of many other statements by and about Ahab in this novel. A moody, solitary cripple can be transformed into the novel's "crazy Ahab" through such a statement, and his other actions now appear in a new light; they turn out to be literally different actions. But is Ahab crazy because he seeks revenge for an action performed by a senseless, irresponsible beast? Or is he crazier still, and so perhaps more human, because he refuses to submit to a power greater than he can master? Is he suffering from the loss of his leg, the loss of his pride, or from the limits to his strength? Each one of these elementary questions conditions our interpretation of the original statement and is in turn conditioned by it; an answer to any one of them commits us to answers to the other questions as well. Ahab emerges through such answers.

Ahab is related to his statement not as a substance is related to its attribute but as a whole is related to its parts; moreover, this relation is interpretive and not causal. Causal accounts of characters are offered precisely when there is no good reason, no good interpretation of a character's actions in terms of the text of which it is a part or which, more accurately, it at least in part constitutes: the relation between a text and its own parts is the same as that between each character and its own elements. Peter Benchley's *Jaws*, for example, is a work that bears remarkable similarities to *Moby-Dick*, narrating as it does the relentless and, in this case, successful pursuit of a killer shark by a marine biologist and the police chief of the coastal town the shark has been terrorizing. In the course of the novel, the biologist has an affair with the policeman's wife, for which we can account only in either of two ways. We can appeal, on the one hand, to the conventions to which novels intended to be read by a very broad public have been subject in the last few years, and which generally dictate that such works contain scenes of what is often described as sexual explicitness. On the other hand, we can claim that the affair occurs precisely so that the tension beween the two men will be greater as they hunt for the shark and save each other's lives in the process. In either case we have abdicated from interpretation. Our account betrays the *absence* of character; it reveals the artless juxtaposition of chance events for a purpose that cannot be justified by the text they are made to constitute, and which iself turns out to be an artificial unity held together by a "mere word"—in this case a title. In a successful interpretive whole, there are no chance events that can be transposed or removed while others remain intact. Coherent characters cannot be related to one another in different ways without themselves changing in the process. Every "object," every part, constitutes all the others and the whole to which they belong.[9]

When we focus on Ahab's statement about the sun, we must not suppose (though we often implicitly do) that Ahab consists of all the other statements pertaining to him in the novel. Nor must we think that Ahab consists of a privileged set of statements, perhaps specifying his essential properties: literary characters have no essential, and therefore no accidental, properties.[10] As is often the case, some of Nietzsche's most startling ideas become intuitively plausible when transposed to literature. To separate Ahab from his cry, the doer from his deed, inevitable as it is in practice, is truly provisional and arbitrary, "mere semeiotics and nothing real" (*WP*, 634). As we continue reading, the cry becomes part of Ahab, and his eventual challenge to Starbuck—"There is one God that is Lord over the earth, and one captain that is lord over the Pequod"—now becomes the specific deed to be interpreted. Its interpretation may cast Ahab's earlier statement in a new light, and this in turn may eventually affect our reading of his present claim in a process that can have no end.

Nietzsche's model for the world, for objects, and for people turns out to be the literary text and its components; his model for our relation to the world turns out to be interpretation. It is a model we can find explicitly in his writing: "Around the hero everything turns into a tragedy; around the demi-god, into a satyr-play; and around God— what? perhaps into 'world'?" (*BGE*, 150). Nietzsche's model is startling and paradoxical. And it is nowhere more so than in his writing of "the world as a work of art that gives birth to itself" (*WP*, 796; cf. 1066). Like an artwork, the world requires reading and interpretation, "good philology," in order to be mastered, understood, and made livable. The "death of God," both as hero and as author, allows Nietzsche to deny that the world is subject to a single overarching interpretation, corresponding to God's role or intention. And its self-creation introduces the most paradoxical idea yet, the fact that the readers of this text are some of its own parts, some of its own characters, who in reading it further its self-creation.

This paradox, I think, does not by itself mar Nietzsche's view any more than the idea that some of a machine's parts are on their own capable of understanding and even of improving that machine by itself mars mechanism. But the paradox involved in Nietzsche's thinking goes to the heart of his attitude and reaches as far back as *The Birth of Tragedy*, where we find it clearly expressed, though in terms he was later, mercifully, to repudiate: "Only insofar as the genius in the act of artistic creation coalesces with the primordial artist of the world does he know anything of the eternal essence of art; for in this state he is, in a marvelous manner, like the weird image of the fairy tale which can turn its eyes at will and behold itself; he is at once subject and object, at once poet, actor, and spectator" (*BT*, 5). The second part of this book discusses Nietzsche's effort to apply this paradoxical idea to his own writing.

As in the literary case, so in the world, according to Nietzsche, to reinterpret events is to rearrange effects and therefore to generate new things. Our "text" is being composed as we read it, and our readings are new parts of it that will give rise to further ones in the future. Even the reinterpretation of existing formulas adds to the world, especially since Nietzsche often thinks of interpretation as "the introduction of meaning—not 'explanation' (in most cases a new interpretation over an old interpretation that has become incomprehensible, that is now itself only a sign)" (*WP*, 604). To introduce new interpretations, therefore, it is necessary to reinterpret old ones. Our text, even though it will someday come to an end, is still and forever incomplete. The mutual adjustment of elements cannot therefore ever be final: "The number of becoming elements is not constant" (*WP*, 617; cf. 520). It is only in this context that we can understand Zarathustra's call, which applies equally to the very children it concerns, "In your children you shall make up for being the children of your fathers; thus you shall redeem all that is past" (*Z*, III, 12; cf. II, 14).

A thing is therefore for Nietzsche not a subject that has effects but simply a collection of interrelated effects, selected from some particular point of view from within a much larger similar set. It is, as he sometimes puts it, a locus of the will to power, a focus of activity within a broader realm, established through the very same activity on the part of some interpreter. It cannot remain unchanged as its effects multiply and enter into new interrelations or as other sets of effects undergo such changes. As with literary objects, every new or reinterpreted incident affects the whole of which it is an immediate part as well as, less directly, everything else.

Nietzsche sometimes writes that healthy life "aims at the expansion of power and ... frequently risks and even sacrifices self-preservation" (*GS*, 349; cf. *BGE*, 13; *WP*, 650, 688). This, I think, must be understood in two ways. First, Nietzsche thinks that increase in what he describes as power does not necessarily lead to increase in strength; on the contrary, it often makes one more susceptible to harm and injury. Power, at its basis, is the proliferation of effects that can be associated with a particular thing, and in the process of this proliferation the "thing" can easily fall apart. Second, Nietzsche also believes that the more one's effects spread, the more one necessarily changes, and the less one remains recognizably who one already was.

Every achievement is then in two ways a destruction. First, it is a destruction of what is replaced by what is newly created: "If a temple is to be erected, a temple must first be destroyed" (*GM*, II, 24; cf. *D*, 9). Second, through a curious and disturbing reversal, it is also the destruction of those whose achievement it is and whom it obliterates even as it creates and constitutes, those whom Zarathustra "loves" because they "do not want to preserve themselves" (*Z*, III, 12).

But we now come face to face with a central problem involved in every presentation of Nietzsche's view of the will to power. The view asserts that things are nothing but their effects, that there are no objects or substances; yet it is stated in language that seems to depend on there being just such entities in the world for its own possibility. As Arthur Danto has written, the will to power "is a difficult view to render wholly intelligible . . . because the terms for intelligibility for us are precisely those the theory cannot fit. To explain the theory in our language is to tolerate a fiction which one wishes to overthrow."[11]

Once again, Danto's position is not unrelated to the view of Jacques Derrida. Like Danto, Derrida notices this paradox. Unlike Danto, however, he does not think that this is a problem that should ideally be overcome. On the contrary, Derrida has made the paradox of the necessity of relying on the very object of one's criticism in order to criticize it absolutely central to his own writing: "There is no sense in doing without the concepts of metaphysics in order to shake metaphysics. We have no language—no syntax and no lexicon—which is foreign to this history; we can pronounce not a single destructive proposition which has not already had to slip into the form, the logic, and the implicit postulations of precisely what it seeks to contest."[12] Derrida's view is itself influenced by Nietzsche's own attack on language as a misleading but ineliminable guide to the structure of the world: "The separation of the 'deed' from the doer . . . this ancient mythology established the belief in cause and effect after it had found a firm form in the functions of language and grammar" (*WP*, 631; cf. *TI*, III, 5).

It would be naive to suppose that we could avoid the paradox generated by the will to power by trying to develop a new language in which this view could be stated in a straightforward way and to which the will to power would be related as the metaphysics of substance and property is related to the language of subject and predicate. Part of the will to power is precisely the view that there is no general structure of the world to which any linguistic system can ever be accurate. Even when Nietzsche suggests that non–Indo-European languages embody different metaphysical views from those to which we have become accustomed, he does not suppose that the speakers of these languages have a better grip on reality (*BGE*, 20). "The demand for an adequate mode of expression," he insists, "is senseless" (*WP*, 625). Zarathustra is not thinking of such change when he says, "New ways I go, a new speech comes to me; weary I grow, like all creators, of the old tongues. My spirit no longer wants to walk on worn soles" (*Z*, II, 1). Linguistic reform is not part of the revaluation of all values.

Nietzsche believes that, however faulty and misleading, our language is inevitably ours: "We cease to think when we refuse to do so under the constraints of language . . . Rational thought is interpretation according to a scheme that we cannot throw off" (*WP*, 522). The will to power may thus appear to lead to a perfect instance of the impasse generated by all efforts to produce a general criticism of language and thought. Since all such attempts necessarily employ the same linguistic modes and metaphysical assumptions they aim to expose, they necessarily perpetuate the very tradition they attack simply by virtue of attacking it. If this is so, the will to power will always remain a paradox. We can neither incorporate it into the scheme it denies nor can we use it to refute that scheme, since it is itself expressed in its terms. On this approach, the will to power offers not a refutation but, to use Derrida's term, a deconstruction of the notions of subject and predicate, substance and attribute, agent and action. The contrast between such pairs of concepts, Derrida writes,

> is never the face-to-face of two terms, but a hierarchy and an order of subordination. Deconstruction cannot limit itself or proceed immediately to a neutralization: it must, by means of a double gesture, a double science, a double writing, practice an *overturning* of the classical opposition [cf. Nietzsche's "the doer is merely a fiction added to the deed" (*GM*, I, 13)] *and* a general *displacement* of the system [cf. Nietzsche's "both the deed and the doer are fictions" (*WP*, 477)].[13]

On this reading, Nietzsche must use metaphysically tainted language in order to show that it is impossible not to use metaphysically tainted language. He does not criticize this language directly, since we cannot do without it, and he does not offer alternatives to it, since there are none. He simply lays its vulnerabilities bare.

A related but more optimistic view is that of Michel Haar, who believes that Nietzsche has succeeded in developing a scheme that is free of all metaphysical commitments of its own. According to Haar, Nietzsche's "*own* vocabulary (Will to Power, Nihilism, Overman, Eternal Return) eludes conceptual logic. Whereas a concept, in the classical sense, comprises and contains, in an identical and total manner, the content that it assumes, most of Nietzsche's key words . . . bring forth a plurality of meanings undermining any logic based on the principle of identity."[14] Like Derrida, Haar believes that logic makes by itself certain metaphysical assumptions and imposes a particular picture of the world upon all those who use it. Unlike Derrida, he also believes that we can somehow do without this logic, though he does not make it clear whether Nietzsche's vocabulary is free of logic altogether or simply free of the logic that is "based on the principle of identity." But though Nietzsche definitely denies that logic or language reflects adequately the structure of the world ("the world appears logical to us because we have made it logical," *WP,* 521), he also writes emphatically that we cannot possibly do without either language or logic. It is therefore very unlikely that he would think that the tradition could be undermined by means of a vocabulary that escaped the assumptions and categories incorporated in "classical" logic.[15]

Nietzsche does think that something can and must be undermined, but this is neither logic nor language as such. Rather, it is an assumption that is shared by Danto as well as by Derrida and Haar and a large number of other philosophers: the view that logic (or language, or mathematics, or physics, or any other particular endeavor) makes by itself such metaphysical commitments and claims to reflect on its own the world as it really is. There is no general agreement about the question whether these commitments are right or wrong; but many writers, including those I am now discussing, share the prior belief that some such assumptions are built into logic or language in the first place. Yet Nietzsche denies that we can ever read the structure of the world from the structure of the means we have developed in order to make it livable by beings like us: "One should not understand the compulsion to construct concepts, species, forms, purposes, laws ('a world of identical cases') as if they enabled us to fix the *real world*; but as a compulsion to arrange a world for ourselves in which our existence is made possible" (*WP,* 521). This is just the assumption which Nelson Goodman has more recently also denied: "Philosophers sometimes mistake features of discourse for features of the subject of discourse. We seldom conclude that the world consists of words just because a true description of it does, but we sometimes suppose that the structure of the world is the same as the structure of the description."[16]

The world we construct, Nietzsche repeatedly insists, is absolutely necessary, and we could not live without it; for us it is as real as can be. We are not in error to live in it, to think and talk about it as we do, and to continue to do so. Our error is to believe that the ways in which we think and talk about it make by themselves any commitment about the real nature of the world, the world that is the common object of all the different perspectives on it. Our error consists in believing that our logic, language, mathematics, or any other practice is metaphysically loaded in the first place, that any such practice can be our guide to the nature of reality. Nietzsche certainly writes, "I am afraid that we are not rid of God because we still have faith in grammar" (*TI*, III, 5). But what he considers necessary for belief in God, who here represents the ultimate substance, is not only grammar but also *faith* in it. And this faith is just the assumption, common to friends and foes of metaphysics alike, that language makes, of its own nature, ontological claims upon its users. This, I think, is precisely the assumption that Nietzsche rejects.

If this is Nietzsche's view, then we may give the paradox involved in the will to power a different interpretation. The will to power constitutes a challenge to the concepts of substance and attribute. Since these concepts, according to Nietzsche, depend on our taking our grammar too seriously, the will to power also constitutes a challenge to our common means of expression. But Nietzsche does not claim that our language is wrong, that instead of the world as we have come to know it we are really faced, paradoxically, as Danto writes, with "a world of effects, but not of effects of anything" (pp. 219-220). He claims not that our language is wrong but that we are wrong in taking it too seriously. He attacks the antithesis between agent and effect which Danto's statement seems to presuppose. He argues that even if the grammatical categories of subject and predicate are categories that are essential to us, this does not imply that the ontological categories of substance and attribute, or any others, are correct. Logic and language are neutral. Nietzsche tries to *reinterpret* them in order to bring this point out, and he tries to accomplish this goal by offering a reinterpretation of these categories themselves, by trying to show that neither substances nor attributes, neither agents nor effects, are as we commonly take them to be.

But the picture of the world presupposed by the will to power, even when it is expressed in terms as positive as those of the statement "A thing is the sum of its effects," is not an alternative to the metaphysics of substance and accident. Nietzsche wants to show that our linguistic categories are compatible with different versions of the ontological structure of the world. That is, he wants to show that the world has no ontological structure. As we shall see by means of an analogy, the world of the will to power is "in itself" radically indeterminate: it can be described in a large number of ways, none of which need, or indeed can, make a claim to constituting its ultimate correct representation. Each way of dealing with the world manifests the will to power of those who engage in it as at the same time it arranges this indeterminate world into a definite object. Nietzsche's task is to reinterpret both our language and our world in order to show that just as language makes no commitments regarding the world, so the world imposes no constraints upon language.

Many of Nietzsche's readers may find that the reinterpretation of existing structures constitutes a very weak reading of the task of the will to power. But in Nietzsche's own view, reinterpretation is the most powerful theoretical and practical instrument. It is the literal analogue of "the hammer" with which he proposes to do philosophy in the Preface to *The Twilight of the Idols*: part tuning fork to sound out hollow idols, part instrument of their destruction, and part sculptor's mallet to fashion new statues out of the forms as well as the materials of the old.

Religion is for Nietzsche one of the greatest if also one of the most objectionable manifestations of the will to power. His discussion of how new religions are established shows how crucially important he takes reinterpretation to be:

> The distinctive invention of the founders of religions is, first: to posit a particular kind of life and everyday customs that have the effect of a *disciplina voluntatis* and at the same time abolish boredom—and then: to bestow on this life style an *interpretation* that makes it appear to be illuminated by the highest value so that this life style becomes something for which one fights and under certain circumstances sacrifices one's life. *Actually, the second of these inventions is more essential.* The first, the way of life, was there before, but alongside other ways of life and without any sense of its special value. The significance and originality of the founders of religions usually consists in their *seeing* it, *selecting* it, and guessing for the first time to what use it can be put, how it can be interpreted. (*GS*, 353)[17]

The will to power manifests itself in offering reinterpretations (cf. *GM*, II, 12). The lives of the ascetic, the poor, and the downtrodden existed before Christianity appropriated them and reinterpreted them from calamities to be avoided into ideals to be pursued. But these lives did not exist as bare facts. The life of the poor already had a definite place and significance in the system of values Nietzsche calls "the noble mode of valuation" (*GM*, I, 10); Christianity gave it a position of importance it had never had before. The ascetic life, construed as the renunciation of some satisfactions in order to better secure others, was already common and invested with authority (*GM*, II, 7–9); philosophy, Nietzsche argues, could not have existed without it (*GM*, III, 11). Similarly, the institution of punishment was continually given new forms and purposes by means of the constant imposition of new interpretations of why people should be punished upon older ones (*GM*, II, 12–13). And even if at times an "old interpretation . . . has . . . become incomprehensible and . . . is now itself only a sign" (*WP*, 604), its elements will often limit the range of possible new interpretations. The principle previously quoted—"If a temple is to be erected, a temple must first be destroyed" (*GM*, II, 24)—suggests that, as is almost universally the case, the form and matter of the destroyed temple will be used for, and will therefore partly determine, the nature of the structure that replaces it.

Reinterpretation is therefore anything but a compromise. Since the institutions that guide our lives are the products of older interpretations, associated with different conditions and embodying other values, reinterpretation is the greatest means for change, for establishing new conditions and creating new values. And if this seems too writerly, too literary, too scholarly for the Nietzsche whom many have learned mindlessly to admire or ignorantly to abhor, so much the better. This most literary of philosophers would be the first to insist that the difference between fighting and writing is at most a difference of degree or, to use one of his own favorite terms, of refinement. The last things ever to be understood, he writes, are "the greatest events and thoughts—but," he continues, "the greatest events are the greatest thoughts" (*BGE*, 285).

All this suggests that, though the will to power urges a reinterpretation of the distinction between the doer and the deed, the surface of our language need in no way change as a result of such revision. "Interpretation reveals its complexity," Gilles Deleuze has written, "when we realize that a new force can only appear and appropriate an object by first of all putting on the mask of the forces which are already in possession of the object . . . A force would not survive if it did not first of all borrow the features of the forces with which it struggles."[18] The claim that our language does not mirror the world does not involve introducing a new language that does; what we need to do in order to see that it does not is to reinterpret the existing structures. In this way philosophy, according to Nietzsche, has always used the ascetic life "as a precondition of its existence" (*GM,* III, 10). "The paths of power," he writes, include the ability "to introduce a new virtue under the name of an old one" (*WP,* 310). This is exactly the accomplishment of "the slave revolt in morality," which came to use the word *good* just for what had previously been considered contemptible, base, and bad (*GM,* I, 10). The single word *punishment* has been so often reinterpreted that even a partial list of the many practices and purposes to which it has been applied occupies a whole section of the *Genealogy* (II, 13).

We cannot therefore stop talking of objects that remain the same through change and that persist in remaining distinct from their effects. But this way of talking, Nietzsche believes, does not reflect the world's underlying reality. From a synchronic point of view, as we have seen, an object is given by an interpretive hypothesis that best allows us, given our particular ends, needs, and values, to group certain phenomena together. Such groupings are often themselves reinterpretations of earlier groupings and enable us to live as best we can. They constitute different phenomena as effects of a particular object or agent, and the object emerges through them: "One should take the doer back into the deed after having conceptually removed the doer and thus emptied the deed . . . one should take doing *something,* the 'aim,' the 'intention,' the 'purpose,' back into the deed after having artificially removed all this and thus emptied the deed" (*WP,* 675).

But how does such reinterpretation apply to things through time, to the concept of the object diachronically? We need to know how we can classify a new phenomenon as the effect of a particular object, how we can establish a relation between this phenomenon and a set of effects earlier grouped together so that we can see the new event as a stage in the ongoing history of that object. In particular, we want to know how, since for Nietzsche everything is in constant change, it is possible to speak of objects diachronically at all.

There can be no antecedent ground of the unity or identity of an object through time any more than there is such ground in the case of an object at a particular time. Over time an object is constituted by the best history of a group of phenomena, a history embodied in the best narrative of the relations among them. Such narratives reveal that different phenomena have served the same purpose or that different purposes have succeeded one another in ways that allow them to be parts of a single history and therefore parts of a single object through time. The crucial point is that for Nietzsche there is no single best narrative and therefore no single best grouping. What is best is always determined in light of different background assumptions, interests, and values; and none of these can make an exclusive claim to being perfectly and objectively valid—valid for all. The will to power is not a "metaphysical" view because, through its emphasis on the indeterminacy of the world and the multiplicity of values, it insists that many views of the world are viable. With the possible exception of those views that refuse to acknowledge this indeterminacy and multiplicity, the will to power does not reject any view of the world on general grounds. Even in the case of such dogmatic approaches, it does not reject automatically the view itself but only its claim to being the only view that can possibly be accepted. Otherwise, a view of the world is rejected only if there is a specific alternative that appears, for particular reasons, to be preferable to it.

Can this very abstract frame be filled out? How are the many narratives of the one world that Nietzsche envisages constructed? In order to answer this question we must proceed by means of an analogy. Consider, then, the case of families. How are families established? What constitutes membership in a particular family? The most obvious condition, and the least that seems necessary, is that one be a descendant of someone who already belongs to that family. And before we turn to the complications that adoption, marriage, and disowning introduce, we must remark that even in the simplest cases the boundaries of families are far from clear: there isn't always a definite answer to the question whether two temporally distant individuals do or do not belong to the same family, even if one can trace a connection of some sort between them. In many cases this answer will depend on the purpose with which the question is asked and on what is at stake. Each individual, in addition, belongs immediately to two families, one on each parent's side, and each of these families in turn branches off into two directions one stage further back, and so on for every ancestor. Even on a biological or, as Nietzsche would have put it himself, a "physiological" level, family connections are immensely more complex than our usual representations of family trees can ever suggest.

When we appeal to family trees, we are concerned to trace, for particular reasons, an individual's origin to a particular source through a particular path and to establish a very specific connection between them. But a moment's thought shows how crucial our "particular reasons" always are in such situations. On one occasion, for example, we may want to exhibit the multiple relationships of Europe's contemporary royalty to Queen Victoria: we therefore leave out the ancestors who lead to different, "unrelated" origins. On another (and here, ironically enough, literature provides a misleading example) we may want to see how all the central characters of *The Forsyte Chronicles* are related to Old Jolyon, the figure Galsworthy quite arbitrarily chose as the family's founder—that is, as the source of its wealth—a choice that reveals a further underlying assumption and value. Galsworthy's neat diagram, which appears in many editions of his novels, makes it easy to forget that Irene has in principle a whole family tree of her own behind her. Her two marriages into the Forsyte family connect not only her but all her ancestors and relatives as well, none of whom appears in the Forsyte family tree, to that family. But this, of course, is of no importance to Galsworthy's narrative. He thus pays no attention and grants no existence, even of a fictive sort, to these possible relatives of the Forsytes.

None of this implies in any way that Galsworthy was "wrong" to omit this information: he could not have included all of it even if for some strange reason he had wanted to do so. In fact it is impossible to say exactly what "all" the information would be in this as well as in every other context in which families are involved. And this is part of the point that this example is designed to show: the specific path traced through what are actually indefinitely complex family interconnections is essentially conditioned by background interests and values. A particular family is constituted only through the presence of such factors, and the paths that are of no interest in each particular case are simply left out of our family trees. But "in the actual world, in which everything is bound to and conditioned by everything else" (*WP*, 584), families are nothing like what these neat representations suggest. It is not just difficult but actually impossible to determine the family to which an individual belongs without assumptions dictated by our conventions, purposes, and values—for example, by the principle that in some social groups paternal descent determines, through primogeniture, the order of inheritance among male heirs.

Marriage introduces a complication on the biological level because it constantly introduces new material into a family's genetic pool. There is therefore no reason to expect that the genetic material of distant ancestors and descendants need overlap to any extent. Even within a very few generations, the probability that an individual will share genetic material with at least one of its great-great-grandparents is no higher than .25. Our concept of the family is tied to the idea of shared behavioral, morphological, or genetic features. But this is only because we are usually concerned with what is really the very short run, with the few generations within which such similarities may be important and obvious. In principle, family membership is totally independent of the notion of common characteristics. And on a legal level, an individual with no apparent biological lines to a particular family may come to be part of it through adoption, while a descendant of a member of that family may be excluded from it for a variety of reasons.

In short, neither the biological nor the legal question of family membership has a clear answer. The neat picture suggested (but not imposed) by the family tree soon gives way to a vastly more complicated network of interrelations among individuals, a network which, in a variety of ways, ultimately connects everyone to everyone else in the world. And therefore descent from a family member is not only the least but also the most that is necessary for being part of that family. Particular families are generated out of this network by means of operations that are essentially conditioned by specific interests and values.

Nietzsche's discussion of punishment suggests that this example is not fanciful. He writes, first, that "the origin and purpose of punishment are two problems that are separate or that ought to be separate." He then generalizes this to the unrestricted view that

> the causes and origins of a thing and its eventual utility, its actual employment and place in a system of purposes, lie worlds apart . . . But purposes and utilities are only *signs* that a will to power has become master of something less powerful and imposed upon it the character of a function; and the entire history of a "thing," an organ, a custom can in this way be a continuous sign-chain of ever new interpretations and adaptations whose causes do not even have to be related to one another but, on the contrary, in some cases succeed and alternate with one another in a purely chance fashion. (*GM*, II, 12)

Nothing about a thing, Nietzsche concludes, need remain constant: "The form is fluid, but the 'meaning' is even more so." Since both its form and its purpose are constantly changing, punishment is constituted by the very history of those forms and practices, those purposes and meanings, that can be seen to belong to a single institution. And all that shows that there is a single institution here in the first place is the narrative that successfully characterizes later forms and purposes as subsequent stages, *as descendants,* of earlier ones.[19] This is just what our analogy with the family had led us to expect.

The analogy showed that a family can consist of individuals who share nothing but biological or legal descent. Our interests and purposes, which certainly are not constant across social groups or over time, condition how families are circumscribed within the indefinitely large set of interrelations that people bear to one another; such interests and purposes actually dictate what constitutes each family. Family trees are conventionally chosen paths within these vast tangles. But just as the qualification *conventionally* does not in any way detract from the reality of families, so the word *arbitrarily,* with which Nietzsche consistently characterizes the way enduring objects are constructed, does not detract from the reality of the world. Families are of course *in* the world, embodied in these complicated relationships, but they are also in a serious sense indeterminate. The possibility of determining new families, as real as those to which we have become accustomed at some particular time, is always present. We can naturally ask whether these new families are already there in the existing interrelations or whether we make them up, create them, when for some reason we follow a new path. The answer to this question is bound to be ambiguous. And its ambiguity corresponds exactly to the ambiguity in Nietzsche's attitude toward the reality of the world as well as toward the relationship between creation and discovery.

In a different context Nietzsche makes a point that applies directly to this discussion: "Every individual," he writes, "consists of the whole course of evolution" (*WP,* 373). And elsewhere he claims: "Human beings are not only single individuals but one particular line of the total organic world. That *they* endure proves that a species of interpretation (even though accretions are still being added) has also endured, that the species of interpretation has not changed. 'Adaptation' " (*WP,* 678; cf. 687). In short, what constitutes the unity and identity, the very fact, of a family is—to use the word that I have perhaps disingenuously been avoiding so far—nothing more and nothing less than the *genealogical* relationship that obtains among its members. Different background assumptions can generate or manifest vastly different genealogical relationships. And it is, I now want to suggest, precisely this sort of genealogical relationship that for Nietzsche constitutes not only families, not only moral and social institutions and schools of thought, but also, quite literally, every single thing in the world.

What I have been calling the effects of things are multiply interrelated in the manner in which, within my analogy, the members of a family are interrelated with everyone else in the world. The unity of each thing, that thing itself, is to be found in the genealogical account that connects one set of phenomena to another. It is to be found in a narrative of the way in which the later set can be seen as the descendant—not as a development, manifestation, or appearance—of the set that came earlier. Genealogy allows for chance occurrences and fortuitous connections, for mutations and for marriages, for violent expansions and intrusions, and it makes change of fortune possible without change in identity. But since the thing itself is to be found in its genealogy, and since there can never be only one genealogy of anything, the very notion of the thing itself, as the will to power has insisted all along, is now no longer necessary or indeed coherent. To ask what the nature of the world is in itself or which description of it is ultimately correct is like asking which family tree depicts the real genealogical connections among everyone in the world. The answer to this question can be uninformative and trivial: it will connect everyone to everyone else in an indefinite variety of ways, and it will therefore generate no family connections at all. It may also be interesting but partial: it will specify a particular family, but will therefore necessarily leave many possible family connections out of account. Nietzsche believes that the question concerning the world can only receive answers of exactly the same sort.

Genealogy, then, is Nietzsche's alternative to ontology. It allows for many alternatives, and it neither discovers nor imposes once and for all a ready-made reality because it depends on the indeterminate picture of the world provided by the will to power. Nietzsche takes the world as if it were a text and the things within it as if they were the characters and other fictional entities of which texts consist. He can thus see them all as a vast sum of essentially interrelated objects. Each one of these is already the product of an earlier grouping or interpretation, and each grouping affects and is affected by all the others. Genealogy concerns itself with these groupings and with the paths that connect them. Every path it traces reveals, where only facts were visible before, an earlier interpretation with its own purposes and values, its own will to power. And in doing so, each genealogical account itself embodies its own interests and manifests its own will to power.

"The will to power interprets," Nietzsche writes (*WP*, 642), and by this he means that his own interpretation, his own genealogy, is aware of its own partiality. One of his central aims is to show that the world we have taken for granted is the product of the Christian interpretation of life, established for the benefit of a particular kind of person with particular needs and desires. These, Nietzsche insists, are not and need not be the needs and desires of everyone, though it has been essential to Christianity to conceal this fact and thus to conceal and deny its own interpretive status. But can Nietzsche's self-conscious genealogical interpretation be both a manifestation of his will to power, of his effort to project his own values and to introduce himself into history, and at the same time *correct*? Or is it at best, as often seems to be the case, an expression of his own personal, privately motivated, and peculiar preferences?

4 | *Nature Against Something That Is Also Nature*

> "Should we be mindful of dreams?" Joseph asked.
> "Can we interpret them?"
>   The Master looked into his eyes and said tersely:
> "We should be mindful of everything, for we can
> interpret everything."
>
> Hermann Hesse, *The Glass Bead Game*

"We are unknown to ourselves, we seekers after knowledge"—*wir Erkennenden* (*GM*, Pref., 1): with its very first sentence *On the Genealogy of Morals* generates the central tension that confronts Nietzsche's own genealogical practice as well as all later discussions and extensions of it. "We have never sought ourselves—," he continues; "how could it happen that we should *find* ourselves?" But at least for the moment he does not say whether this search could be undertaken and what, once undertaken, it could ever hope to find.

A similar tension lurks in his description of "philosophers" in *The Gay Science*. They are so totally devoted, Nietzsche writes, to the pursuit of truth that they are consumed by "the great *passion* of the seeker after knowledge who lives and must live continually in the thundercloud of the highest problems and the heaviest responsibilities (by no means as an observer, outside, indifferent, secure, and objective)" (*GS*, 351). The parenthesis within which Nietzsche places the last crucial qualification suggests that these seekers after knowledge themselves bracket and overlook, and are therefore in one sense ignorant of, the partiality of their own enterprise. Even if the partisan and nonobjective nature of their search intimates itself to them, the full awareness of its character seems to correspond to a blind spot in their field of vision. They cannot look for it, and consequently they cannot see it. Nietzsche concludes the first section of the Preface to the *Genealogy*: "So we are necessarily strangers to ourselves, we do not comprehend ourselves, we *have* to misunderstand ourselves, for us the law 'Each is farthest from one's own self' applies to all eternity—we are in no way 'seekers after knowledge' with respect to ourselves" (*GM*, Pref., 1).

Those who pursue knowledge, Nietzsche seems to claim, are, and perhaps must remain, ignorant of themselves if they are to pursue knowledge at all. This refusal of individuals, types, or, more generally, institutions to acknowledge an aspect of themselves in order to survive as the individuals, types, or institutions they happen to be is at the heart of Nietzsche's genealogical writing and of the objects and mechanisms with which this writing is concerned. Various backward-turning tensions of this sort, and the relations between them, form the subject matter of the discussion that follows.

On the Genealogy of Morals asks two main questions, starkly put in section 3 of its Preface: "Under what conditions did human beings devise these value judgments good and evil? and what value do they themselves possess?" Nietzsche discusses these judgments explicitly in the first of the three essays of which this work consists, but it is clear that he aims to attack not simply these particular terms but, more important, moral valuation and the moral point of view in general. He believes that these two questions are deeply connected with one another: "We need a *critique* of moral values, *the value of these values themselves must first be called in question*—and for that there is needed a knowledge of the conditions and circumstances in which they grew, under which they evolved and changed" (*GM*, Pref., 6). But before we try to determine if and how the investigation of the descent *(Herkunft)* of moral values can affect our own evaluation of the moral point of view, we must first look at some of the broader methodological features of genealogy.[1]

It is essential to Nietzsche's conception of genealogy that it is explicitly modeled on the interpretation of texts. The genealogy of moral institutions is an interpretation that aims to show that they too, like all other institutions, exhibit the contingent, complicated, and even motley character discussed in the preceding chapter. Nietzsche is very eager to distinguish his own approach from the speculative psychological history he vaguely associates with some nameless "English psychologists" (*GM*, I, 1).[2] And he warns his readers "against gazing around haphazardly in the blue after the English fashion. For it must be obvious which color is a hundred times more vital for a genealogist of morals than blue: namely *gray*, that is, what is documented, what can actually be confirmed and has actually existed, in short the entire long hieroglyphic record, so hard to decipher, of the moral past of humanity!" (*GM*, Pref., 7).

Genealogy is interpretation in the sense that it treats our moral practices not as given but as "texts," as signs with a meaning, as manifestations of a will to power that this interpretation tries to reveal. Nietzsche emphasizes the interpretive nature of his enterprise by announcing at its outset that the third essay of the *Genealogy* is itself an interpretation (*Auslegung*) of the aphorism he has prefixed to it: in this way, he writes, he intends to provide an instance of what it is "to practice reading as an *art*" (*GM*, Pref., 8). The obscure relationship between Nietzsche's essay and the aphorism of which it is the interpretation has received remarkably little attention. But before I try to make some tentative comments on it, I want to draw out some of the more obvious implications involved in the idea of interpretation in general.

Jean Granier has written that the task of interpretation is "to decode scrupulously the text before us, even if its message shatters our dearest hopes. The norm of knowledge is the ideal of the philological method."[3] Intuitively at least, interpretation implies attention to and respect of the text. It depends on the effort to read correctly and on the presupposition that this is possible. It generates the hope of getting matters right. And indeed, in the opening pages of this work, Nietzsche returns again and again to the claim that his genealogy, his interpretation of the history and value of morality, aims at nothing less than the truth; and he insists that, unlike the efforts of others, his own hits its mark.[4] In *The Gay Science* (357) he had written, "We . . . reject the Christian interpretation and condemn its 'meaning' as counterfeit" and had gone on to characterize philologists, who for him are the paradigmatic textual interpreters, as "the destroyers of every faith that rests on books" (*GS*, 358). Now, in the *Genealogy*, after the cryptic and puzzling opening section of the Preface, he introduces his subject with an almost overwhelming emphasis on the importance of truth. He even concludes the first essay's first section by expressing his determination (which he hopes is shared by his opponents) "to sacrifice all desirability to truth, *every* truth, even plain, harsh, ugly, repellent, unchristian, immoral truth.—For such truths do exist—" (*GM,* I, 1).

Nietzsche, then, begins his own interpretive project by paying tribute to interpretation as tradition conceives it. He does not present his own view until he has exposed what he takes to be the main error of his rival genealogists; this error, he claims, consists in giving the wrong account of the values with which they are concerned: some of them identify goodness with selflessness (*GM,* I, 2) and others with utility (*GM,* I, 3). But though Nietzsche thinks that these identifications are wrong, he does not reject them outright, and it is important to see how he construes his opponents' mistake. He seems to me perfectly willing to agree that many, perhaps most people today do in fact praise agents and actions as good on account of their being altruistic or practical. That they do so is the achievement of "the slave revolt in morality: that revolt that has a history of two thousand years behind it and which we no longer see because it—has been victorious" (*GM,* I, 7). Like everyone else, Nietzsche's rivals make the mistake of remaining blind to the slave revolt; they do not realize that, at some particular time, it created the values by which most people regulate their lives today, and that these values are not given us by nature. Considering the most common current interpretation of our values as the only one they have had, they fail to see that selflessness or utility is in fact an interpretation in the first place. They therefore believe that there is a natural connection between being good and being selfless, and therefore that this connection is not subject to history and to change, to appropriation and manipulation by particular groups with particular interests at different times. They see our values as given objects rather than as created products, and they make a straightforward, unthinking projection of the categories of the present onto the past. This is why Nietzsche writes that "it is, unhappily, certain that the *historical spirit* itself is lacking in these historians of morality, that precisely all the good spirits of history itself have left them in the lurch! As is the hallowed custom with philosophers, the thinking of them is *by nature* unhistorical" (*GM,* I, 2; cf. *TI,* III, 1).

For Nietzsche, by contrast, the connection between goodness and altruism or utility is anything but natural, and there is no question of tracing it to the origin of valuation. He claims that this connection is the specific creation of the slave revolt in morality, which he associates with the emergence of Christianity, and he takes the connection to result from reversing an earlier and very different mode of valuation. People have become convinced that goodness is selflessness because the standards of valuation that were most advantageous to a particular group within society, "the wretched . . . the poor, impotent, lowly . . . the suffering, deprived, sick, ugly" (*GM*, I, 7), have been imposed on almost everyone else as well.

Now Nietzsche's view of the origin of our current values, even if it is correct, does not show that we should not identify goodness with altruism or utility. Nothing is objectionable simply because it has an objectionable origin. Had Nietzsche made this argument he would indeed have been, as he sometimes seems to be, guilty of falling into the genetic fallacy, which amounts to confusing the origin of something with its nature or value.[5] But Nietzsche is quite aware that such an argument is unacceptable: he himself exposes it in section 345 of *The Gay Science*, and in *Daybreak* he had written that "the more insight we possess into an origin the less significant does the origin appear" (*D*, 44). His argument, as we shall see, is in any case more subtle and more complicated.

Nietzsche's account of the origin of the current conception of goodness shows, however, that his rivals' error is itself quite complicated. It consists, first, in assuming that the dominant sense of a word, the accepted interpretation of a value, or the current function of an institution is naturally appropriate to it and never the product of earlier operations, of reversals, impositions, and appropriations. That is, their error consists in being ignorant of the specific historical and genealogical tangles that produce the contingent structures we mistakenly consider given, solid, and extending without change into the future as well as into the past.

In addition to overlooking history, however, Nietzsche also thinks that this approach refuses to acknowledge that even today the term *good* does not have a single sense or univocal interpretation. He appeals to a form of argument that goes back to Plato's *Protagoras* (332d–333b). According to this argument, if we can show that a single term has two distinct contraries, as the term *even* is contrasted with both *rough* and *odd*, then it follows that this term has two distinct senses, that it is not a single term at all. And Nietzsche claims that even today the term *good* is more complicated than we commonly suppose, since it actually has two distinct contraries: *evil (böse),* rough-ly equivalent to *wicked* or *malevolent,* and *bad (schlecht),* closer to *base* or *contemptible.* To baseness there corresponds the notion of good-ness as nobility, while goodness as utility or selflessness contrasts with wickedness. I cannot reproduce here Nietzsche's well-known and complicated discussion of the intricate relations between these two modes of valuation. But I must mention one idea that will become in-creasingly important to our purposes. According to Nietzsche, the view that goodness is identical with nobility, which is itself an inter-pretation congenial to one particular social group, is as a matter of fact temporally prior to the view that goodness is selflessness or utility to society as a whole. This second interpretation, he argues, comes about by a reversal of the values of the noble code. The qualities the noble valuation admired were actually bad and disadvantageous for most people: the slave revolt declared them to be bad in themselves, or evil; the qualities the noble valuation excluded were actually in the interest of the larger group within society: the slave revolt declared them to be good in themselves—that is, good for everyone without exception. Nevertheless, this reversal is not complete. The qualities and, even more important, the attitudes associated with the noble mode of valu-ation are still present within our current schemes of thought and ac-tion. Nietzsche can close the first essay of the *Genealogy* (I, 17) on a hopeful note at least partly because the slave revolt is not yet an abso-lute master: "The two opposing values 'good and bad,' 'good and evil' have been engaged in a fearful struggle on earth for thousands of years; and though the latter value has certainly been on top for a long time, there are still places where the struggle is as yet undecided" (*GM,* I, 16; cf. *BGE,* 260). The last chapter of this book discusses the nature of this struggle and the results of the outcome Nietzsche hopes it will have. For the moment we are concerned with the nature of the error of Nietzsche's rival genealogists, which is in part to overlook this complexity of our current system of valuation. They pick out the one strand within it which Nietzsche, for reasons I shall soon discuss, con-siders specifically moral, and they identify it with the very essence of valuation itself.

At this point, having assumed that the strand they have unthink-ingly privileged has always been, as it is now, the essence of valuation, Nietzsche's rivals also assume that it must have been present at, and responsible for, the emergence of valuation in the first place. Their approach is an effort to show that one specific interpretation of evaluative practices and institutions (the values good and evil, the notions of sin, guilt, and the bad conscience, the mode of life encapsulated in asceticism) is to be found at the origins of all social life. Theirs is therefore an effort to show that our moral institutions do not involve an interpretation at all, that social life emerged in all essentials as it now is, and that it has remained intact through history.

Nietzsche's opposition to traditional histories of morality and his sometimes extravagant claims for the novelty and importance of his own approach (GS, 345) are primarily caused by his aversion to this linear or static conception of the nature of values and institutions. Genealogy is not, as it sometimes seems to be, a new method of doing history with its own rules and principles; it is rather an effort to take history itself very seriously and to find it where it has least been expected to be. Genealogy takes as its objects precisely those institutions and practices which, like morality, are usually thought to be totally exempt from change and development. It tries to show the way in which they too undergo changes as a result of historical developments. And it also tries to show how such changes escape our notice and how it is often in the interest of these practices to mask their specific historical origins and character. As a result of this, genealogy has direct practical consequences because, by demonstrating the contingent character of the institutions that traditional history exhibits as unchanging, it creates the possibility of altering them. Nietzsche denies both the view that institutions regularly arise in the form in which we now know them and the correlative idea that we can determine what such institutions really aim at, what they really are, and what they always have been by tracing them to their origins. On the contrary, from his earliest writings on, Nietzsche had claimed that such tracings inevitably reveal conditions and purposes totally different from those to which they eventually gave rise, and that the mode in which later stages emerge from earlier ones is anything but logical or rational: "Everywhere in all beginnings we find only the crude, the unformed, the empty and the ugly . . . Everywhere, the way to the beginning leads to barbarism" (PTG, 1).[6]

Morality too has developed in a complex, haphazard, and often violent manner. Earlier modes of valuation (GM, I, 7, 8, 10), of indebtedness and punishment (GM, II, 4–6, 12–14), and of life (GM, III, 11) were appropriated, reversed, reinterpreted, and transposed in order to fabricate the general system according to which most lives today are ordered. The worst assumption a genealogist can make is to think that the present purpose and significance of these operations, their end product, was the factor that brought them about in the beginning. On the contrary, as the history of punishment has suggested, the development of institutions often consists of fortuitous and rationally inexplicable events. Even "when one has demonstrated that a thing is of the highest utility, one has however thereby taken not one step toward explaining its origin: that is to say, one can never employ utility to make it comprehensible that a thing must necessarily exist" (*D*, 37; cf. 44). Nietzsche even puts this point in biological terms: "The utility of an organ does not explain its origin" (*WP*, 647): we cannot project the current function of anything backward as the cause of its emergence. Though it is crucial to know the history of something in order to understand what it is, a thing's origin can never by itself explain its nature: "*In the beginning was.* To glorify the origin—that is the metaphysical after-shoot which sprouts again at the contemplation of history, and absolutely makes us imagine that *in the beginining* of things lies all that is most valuable and essential" *(WS*, 3).

"The genealogist," Michel Foucault has written, "finds that there is 'something altogether different' behind things: not a timeless and essential secret, but the secret that they have no essence or that their essence was fabricated in a piecemeal fashion from alien forms" (p. 142). This is exactly what Nietzsche tries to show in *On the Genealogy of Morals*, a text we might accurately describe as his history of the *moralization* of various values, practices, and modes of life, all of which existed in related forms and with different significance before they were appropriated by Christianity and turned into the guiding principles of contemporary individual and social life.

The first essay of the *Genealogy* argues that a premoral set of values, expressed by the terms *good* (noble) and *bad* (base), was reversed by Christianity so that the features previously associated with nobility now came to constitute evil (wickedness) while those associated with baseness came to represent a new sort of goodness (meekness). In the second essay Nietzsche claims that the contractual notions of debt and exchange and the legal notion of punishment, by means of which accounts between different parties were settled then and there, once and for all, were radicalized and gave rise to our concepts of guilt, sin, and the bad conscience as well as to the idea that atonement for guilt can be made, if at all, only in an afterlife. The third and most complex essay is his effort to account for the power of "the ascetic ideal," the denial of, and the attempt to distance oneself from, the activities and values that are most central to everyday life. The ascetic, Nietzsche writes, treats "life as a wrong road on which one must finally walk back to the point where it begins, or as a mistake that is put right by deeds—that we *ought* to put right" (*GM*, III, 11). Nietzsche's analysis of the ascetic life, its origins, its apparent function, and its real significance, is complicated enough to make even the exclusive attention I propose to give it in what follows seriously inadequate. My discussion will be partial and will have the specific aim of exhibiting some of the distinctive features of genealogy as well as the problems generated by the family of tensions to which I referred at the opening of this chapter.

The third essay of *On the Genealogy of Morals*, "What Is the Meaning of Ascetic Ideals?" is, as Nietzsche himself writes, an interpretation of an aphorism that had appeared in slightly different form in *Thus Spoke Zarathustra*: "Unconcerned, mocking, violent—thus wisdom wants *us*: she is a woman *(ein Weib)* and always loves only a warrior" (*Z*, I, 7). The section in which this sentence occurs is entitled "On Reading and Writing." This reinforces the obvious point that Nietzsche is in no way concerned with armed warfare but with the passion and partiality of the intellectual enterprise itself: he praises not the wisdom of soldiers but the strength of thinkers. The conception of the writer as warrior, and not the identification of wisdom with woman, is the crucial feature of this aphorism, for it generates a tension between this part of the *Genealogy* on the one hand and its opening sections, which emphasize the disinterested and objective pursuit of the truth, on the other. The "seekers after knowledge" cannot be easily thought of as warriors. And even if such terms can be applied to them, it still is difficult to reconcile the scholar's serious and unflinching devotion to truth with the characterization implicit in the words *unconcerned, mocking, violent*. The terms of reference seem to have changed: according to this aphorism, the writer is primarily after victory and not after truth.

But in what way is this essay an interpretation of the aphorism? It does not mention it again. It does not offer to explicate it. It does not even *concern* itself with it at all. In fact the essay almost seems designed to make its readers forget that it is intended as an interpretation of the sentence that stands at its head. Nietzsche, however, does not consider interpretation to be only commentary, elucidation, or, as he once put it, "conceptual translation" (*WP,* 605). On the contrary, since he believes that "all subduing and becoming master involves interpretation" (*GM,* II, 12), he can also write that "interpretation is itself a means of becoming master of something" (*WP,* 643). The third essay of this work is therefore primarily a self-reflexive application of the aphorism that precedes it, and it is by applying it that it interprets—that is, extends, draws out, and complicates—it. The essay also in a way masters, or appropriates, the aphorism in that it gives this general and vague sentence a very specific sense and direction, which may or may not have been part of its original intention. The application is self-reflexive because Nietzsche interprets the aphorism by applying it within a text that is itself an interpretation of something else. The object of this interpretation is the ascetic ideal, against which this essay is explicitly a declaration of war. In fact Nietzsche argues that the ascetic ideal itself is an interpretation of certain phenomena which it has tried to master by establishing its own aims, purposes, and values. Nietzsche wants to expose these values for what they are, and his essay is therefore a reinterpretation of the interpretation involved in the ascetic ideal. As such, his own text embodies aims, purposes, and values of its own; his effort to establish them in place of the values of asceticism is therefore an effort to master that ideal in the very process of understanding its nature.

What are the values embodied in Nietzsche's own interpretation? The opening pages of the *Genealogy* lead its readers to believe that the genealogist's main motivation is the pursuit of truth. And in fact, when Nietzsche turns to asceticism, he consistently accuses its moral version, the morally grounded devotion to "poverty, chastity, humility" (*GM,* III, 8), of being based on error and falsehood. But in order to understand the significance of this accusation and the paradoxes it creates for Nietzsche, we must first determine what he understands by "the moral version" of asceticism—a mode of life which, in his eyes, constitutes a serious paradox in its own right. We shall eventually see that these two sets of paradoxes, one in the object investigated by genealogy and the other in the genealogical investigation itself, are ironically versions of one another.

Moral or Christian asceticism is for Nietzsche one aspect of a broader phenomenon. Apart from the asceticism sometimes exhibited by artists (*GM,* III, 2–4), he argues, philosopohers too have always had a tendency toward it: "As long as there are philosophers on earth, and wherever there have been philosophers . . . there unquestionably exists a peculiar philosophers' irritation at and rancor against sensuality . . . There also exists a peculiar philosophers' prejudice and affection in favor of the whole ascetic ideal; one should not overlook that. Both . . . pertain to the type" (*GM*, III, 7). Nietzsche seems to me to overstate his case here. Though there may well be a philosophical type to whom asceticism is central, not all philosophers belong to it.[7] But Nietzsche's general point is important, for his purpose is to distinguish philosophical from moral asceticism. For many people, and even for some philosophers, abstention from some of the pleasures of life is a way of being better able to secure certain other similar pleasures which they value more highly. Even though Nietzsche's comments on the bad effects of sexuality on creativity are painfully naive (*GM*, III, 8), it is still true that asceticism, interpreted very broadly as the desire to be free of some worldly pleasures, does "reveal . . . many bridges to independence" and to individual intellectual achievement (*GM*, III, 7). But this is really nothing but prudentially motivated self-control: one gives up a particular good in exchange for a further, greater advantage. Nothing but utility is involved: morality plays no part in the calculation. The attitude involved is perfectly egoistic. The philosophers find in the ascetic ideal "an optimum condition for the highest and boldest spirituality and smile—they do *not* deny 'existence,' they rather affirm *their* existence and *only* their existence, and this perhaps to the point at which they are not far from harboring the impious wish: *pereat mundus, fiat philosophia, fiat philosophus, fiam!*" (*GM*, III, 7).

Nietzsche writes that if you "take a close look at the lives of all the great, fruitful, inventive spirits . . . you will always encounter . . . to a certain degree" the three ascetic ideals: poverty, chastity, and humility. But, he continues, such people consider these ideals neither duties nor virtues. On the contrary, they take them to be simply "the most appropriate and natural conditions of their *best* existence, their *fairest* fruitfulness" (*GM*, III, 8). Nietzsche goes on to discuss some further, less innocent connections between philosophy and asceticism. Philosophy, he writes, "for a long time lacked the courage for itself" (*GM*, III, 9) and therefore had to assume the aspect of the much more radical asceticism of the priest so that it could be practiced at all: "The *ascetic priest* provided until the most modern times the repulsive and gloomy caterpillar form in which alone the philosopher could live and creep about" (*GM*, III, 10).[8] But the crucial idea for our purposes is that behind this mask the philosopher's asceticism is practiced for the sake of a better present life; it is neither a denial of life nor an atonement for past sin, and it is not a preparation for a future existence. Nonmoral asceticism glorifies one specific type of earthly life among others; it does not condemn the pleasures it avoids. It does not consider that there is something inherently wrong with them and that they should therefore be avoided by all. Nonmoral ascetics need not dogmatically expect that others will benefit if they too deny the pleasures they themselves avoid. They have no reason for such an expectation since they have no reason to believe that the life of the philosopher, which they want to secure for themselves, is good for everybody. Such ascetics, therefore, need not be interested in legislating what is and what is not proper for others to seek and avoid.

It is not clear whether Nietzsche believes that any of the great philosophers has consciously seen asceticism in this light. If not, then priestly asceticism must have been more than a "caterpillar form" of philosophy. But the point remains that in such cases the "meaning" of ascetic ideals is that they secure for some people the best life they can achieve. Asceticism can therefore provide the means for enhancing one's actual life and for coming to be able, in Nietzsche's words, to affirm it more strongly. It is produced by a desire and a tendency, perhaps even a compulsion, to engage in what one is best suited for, regardless of the consequences: it is the product and expression of the will to power; its meaning is the will to power.

But Nietzsche believes that "all meaning is will to power" (*WP*, 590). Moral asceticism, therefore, seems to constitute an almost insurmountable paradox for his view. Moral ascetics, according to his own characterization, appear to be involved in the effort to distance themselves from life as much as they possibly can and to renounce the goods they already possess for the otherworldly rewards which, from Nietzsche's naturalistic viewpoint, are nothing at all. In denying the whole of life and not simply one of its aspects, moral ascetics seem, therefore, to be trying to renounce their will to power. But Nietzsche does not simply believe that this effort can never succeed; he is also convinced that it cannot ever begin, since every effort is itself a manifestation of the will to power in the first place. Moral asceticism, therefore, is a manifestation of a will to power that aims at its own annihilation.

The moralization of asceticism occurs when the preexisting prudential structure of behavior which I have been discussing is radicalized and interpreted not as a way of securing certain human pleasures by means of avoiding others, but as the desire to avoid all human pleasures in general. Asceticism, which earlier was a very specific attitude toward some aspects of each individual life, now pronounces judgment regarding life as a whole: "The idea at issue here is the *valuation* the ascetic priest places on our life; he juxtaposes it (along with what pertains to it: 'nature,' 'world,' the whole sphere of becoming and transitoriness) with a quite different mode of existence which it opposes and excludes, *unless* it turn against itself, *deny itself*: in that case, the case of the ascetic life, life counts as a bridge to that other mode of existence" (*GM*, III, 11). But, assuming that the metaphysics of Christianity is not acceptable and that there is no eternal world and no eternal life, how can such an attitude emerge at all? If one insists, as Nietzsche does, on offering purely naturalistic accounts of everything, the mere existence of a mode of life that turns itself against nature is a very serious problem, for this mode of life too must be accounted by the same naturalistic mechanisms that account for everything else. But then it appears that the ascetic life, which must be as natural a phenomenon as everything else,

> is a self-contradiction; here rules a *ressentiment* without equal, that of an insatiable instinct and power-will that wants to become master not over something in life but over life itself, over its most profound, powerful, and basic conditions . . . All this is in the highest degree paradoxical: we stand before a discord that *wants* to be discordant, that *enjoys* itself in this suffering and even grows more self-confident and triumphant the more its own presupposition, its physiological capacity for life decreases. (*GM*, III, 11)

How has it been possible, and why has it been necessary, for nature to turn against itself? This, Nietzsche insists, is precisely what has occurred through the Christian and moral degradation "of the human, and even more of the animal, and more still of the material" (*GM*, III, 28): "What, then, is this struggle of the Christian 'against nature'? Do not let us be deceived by his words and explanations! It is nature against something that is also nature" (*WP*, 228). Nietzsche had always been interested in such peculiar self-reflexive situations and had tried from early on to develop a mechanism that would account for them. Apparently unnatural conditions, he argued, are always in the final analysis means for accomplishing natural ends. Though his attention toward this issue underwent radical changes over the years, we can still see a deep continuity between his later views and his having written, much earlier, of "those illusions which nature so frequently employs to achieve her own ends. The true goal is veiled by a phantasm: and while we stretch out our hands for the latter, nature attains the former by means of an illusion" (*BT*, 3). This mechanism, Nietzsche had argued, could be observed in the functioning of tragedy itself. Too much ("Dionysian") insight into the reality of life leads to despair and inaction: "Knowledge kills action; action requires the veils of illusion: that is the doctrine of Hamlet" (*BT*, 7). The action of tragedy shows the most powerful individuals trying, and failing, to have an effect on the "eternal nature of things." But juxtaposed with this most powerful representation of the vanity of all effort is the tragic chorus, assuring its spectators that even in their efforts to change nature, the tragic heroes, like those spectators themselves, are its products and elements, and the realization that one is a part of everything that lives makes life "indestructibly powerful and pleasurable" and therefore worth living after all. But tragedy cannot be contrasted to life, of which it is the creation and part. "With this chorus the profound Hellene, uniquely susceptible to the tenderest and deepest suffering, comforts himself, having looked boldly right into the terrible destructiveness of so-called world history as well as at the cruelty of nature, and being in danger of longing for a Buddhistic negation of the will. Art saves him, and through art—life" (*BT*, 7). Tragedy apparently discourages all effort, but actually promotes it. Its real end is quite opposed to the end it seems to have, and both together serve the interests of life (cf. *BT*, 15, 18). A main reason for Nietzsche's continuing admiration of the Greeks is what he takes as their ability to exploit mechanisms of this sort. Having glimpsed the truth, personified in *The Gay Science* as Baubo, they were, according to his unsettling view, revolted by it. Accordingly, they turned away from its pursuit. They made the preliminary stages of its conquest their final purpose: "Oh, those Greeks! They knew how to live. What is required for this is to stop courageously at the surface, the fold, the skin, to adore appearance, to believe in forms, tones, words, in the whole Olympus of appearance. Those Greeks were superficial—*out of profundity!*" (*GS*, Pref., 4; cf. *BT*, 24).

But how are mechanisms that promote what they deny related to moral asceticism? According to Nietzsche, the ascetic priest insists on downgrading, and turning completely against, aspects and functions of life that are nevertheless essential to it (cf. *TI*, V, "Morality as Anti-Nature"). He therefore seems to encourage those who follow him to want to cease being alive. Now, genealogy shows that moral asceticism emerges by radicalizing the modest and worldly asceticism of the philosophers. Philosophical asceticism presents no paradox. But its descendant, in which life appears to turn against itself, does. Nietzsche wants to resolve this paradox and also explain why this radicalization ever occurred. The formula of his resolution is this: "It must be a necessity of the first order that again and again promotes the growth and prosperity of this *life-inimical* species—it must indeed be in the *interest of life itself* that such a self-contradictory type does not die out" (*GM*, III, 11).

Astonishingly, and despite his deep aversion to it, Nietzsche finally comes to attribute to moral asceticism a function quite similar to the function he had earlier ascribed to art in *The Birth of Tragedy:* art appears to draw people away from life, to depict utter failure, only to show that life is worth living nonetheless. The ascetic priest denies life and turns against it, only in order to seduce his flock as well as himself into continuing to live. "Such a self-contradiction as the ascetic priest appears to represent, 'life *against* life,' is, physiologically considered and not merely psychologically, a simple absurdity. It can only be *apparent* . . . Let us replace it with a brief formulation of the facts of the matter: *the ascetic ideal springs from the protective instinct of a degenerating life* which tries by all means to sustain itself and to fight for its existence" (*GM*, III, 13).

"The human animal," Nietzsche writes, "is more sick, uncertain, changeable, indeterminate than any other animal, there is no doubt about that—it is *the* sick animal" (*GM*, III, 13). He often imagines, in a naive and sometimes crude way, that the causes of this "illness" are straightforwardly physiological.[9] I see no reason for accepting this aspect of his view. But it still seems to me that we must take very seriously the phenomenon he describes as an illness: the fact that the lives of most people are, and are felt by them to be, miserable. The world for Nietzsche is full of people who are incapable of accomplishing what they hope to accomplish, people who want in vain to be brave, generous, strong, perhaps even cruel, or at least notorious in some way—people who want to, but cannot, leave a mark on history. These are "the suffering," those who, as he argues in the first essay of the *Genealogy*, have finally convinced themselves that their weaknesses are actually their virtues, the results of their choice rather than the short-comings of their nature; they even take their weaknesses to be reasons why they will someday be rewarded "in another life." Unable to distinguish themselves from the rest of the world, they come to consider uniformity a virtue and impose it on everyone: this is how "the herd" is created. The values of the suffering are created by reversing the values of the noble, according to which strength and distinction, not meekness and uniformity, are the dominant virtues—virtues which not everyone was expected to be capable of possessing. The values of the weak, which Nietzsche considers moral at least in part because they are intended to be virtues that all must exhibit, aim to ease suffering caused by impotence by construing such impotence as an achievement. But this code, Nietzsche writes, "combats only the suffering itself, the discomfiture of the sufferer, *not* the real sickness" (*GM*, III, 17). And so long as its causes are not eliminated, suffering itself cannot be eliminated and will keep reappearing in different guises. Nietzsche, I shall argue in the final chapter, does not believe that such suffering can ever be completely eliminated and offers no suggestions for curing it.

The weak actually suffer from envy, from *ressentiment*, of the few "fortunate accidents of great success" (*A*, 4) who are not like them and who are unaffected by the morality of the herd. Like all the envious, therefore, the weak are suffering from themselves: "Where does one not encounter that veiled glance which burdens one with a profound sadness, that inward-turned glance of the born failure which betrays how such people speak to themselves—that glance which is a sigh! 'If only I were someone else,' sighs that glance: 'but there is no hope of that. I am who I am: how could I ever get free of myself? And yet—*I am sick of myself!*' " (*GM*, III, 14). But as Stein, in his convoluted English, says in Conrad's *Lord Jim*, "One thing alone can us from being ourselves cure." It is just at this point, when people are on the verge of giving up the most elementary desire to go on living, that the ascetic priest enters the picture. And it is also at this point that his guise as life's enemy falls away and reveals his real nature: "this ascetic priest, this apparent enemy of life, this *denier*—precisely he is among the greatest *conserving* and yes-creating forces of life" (*GM*, III, 13). How is that possible?

What is most horrible about physical or psychological suffering in Nietzsche's eyes is not the suffering itself, horrible as it may be. This, he believes, can be tolerated; it can even be pursued if a reason for it exists, if it is the means to further achievement (cf. *GM*, III, 28). The most repellent feature of human misery for Nietzsche is just the fact that there is no reason for it. Since senseless misery forces the question why one should bother to undergo it at all, it is crucial to offer an interpretation that explains it and perhaps even justifies it. The great achievement of the ascetic priest is that he explains suffering and that his explanation appeals to a "*guilty* agent who is susceptible to suffering." In this way he supplies a cause, someone who is responsible for suffering, and also an object on whom those who suffer can vent their affects and so "*deaden,* by means of a violent emotion . . . a tormenting secret pain that is becoming unendurable" (*GM*, III, 15). But the ascetic's interpretation involves one further essential twist: " 'I suffer: someone must be to blame for it'—thus thinks every sickly sheep. But its shepherd, the ascetic priest, says: 'Quite so, my sheep! Someone must be to blame for it: but you yourself are this someone, you alone are to blame for it—*you alone are to blame for yourself!*' " (*GM*, III, 15).

As a matter of fact, Nietzsche argues, people suffer because they cannot realize their ambitions or satisfy their desires. The ascetic takes suffering as given, and interprets it not as the product of unrealized ambition but as the punishment of guilt: people suffer because they may have been sensual, proud, cruel, or even just ambitious—not because such drives were not satisfied. More important, they suffer because they may have *wanted* to act in some such way: this is why the moral quality of actions is often located in the intention or motive with which they are performed. In this way, asceticism creates a sin out of wanting to have features that, according to the noble mode of valuation, might have constituted virtues. But whether these features would have been virtues or not, the desire to exhibit them, according to Nietzsche, cannot possibly be eliminated. Both such features and the tendency to act according to them are essentially and indispensably part of what we are. The punishment, therefore, will necessarily continue. Asceticism can never eliminate suffering, but it succeeds in creating an interpretation that explains why it is inevitable:

> Human beings, suffering from themselves in one way or other . . . ,
> uncertain why or wherefore, thirsting for reasons—reasons re-

lieve—thirsting, too, for remedies and narcotics, at last take counsel with one who knows hidden things, too—and behold! they receive a hint, they receive from their sorcerer, the ascetic priest, the *first* hint as to the "cause" of their suffering; they must seek it in *themselves*, in some *guilt*, in a piece of the past, they must understand their suffering as a *punishment*. (*GM*, III, 20)

There are many reasons why the ascetic interpretation of suffering is an invention of genius. Nietzsche believes, as we have seen, that suffering is inevitable (perhaps for physiological or psychological reasons; perhaps, we might add, for social and economic ones as well). In blaming suffering on the sufferer himself and on features that cannot possibly be eliminated, this interpretation does not promise to accomplish what cannot be accomplished: it does not promise to eliminate suffering itself, at least during the course of this life. It is therefore protected against recalcitrant fact. But it does promise that suffering may decrease if one distances oneself as far as possible from the features asceticism takes to be responsible for it. But, as I have said, we cannot do away with these features; to want to do away with them is to want to do away with ourselves. This is why Nietzsche insists that the ascetic ideal, "this horror of the senses, of reason itself, this fear of happiness and beauty, this longing to get away from all appearance, change, becoming, death, wishing, from longing itself—all this means—let us dare grasp it, *a will to nothingness*, a counter-will to life, a rebellion against the most fundamental presuppositions of life" (*GM*, III, 28; cf. III, 1). Desire in general may always lead to a specific sinful desire; in any case, "sinful" desires, being essential to human beings, are unavoidable. In its most extreme form, therefore, the ascetic ideal is a desire to stop desiring, a will to cease willing. But Nietzsche contrasts even this self-defeating project with merely abdicating from effort, which he considers the most dangerous "nihilistic" consequence of the realization that there is no reason for suffering; the "will to nothingness," by contrast, "is and remains a *will!*" (*GM*, III, 28). To will not to will is still to will. In particular, it is to will to be other than one has been so far. But to will to be other than one has been so far is to will to "overcome" oneself, and that is a characteristic way of manifesting the will to power, which Nietzsche also calls "the will to life" (*GS*, 349). This circle is now complete.

The ascetic hatred of life is therefore a mechanism for giving the weak as well as the ascetic priests themselves (for they too are sick in just the same way, *GM*, III, 15) a reason to go on living. Through the priestly denial of nature, "the curative instinct of life has at least attempted . . . to exploit the bad instincts of all sufferers for the purpose of self-discipline, self-surveillance, and self-overcoming" (*GM*, III, 16). Though this is not the self-overcoming Zarathustra praises in his speeches, and though the effort it involves may be doomed from its beginning, "the will to nothingness" is still an effort to become master of oneself. It is therefore, once again, a manifestation of the single activity which, according to Nietzsche, keeps everything alive: "Only where there is life is there also will: not will to life—thus I teach you—but will to power" (*Z*, II, 12).[10]

The ascetic ideal, having been shown to be itself an aspect of the will to power, is no longer the paradox it appeared to be. Nietzsche claims that sin is not a fact but an interpretation of the fact "of physiological depression" (*GM*, III, 16). We may well disagree with Nietzsche's own diagnosis of that fact, but we are still free to accept his view that human misery, however caused, has prompted its religious interpretation and that this interpretation has, on one level, alleviated the misery that prompted it.[11] "The preponderance of feelings of displeasure over feelings of pleasure is the cause of this fictitious morality and religion; but such a preponderance provides the very formula of decadence" (*A*, 15). The ascetic ideal, confronted with this decadence, ultimately functions positively: it preserves life, even if it does this at the cost of furthering that decadence by constantly increasing feelings of displeasure, by making people inevitably less and less satisfied with themselves: saints always see themselves as the greatest sinners. In willing to deny their nature, in willing "nothingness," weak human beings "could now *will* something: no matter at first to what end, why, and with what they willed: *the will itself was saved*" (*GM*, III, 28). Nonmoral asceticism is an affirmative phenomenon because it denies some pleasures only in order to acquire others and to secure a better life in this world. Moral asceticism radicalizes this denial, negates all pleasure, and downgrades the whole world. Even so, moral asceticism is not negative in every way, for it is an effort to enable a certain kind of person to live the best life possible, even if that best turns out to be miserable indeed. Like every ideal, moral asceticism is, as Sarah Kofman writes, "affirmative; negative ideals affirm the being that evaluates; they are means for its remaining alive, even if this is at the cost of harming stronger lives and the future of humanity."[12] But if Nietzsche's genealogical interpretation of the ascetic ideal shows that it too is affirmative and a manifestation of the will to power, on what grounds can he possibly criticize it? Why does he write that "one may without exaggeration call it *the true calamity* [*Verhängniss*] in the history of European health" (*GM*, III, 28)? This is the problem with which we are now faced.

Part of the answer to this question is suggested by the last part of Kofman's statement. The ascetic ideal does not rest content with ordering the lives of those who may actually need it. Nietzsche himself has prepared the ground for this answer by means of a verbal anticipation of the statement just quoted: "What is to be feared, what has a more calamitous effect than any other calamity [was verhängnissvoll wirkt wie kein andres Verhängniss], is that human beings should inspire not profound fear but profound *nausea;* also not great fear but great pity" (*GM*, III, 14). But this, Nietzsche thinks, is precisely the purpose of the purveyors of the ascetic ideal. Their *ressentiment,* and in fact the very structure of their project, requires them to convince even those who belong to the "higher type," which "has appeared often—but as a fortunate accident, never as something *willed*" (*A*, 3), to look at the world and at themselves with the ascetic's eyes. They too must be made to suffer even though they are not disposed to do so on their own. When would the weak, Nietzsche asks, "achieve the ultimate, subtlest, sublimest triumph of revenge?" And he answers: "Undoubtedly if they succeeded in *poisoning the consciences* of the fortunate with their own misery, with all misery, so that one day the fortunate began to be ashamed of their good fortune and perhaps said one to another: 'It is disgraceful to be fortunate: *there is too much misery!*' " (*GM*, III, 14).

The will to power Nietzsche uncovers in the ascetic ideal exhibits a particular feature that cannot be found, for example, in the will to power manifested in the noble mode of valuation he discusses in the first essay of the *Genealogy.* The idealized nobles of that text, along with the few individuals who, like Napoleon and Goethe, have luckily escaped the slave morality, delight in what they perceive to be their own goodness and have no expectation that anyone else can be like them. The "pathos of distance" makes them take the greatest delight precisely in their difference from everybody else (*GM*, I, 2). Nietzsche believes that they could not even begin to imagine that the "bad"—that is, the base and weak—could ever come to be noble and strong like them. The will to power of the noble individuals is manifested as an affirmation of their difference: they do not want others to be like them (even if that were possible) any more than they want to be like others. They want to remain the distinct and distinguished individuals they are. For the rest of the world, however, it is essential that the differences between individuals become as small as possible. Nietzsche considers noble individuals to be, at least potentially, as dangerous to the weak as they are actually envied by them. The central purpose of the slave morality, therefore, is to make such people ashamed of their distinction and willing to deny it. It aims to bring them down to the level of those below them and thus to eliminate, in one stroke, both the fear and the envy of the weak. This is the slave morality's final victory: "The will of the weak to represent *some* form of superiority, their instinct for devious paths to tyranny over the healthy—where can it not be discovered, this will to power of the weakest?" (*GM*, III, 14).

Nietzsche's terms "strong and weak," "noble and base," "healthy and sick" are among the vaguest in his vocabulary. But one clear difference between these two groups is that the slave morality aims to make everyone conform to a single code of behavior, while those who subscribe to the noble mode of valuation find any such goal ludicrous, if at all conceivable. How, then, could the project of making such people accept the slave morality and the ascetic ideal as their own have been successful? An interpretation can appear to be binding on everyone only if the fact that it is an interpretation remains hidden. And this can be achieved only if the interpretation in question is presented as a view that is objectively true of the world and is addressed to all human beings simply as human beings, as rational agents, or in this case, as children of God. To appeal to features that appear to be universally shared and that do not distinguish any particular group from any other is to conceal this partiality of the interpretation, to mask the specific interests and values it addresses and promotes, to deny its will to power. The ascetic ideal aims to rule the lives of those who do not need it and who will in fact do better without it. But in addition it can accomplish its goal only by pretending to be something that it is not, by presenting itself as fact and not as interpretation. The will to power that is manifested in it is therefore not only harmful but also essentially deceptive, and this constitutes the second reason why Nietzsche, though he acknowledges it as a natural and even positive phenomenon, is eager to condemn it.

To say of a view that it is an interpretation is not to say that it is false. It is, rather, to say that it is a view that, like all views, is produced by specific interests, for specific purposes, and that it is appropriate for specific types of people. And though this does not make the issue of truth irrelevant, the ultimate question to be asked of an interpretation concerns the interests it promotes: for what type of person is it appropriate? Whom does it benefit? It is for this reason, I think, that Gilles Deleuze writes that when we examine our institutions and the interpretations that produce them, we should not ask the "metaphysical" question "What is?" but instead the "genealogical" question "Which one . . . ?" (*qui*). Deleuze refers to a sketch for a preface to *The Wanderer and His Shadow* in which Nietzsche writes: "What is it? I cried out with curiosity—*Which one is it?* you ought to ask! Thus spoke Dionysus, then kept quiet in his own special way, that is to say, in an enticing way." Deleuze explicates this by claiming that for Nietzsche "the question 'which one' means this: What are the forces that take hold of a given thing, what is the will that possesses it?" (pp. 76–77). This question does not concern individuals, for, as Deleuze concludes, "We should not ask 'Which one wills?', 'Which one interprets?', 'Which one evaluates?' for everywhere and always the will to power is *the one that*" (p. 77). I take this to mean that interpretation is always an effort to reveal and make obvious the character, the type of person, and the type of life which a view promotes and elevates. This type may be quite different from what was intended by the individuals who devised the view in question and who may not, at least not knowingly, have been such types themselves. The genealogy of a view or an institution is therefore not an inquiry into the explicit goals of its originators. And this fact gives us a reason why the search for origins as traditionally conceived, the search for what particular authors or agents took their creations to be, for what such objects meant to their original audiences, is not part of the genealogical enterprise. Genealogy is the study of the various unforeseen and often unrelated accomplishments that different institutions make possible during their variable lives.

In a famous passage Nietzsche writes: "Gradually it has become clear to me what every great philosophy so far has been: namely, the personal confession of its author and a kind of involuntary and unconscious memoir; also that the moral (or immoral) intentions in every philosophy constituted the real germ from which the whole plant has grown" (*BGE*, 6). It has often been thought that this statement expresses a naive psychohistorical reductionism[13]: that is, that Nietzsche believes that to understand what a philosophical view "really" means is to locate some specific events in its author's life which, in some sense, explain why that author held that particular view. An especially crude version of this approach, for example, would claim that Nietzsche came to his famous view of the death of God because he always resented his father's early death and the fact that he had no male authority figure to look up to while he was a child—a fact that has also been held to account for his early admiration for Wagner. But Nietzsche, who often described himself as a "psychologist," was not concerned with that sort of investigation, in which, as a matter of fact, he never engaged. The important part of his statement concerns the relation between the moral intentions with which a philosophical view is presented, whether its author is aware of them or not, and the other components of that view. Nietzsche believed that the goal of every philosophical view is to present a picture of the world and a conception of values which makes a certain type of person possible and which allows it to prosper and to flourish. As we have already seen, he wrote: "We seek a picture of the world in that philosophy in which we feel freest; i.e., in which our most powerful drive feels free to function. This will also be the case with me!" (*WP*, 418). He believed that the evaluation of philosophical views is to a very great extent an evaluation of this type of agent. And he thought that, though all philosophers aim at presenting such a type, only he was aware of that fact.

In order to make a claim to unconditional acceptance, the ascetic ideal conceals its will to power and its partial and specific origins and goals. It presents itself as text and not as interpretation, whereas in fact it is one interpretation of the "text" constituted by the lives of the poor and downtrodden, which is itself the product of countless earlier interpretations and reversals of previous modes of life. Morality, Nietzsche writes, "permits no other interpretation, no other goal; it rejects, denies, affirms, and sanctions solely from the point of view of *its* interpretation (and has there ever been a system of interpretation more thoroughly thought through?)" (*GM*, III, 23; cf. *BGE*, 202). This deception, which is also a self-deception, characterizes all dogmatism and constitutes the grounds for yet another objection against the ascetic ideal. This is that asceticism denies the radical contingency of history, the fact that every institution is subject to change, revision, and even elimination. But even more important, it denies that many modes of life are possible at the same time, and that this pluralism, despite its undeniable dangers, holds greater promise than the uniform leveling that Nietzsche finds to be implicit in Christianity and in all other absolutist codes. Moralities, Nietzsche writes, must "finally reach agreement that it is *immoral* to say: 'What is right for one is fair for the other' " (*BGE*, 221).

The interpretations Nietzsche praises, unlike the ascetic ideal, declare that this is what they are, proclaim that they are in two senses partial, and invite their own questioning. The last feature is crucial because it is only in light of a new interpretation, produced through such questioning, that the general knowledge that a view is an interpretation becomes a specific awareness of its particular sources, values, and ends. Nietzsche is particularly conscious of this point in the *Genealogy*. This makes him also aware that his own investigation may generate a paradox that is similar to the paradox it uncovers in the ascetic ideal. And the paradox involved in Nietzsche's method of investigation may be more difficult to resolve than the paradox implicit in the object he investigates.

Nietzsche denounces the ascetic ideal, but for complex reasons that I shall discuss in the last chapter of this book, he does not offer to replace it with a positive morality of his own. Nietzsche considers that his interpretation of traditional moral institutions is in itself a war against them: to show them for what they really are is sufficient to turn people away from them. Yet the very words "to show them for what they really are" generate the serious problem that we must now face. The ascetic ideal is for Nietzsche a "lie." It looks "for error precisely where the instinct of life most unconditionally posits truth" (*GM*, III, 12; cf. *A*, 56). It is based on erroneous causal presuppositions regarding freedom of choice, guilt, and punishment, which he undertakes to expose (cf. *TI*, VI; *A*, 38). As Nietzsche knows, his fight against Christianity is motivated by his desire to get to the truth about these matters. But at the same time he knows that his attack is an interpretation in the sense that I have been discussing and that it cannot therefore be a refutation of a traditional sort. "What have I to do with refutations!" he writes (*GM*, Pref., 4). His attack is a demonstration that, despite its claims to the contrary, the ascetic ideal too is only an interpretation and therefore lacks the objectivity and universality to which it pretends. He still, however, offers this demonstration in the belief, which he cannot question, that it is true. And this belief involves him in paradox.

Nietzsche discusses the faith in truth in sections 23–26 of the third essay of the *Genealogy.* His startling conclusion is that its modern expressions, science *(Wissenschaft)* and historiography *(Geschichtsschreibung),* which have exposed asceticism as the false view that it is, are themselves not opponents of the ascetic ideal "but rather the latest and noblest forms of it" (*GM*, III, 23). In section 24 he refers his readers to the fifth book of *The Gay Science,* where he discusses science at length, and even quotes one of its central passages: "It is still a *metaphysical faith* that underlies our faith in science—and we seekers after knowledge of today, we godless ones and anti-metaphysicians, we, too, derive *our* flame from the fire ignited by a faith millennia old, the Christian faith, which was also Plato's, that God is truth, that truth is divine" (*GS,* 344). If this is so, however, then in fighting the ascetic ideal, Nietzsche (and everyone who follows him) is actually perpetuating it, much in the way that the ascetic ideal itself preserved life by means of denying it.

The reasons why faith in truth is a part and not an opponent of asceticism are complex. One of them is that "it is precisely in their faith in truth that its adherents are more rigid and unconditional than anyone" (*GM*, III, 24). Nietzsche certainly thinks that the fact that science rests on the "faith" that "*nothing* is needed *more* than truth, and in relation to it everything else has only second-rate value" (*GS,* 344) shows that science rests on unquestioned presuppositions that make it continuous with the dogmatic tradition it opposes and fights. But he also gives other reasons.[14] In the same section of *The Gay Science* he offers the curious and puzzling argument that the devotion to truth on which science depends must be either the will not to allow oneself to be deceived or the will not to deceive. The former principle, he claims, is clearly prudential: "One assumes that it is harmful, dangerous, calamitous to be deceived." But this, he continues, is groundless. On many occasions it is much more advantageous to be deceived about the facts than to know the truth about them. Therefore, the unconditional faith "that truth is more important than any other thing, including every other conviction . . . could never have come into being if both truth and untruth proved to be useful, which is the case." The unconditional pursuit of truth, Nietzsche concludes, cannot rest on this prudential principle: " 'Will to truth' does *not* mean 'I will not allow myself to be deceived' but—there is not alternative—'I will not deceive, not even myself'; *and with this we stand on moral ground*" (*GS,* 344). Life, he claims, is full of semblance, error, deception, and delusion: why should human beings be different from the rest of the world? But we do think that we are different; and this belief, which contrasts human beings with the rest of nature, repeats the dialectical moves of self-denial which Nietzsche discusses in his interpretation of the ascetic ideal. The unconditional will to truth springs from an effort on our part to deny nature in general, and our nature, to which deception and error are essential, in particular. It is therefore another version of asceticism.

It is very difficult to evaluate this suggestive argument, if only because it is so compressed and abstract. Nietzsche would have done well, at least in this one case, to go against his own nature and stay with this problem, expand his claim, elucidate his attitude, and even spell out his premises. Fortunately, however, we can leave this argument at this intriguing but far from telling stage. Nietzsche's main reason for thinking that science is a version of asceticism is different from the two I have mentioned so far.

Nietzsche does not explicitly discuss this consideration, which, if the argument of this book is at all correct, is one of the central difficulties his own writing generates and which it aims to resolve: implicit as it is in the structure of his project, it keeps emerging in his texts without having to be the object of direct discussion. This difficulty is the following. An interpretation, simply by virtue of being offered, is inevitably offered in the conviction that it is true. But then, despite any assurances to the contrary, it is presented as a view which everybody must accept on account of its being true. When we show that some other enterprise is partial, even as we assert that ours is partial as well, we implicitly and perhaps against our will commend what we do to universal attention. Every effort to present a view, no matter how explicitly its interpretive nature is admitted, makes an inescapable dogmatic commitment. The point is not that the faith in truth is not questioned enough but that a view cannot be questioned at all while it is being offered. Even a view that denies that there is such a thing as truth must be presented as true. Asceticism, we have seen, tries to conceal that it is an interpretation. Attacking it and demonstrating that it is after all an interpretation is still done in the name of truth. And as long as this commitment is made, the dogmatism on which asceticism depends has not yet been eliminated.

Perhaps it might be possible, as Nietzsche wrote, to "conceive of such a pleasure and power of self-determination, such a *freedom* of the will that the spirit would take leave of all faith and every wish for certainty, being practiced in maintaining itself on insubstantial ropes and possibilities and dancing even near abysses. Such a spirit would be the *free spirit par excellence*" (*GS*, 347). Perhaps one could conceive of such a free spirit, though Nietzsche's own conception stops short of being very specific. He himself may have come close to exemplifying that conception in the *Genealogy*, but he still knows, I think, that he falls short of this perhaps impossible ideal. His genealogical account of morality may raise the question of its own status, but it cannot answer it—not, at least, without another genealogy of Nietzsche's own practice, which would itself raise the same question again. It is no wonder, after all, that the seekers after knowledge remain unknown to themselves. "The will to knowledge," Nietzsche writes, "requires a critique—let us define our own task—the value of truth must for once be experimentally *called into question*" (*GM*, III, 24). But is it possible to undertake this task in the name of anything other than the will to truth itself? Will not such a critique, along with the whole of genealogy, constitute one more case of nature against something that is also nature? And is not this precisely what genealogy revealed asceticism itself to be?

Surprisingly, however, the will to truth, though not simply a "remnant" but the very "kernel" of asceticism, may still be that ideal's worst enemy. Perhaps, that is, asceticism will be undermined from within: "You see what it was that really triumphed over the Christian god: Christian morality itself, the concept of truthfulness that was understood even more rigorously, the father confessor's refinement of the Christian conscience, translated and sublimated into a scientific conscience, into intellectual cleanliness at any price" (*GS*, 357). Science is itself the descendant of the Christian emphasis on truthfulness, and the discipline of "two thousand years of truthfulness . . . finally forbids itself the *lie involved in belief in God*" (*GM*, III, 27). Christianity in this way undermines itself; it causes, as Nietzsche puts it, its own self-overcoming:

> All great things bring about their own destruction through an act of self-overcoming: thus the law of life will have it . . . In this way Christianity *as a dogma* was destroyed by its own morality; in the same way Christianity *as morality* must now perish, too: we stand at the threshold of *this* event. After Christian truthfulness has drawn one inference after another, it must end by drawing *its most striking* inference, its inference *against* itself; this will happen, however,

when it poses the question *"What is the meaning of all will to truth?"* (*GM*, III, 27)

But one may suspect that even this question must be posed in the name of the will to truth. This "event," therefore, may be yet another case of nature against something that is also nature. It may be yet another instance of the circle that animates the very structure of the *Genealogy* as well as the practice this work demonstrates and the objects it investigates. Can such an "event" ever be completed?

This question may be urgent if the issue of truth is raised with Nietzsche's seriousness; for precisely this seriousness still prevents us from deciding (provided we care to do so) whether Nietzsche did or did not liberate himself from "metaphysics" or "philosophy." In my opinion there can be no straightforward answer to either of these questions, and Nietzsche was aware of it. Every attempt to escape "metaphysics," precisely because of the circle I have been discussing, always runs the risk of being taken as, and therefore of being, a part of metaphysics in its own right. By calling for an end to philosophy, Nietzsche, perhaps knowingly, has added to it—if only because his successors have proposed progressively more radical ends for it than the end envisaged by this first of the last metaphysicians. And in trying to place Nietzsche back within philosophy and themselves outside it, his successors have also, in their own turn, produced more philosophy. Ironically, as the ascetic ideal was life's ploy to make people continue to live, so the death of philosophy may be philosophy's own ploy to make people continue to write.[15]

"A depreciation of the ascetic ideal unavoidably involves a depreciation of science," because both depend essentially on the unconditional faith that "truth is inestimable and cannot be criticized" (*GM*, III, 25). But it is not easy to see how science can be depreciated without doing more science and therefore without perpetuating it. Nietzsche knows these difficulties. This is why he denies that science is the ultimate enemy of the ascetic ideal and why he writes that "in the most spiritual sphere, too, the ascetic ideal has at present only *one* kind of real enemy capable of *harming* it: the comedians of this ideal— for they arouse mistrust in it" (*GM,* III, 27). Nietzsche tries to be such a comedian—which does not necessarily involve being funny. Rather, it involves the effort to reveal the inner contradictions and deceptions of asceticism, to denounce it, and yet not produce a view that itself unwittingly repeats the same contradictions and deceptions, for to repeat these is to fail to arouse mistrust in the ascetic ideal; on the contrary, it is to offer a demonstration that it is inescapable. This is the task Nietzsche sets for himself, and with a short discussion of which I shall close this chapter. His attempt to resolve it is the subject of the next part of this book.

We know that Nietzsche denounces Christian morality because of its negative attitude toward life. This view is at the heart not only of the *Genealogy* but of all his late writings as well. The church, he writes, "has at all times laid the stress of discipline on extirpation (of sensuality, of pride, of the lust to rule, of avarice, of vengefulness). But an attack on the roots of passion means an attack on the roots of life: the practice of the church is *hostile to life*" (*TI,* V, 1). This dissonant, discordant effort on the part of a living creature to do away with part of itself is the main reason for Nietzsche's own hostility to Christianity, which he accuses of trying to impose upon everyone an inverted picture of the world: "Wherever the theologians' instinct extends, *value judgments* have been stood on their heads and the concepts 'true' and 'false' are necessarily reversed: whatever is most harmful to life is called 'true'; whatever elevates it, enhances, affirms, justifies it, and makes it triumphant, is called 'false' " (*A, 9*). But we also know that Nietzsche believes that even the most apparently negative ideal still affirms the particular kind of life that is most suited for its adherents. Every interpretation of the world affirms such a life, and the genealogist aims to find what that life is in each individual case. Every denial presupposes some positive values: "Life itself forces us to posit values; life itself values through us when we posit values." An ideal, therefore, that condemns life as we commonly live it must be the ideal of those who cannot live that way, those who themselves are instances "of declining, weakened, condemned life" (*TI,* V, 5). Such an ideal commends declining life and is its means of clinging to itself after all. Those who cannot live life as it is denounce it and invent another mode of living through which they can at least survive if not thrive.

Statements like these suggest that, faced with the Christian reversal of values, Nietzsche advocates a further reversal, an overturning of the Christian ideals. Nietzsche often seems to urge that life must be unequivocally celebrated because, in contrast to the Christian view he rejects, he thinks that life is essentially pleasant, joyful, and good. Some of Nietzsche's earlier writings express such a view (see *BT,* 7, 9, 24). But in his later works he develops a subtler and more sophisticated approach. Instead of attacking negative judgments of life directly, he treats them as hints or signs of the types of people who make them and who are enabled to live by them. But he also treats positive judgments in just the same way. He asks not only whether a judgment is affirmative or negative, since all are ultimately affirmative, but also what specifically it is that each judgment affirms. What Nietzsche eventually comes to attack directly is not any particular judgment but the very tendency to make general judgments about the value of life in itself, as if there were such a single thing with a character of its own, capable of being praised or blamed by some uniform standard. But his perspectivism forbids any general evaluation of this sort, positive or negative: "Judgments, judgments of value, concerning life, for it or against it, can, in the end, never be true; they have value only as symptoms, they are worthy of consideration only as symptoms; in themselves such judgments are stupidities. One must by all means stretch out one's fingers and make the attempt to grasp this amazing finesse, *that the value of life cannot be estimated*" (*TI*, II, 2). There can be no overall evaluations of life, because life in itself, if such a thing exists at all, has no value whatever: "Becoming is of equivalent value every moment; the sum of its values always remains the same; in other words, it has no value at all, for anything against which to measure it, and in relation to which the word 'value' would have meaning, is lacking. *The total value of the world cannot be evaluated;* consequently philosophical pessimism belongs among comical things" (*WP*, 708). This very same argument, of course, implies that philosophical optimism is no less comical. Nietzsche cannot take any general attitude toward life and the world seriously. Consequently his own positive view cannot consist in a simple reversal of the Christian negative evaluation he rejects and in an unqualified celebration of all life.

Yet it is impossible to live without values: "No people could live," Zarathustra says, "without first esteeming." But these values and the judgments in which they are expressed need not (and could not) be universal in the sense just discussed. Zarathustra continues: "But if they want to preserve themselves, then they must not esteem as the neighbor esteems" (*Z*, I, 14). Life itself has no value, but the life of an individual or a group has as great a value as that individual or group can give it. Some lives are mean or horrible, others magnificent. Life's value depends on what one makes of it, and this is a further sense in which Nietzsche believes that value is created and not discovered.

Most people, however, are in his view incapable of seeing this point. They pronounce the same general judgments they have inherited and consequently think that values are already in the world: "Whoever is incapable of laying one's will into things, lacking will and strength, at least lays some *meaning* into them, i.e., the faith that there is a will in them already. It is a measure of the degree of the strength of will to what extent one can do without meaning in things, to what extent one can endure to live in a meaningless world *because one organizes a small portion of it oneself*" (*WP*, 585A).

But what is it to give meaning, organization, and value to the world? It is first, as we shall see in detail in the remainder of this book, to become able to accept the fact that pain and suffering are inelimina-ble parts of life and that they are, like everything else in the world, neither good nor bad in themselves. Their value depends on what, if anything, is made of them: "Human beings, the bravest of animals and those most accustomed to suffering, do *not* repudiate suffering as such; they *desire* it, they even seek it out, provided they are shown a *meaning* for it, a *purpose* of suffering" (*GM*, III, 28). Second, it is to cre-ate for oneself a life that, despite and perhaps because of the pain and suffering it will inevitably contain, will constitute such an achieve-ment that one would be willing to live through it again, down to its smallest detail, exactly as it has already occurred, if one were given that opportunity. It is to want one's life to be exactly what it has been and to be unwilling and even unable to conceive that a life in any way different would be a life of one's own.

This is the thought of the eternal recurrence. It presupposes, as we shall see, that one has shaped oneself into an object so organized that every single part of it is equally essential and in which, therefore, any alteration would bring about a breakdown of the whole. What is pri-marily important for such a type of person is the organization of its experiences and actions and not their intrinsic or moral character. This essentially aesthetic attitude toward life and the world involves a radical formalism, of which Nietzsche was perfectly aware; as we have seen, he wrote, "Content henceforth becomes something merely formal—our life included" (*WP*, 818).

To be, then, a comedian of the ascetic ideal is to give up the very idea of trying to determine in general terms the value of life and the world. It is to turn to oneself in order to make one's life valuable with-out claiming that one's particular method for accomplishing this end should, or even could, be followed by others. It is to be a moral perspectivist.

But the ability to exemplify greatness without demonstrating the means of achieving it, and without even caring to require that anyone else achieve it, is one of the most essential features of great artworks. Nietzsche knows the opposition between art and morality very well indeed: "Art, in which precisely the *lie* is sanctified and the *will to deception* has good conscience, is much more fundamentally opposed to the ascetic ideal than is science: this was instinctively sensed by Plato, the greatest enemy of art Europe has yet produced" (*GM,* III, 25). Nietzsche's problem is that he wants to attack the tradition to which he belongs and also escape it. An explicit attack, as we saw, would perpetuate that tradition. A complete escape from it directly into art (something he did at times consider) would simply change the subject but leave that tradition intact. Nietzsche wants to warn others against dogmatism without taking a dogmatic stand himself. His unparalleled solution to this problem is to try consciously to fashion a literary character out of himself and a literary work out of his life. In what follows we shall examine his solution. We shall ask what is involved in the creation out of one's own self of a literary character whose views are exclusively philosophical; what philosophical views about the world and life make this project possible; and whether the effort of turning life into literature escapes the problem of dogmatism and the necessity of turning nature against something that is also nature.

II | THE SELF

5 | *This Life— Your Eternal Life*

It's the difference between making the most out of life and making the least, so that you'll get another better one in some other time and place. Will it be a sin to make the most out of that one too, I wonder; and shall we have to be bribed off in the future state as well as in the present?

Henry James, "The Author of Beltraffio"

Whatever else we may be tempted to say of Nietzsche's ideas, it is unlikely that we shall describe many of them as sensible. Time after time, Nietzsche tears at the fabric of common sense, at the sense of ordinary language, at the language of reasonable thought. This is a feature of his writing on which he insists and of which he is proud. "How *could* I mistake myself," he asks, "for one of those for whom there are ears even now? Only the day after tomorrow belongs to me. Some are born posthumously" (*A*, Pref.). And in a letter to Carl von Gersdorff he writes with arrogant simplicity, "There's no one alive today who could write anything like *Zarathustra*."[1]

By insisting so strenuously on his unique position in the history of thought, essential as this may be to his project, Nietzsche may actually have done himself a great disservice, for he has made it easier to attribute to him views that are often impossible to accept and then either to defend them without good reason as views whose time has not yet come or to dismiss them without proper attention as the thoughts of someone more interested in shocking than in teaching. But though Nietzsche was undoubtedly eager to shock, he never considered shocking incompatible with teaching, which he was equally eager to do. And yet none of his views has made this more difficult to believe than the very one of which he says that both Zarathustra (Z, III, 13) and he himself (TI, X, 5) are the teachers: this is that most peculiar among his many peculiar ideas, the eternal recurrence.

Most commonly, the eternal recurrence is interpreted as a cosmological hypothesis. As such, it holds that everything that has already happened in the universe, and everything that is happening at this very moment, and everything that will happen in the future, has already happened and will happen again, preceded and followed by exactly the same events in exactly the same order, an infinite number of times. Each of these cycles is absolutely identical with every other; in fact, it would be more correct (if anything could be correct in this context) to say that there is only one cycle, repeated over and over again to infinity. One might then write of "the world as a circular movement that has already repeated itself infinitely often and plays its game in infinitum" (WP, 1066). There can be no variations, and hence no interactions, between these repetitions. Everything that we are now doing we have already done in the past, though it is impossible to remember, since that would constitute an interaction between two of the cycle's repetitions. And we shall do everything again, exactly as we are doing it now, infinitely many times in the future.[2]

Though some interpreters simply cannot believe that Nietzsche could actually have accepted a theory of this nature,[3] it is not impossible to find support for such a reading in his texts. The evidence, however, is far from telling. For one thing, this cosmological doctrine is not be be found in a number of passages where Nietzsche discusses the recurrence. For another, much of what Nietzsche actually writes about the recurrence and its psychological impact does not commit him to this cosmological hypothesis. The psychological use to which he so crucially puts the eternal recurrence presupposes only a weaker view which is quite independent of any theory of the physical universe. This weaker view makes a much more serious claim on our attention than the cosmological theory with which Nietzsche's commentators, and sometimes perhaps even Nietzsche himself, have identified it.

Nietzsche may have suspected at times that this cosmology was useless to him. If this is true, it would explain why he never tried to publish any of his "proofs" of the recurrence, despite the fact that, if it is interpreted cosmologically, the theory is inseparable from some such proof. Since it is essentially a theory for which no empirical support can possibly be given, the recurrence cannot even begin to appear credible independently of an a priori demonstration of some sort.[4] This is not a minor matter, for in a famous passage Nietzsche describes the recurrence as "the fundamental conception of" *Thus Spoke Zarathustra* (*EH*, III, on *Z*, 1), and he considers that Zarathustra himself, as we just saw, is its teacher. But to teach a theory of the universe is at least to make some effort to show that it is true, and Nietzsche never makes this effort in his published work. It might be claimed that the style in which *Zarathustra* is written does not tolerate an attempt at a scientific proof of the theory. And one might argue that the section "On the Vision and the Riddle" (*Z*, III, 2), which I shall soon discuss in detail, comes as close to offering such a proof as is compatible with the work's lyrical style. But we have also seen that Nietzsche describes himself as the teacher of the eternal recurrence in *The Twilight of the Idols.* The style and force of this work differ drastically from the tone of *Zarathustra* and could easily tolerate a rigorous proof of the cosmological doctrine; nevertheless, Nietzsche chose not to include such a proof in that text either.

Nietzsche did leave some sketches of a proof of a cosmology in his notes, and Elizabeth Förster-Nietzsche included some of these in *The Will to Power,* giving them great weight by placing them at the end of the volume (*WP,* 1053–1067). But it is very difficult to determine what the purpose of these sketches is. This, and not their unpublished status, makes it difficult to take them as the heart of Nietzsche's view. Did Nietzsche plan to include them in a work which he was never able to write (see *WP,* 1057)? Was he so dissatisfied with the proof he had devised that he decided not to publish it until he was convinced by it? Or did he think that, despite the importance the recurrence has for his thought, a proof of the doctrine was not after all necessary?

Whatever the answer to these questions, Nietzsche should have been deeply dissatisfied with his "proof," which is incomplete and invalid. Without going into this question in great detail, we can see that in order to reach the conclusion that the history of the universe is eternally repeating itself, at least two premises are necessary:

(1) the sum total of energy in the universe is finite
(2) the total number of energy states in the universe is finite

Nietzsche, who discusses these premises explicitly, seems to think that the first entails the second (*KGW,* V2, 421). But this is not correct. A system may have only a finite amount of energy, and yet that total can be distributed in an infinite number of ways; this would then prevent the repetition which Nietzsche may have had in mind.[5] Premise 2 must be given an independent justification, and it is not at all clear what such a justification would be. In any case, behind this and other similar considerations there lurks Georg Simmel's classical refutation which grants that premise 2 is true and that there is only a finite number of states in the system (three, to be precise) and which still shows that a particular combination of these states will never recur.[6]

A careful reading of the passages that are commonly taken to support the cosmological interpretation of the recurrence, even though they do not offer to prove it, shows that it is not even clear that they assert that theory. One such passage, for example, is note 55 of *The Will to Power,* which actually consists of passages collected from different notebooks, in which Nietzsche describes the eternal recurrence as "the most *scientific* of all possible hypotheses." Assuming that by "scientific" Nietzsche must mean "objective" and that by this he must mean "physical," it is argued that therefore he must think of the hypothesis in question as a cosmology (cf. Kaufmann, p. 326). But this assumption is unjustified. First, apart from the commonplace that the connotations of *wissenschaftlich* are much broader than those of the English word *scientific,* we must recall Nietzsche's fundamental suspicion of natural science: "It is perhaps dawning on five or six minds that physics, too, is only an interpretation and exegesis of the world (to suit us, if I may say so!) and *not* a world-explanation" (*BGE,* 14); "most of what today displays itself as 'objectivity,' 'being scientific,' ... 'pure knowledge, free of will,' is merely dressed up skepticism and paralysis of the will" (*BGE,* 208). We cannot therefore assume without argument that the eternal recurrence represents Nietzsche's effort to outdo physics at its own game, a game which, in any case, he does not recognize in its traditional version. Also, if we are to interpret this phrase, we must pay attention to the context within which it occurs. The passage within which it is found begins as follows: "Let us think this thought in its most terrible form: existence as it is, without meaning or aim, yet recurring inevitably without any finale of nothingness: 'the eternal recurrence.' This is the most extreme form of nihilism: the nothing (the 'meaningless') eternally!" (*WP*, 55). What is at issue here is clearly only the thought that the universe is not progressing in any way, that there is nothing specific toward which it tends, and that it will continue as it is now indefinitely—not the view that the very same individual events in it will be eternally repeated. Nietzsche is discussing the collapse of Christianity and of the idea that every individual life as well as the whole world has a purpose of its own. This collapse now makes it seem "as if there were no meaning at all in existence, as if everything were in vain . . . Duration 'in vain,' without end or aim, is the most paralyzing idea" (*WP*, 55).

In this whole passage Nietzsche does not once allude to the specific cosmological view with which the recurrence is usually identified. He is interested only in the realization that the world will continue to be more or less as it has always been so long as it exists, that no final state will redeem those who have gone before. This becomes more obvious when we realize that this passage supplies its own interpretation of the term that concerns us. Having written that the recurrence, as described above, is "the most *scientific* of all possible hypotheses," Nietzsche continues immediately, "We deny end goals; if existence had one, it would have been reached" (*WP*, 55). This shows that instead of being objective or in correspondence to the facts, notions which Nietzsche finds in any case to be incoherent, the eternal recurrence is "scientific" in that it is strictly nonteleological; this is after all the central theme with which this note is concerned. The interpretation of the recurrence which this chapter presents is clearly "scientific" in this sense of the term.

In fact, it is very difficult to find any clear references to cosmology in Nietzsche's published discussions of the recurrence. At one point he praises "the ideal of the most high-spirited, alive, and world-affirming human being who has not only come to terms and learned to get along with whatever was and is, but who wants to have *what was and is* repeated into all eternity, shouting insatiably *da capo*" (*BGE*, 56). But all that is involved here is the *desire* that "what was and is" be eternally repeated. The passage is quite vague as to exactly what it is that is to be repeated, as to whether the cosmology associated with the eternal recurrence is true, and even as to whether it is at all coherent. The truth of this hypothesis is no more presupposed in the following passage: "My formula for greatness for a human being is *amor fati:* that one wants nothing to be different, not forward, not backward, not in all eternity. Not merely bear what is necessary, still less conceal it—all idealism is mendaciousness in the face of what is necessary—but *love* it" (*EH*, II, 10).

Even the following text, which may appear absolutely telling, may leave a careful reader with doubts:

> The affirmation of passing away *and destroying*, which is the decisive feature of a Dionysian philosophy; saying Yes to opposition and war; *becoming*, along with a radical repudiation of the very concept of *being*—all this is clearly more closely related to me than anything else thought to date. The doctrine of the "eternal recurrence," that is, of the unconditional and infinitely repeated circular course of all things [*alle Dinge*]—this doctrine of Zarathustra *might* in the end have been taught already by Heraclitus. (*EH*, III, on *BT*, 3)[7]

We would be wrong, I think, to assume without question that the expression *alle Dinge* refers to each and every individual occurrence in the history of the world, for Nietzsche connects the recurrence with Dionysianism, a religion that emphasizes the infinite repetition of the cycles of nature, not the individual events that constitute world history. What Nietzsche himself underscores here is the fact that Dionysianism celebrates every aspect of these cycles, even the phases that consist in degeneration and decay. And the relation of his view to that of Heraclitus is effected not through cosmology but through Heraclitus' writing that war and death are the other sides of peace and life, that none of them could exist without any of the others. In fact, Nietzsche sometimes seems to deny precisely the cosmology that is so often attributed to him: "Let us beware," he writes, "of positing generally and everywhere anything as elegant as the cyclical movements of our neighboring stars" (*GS*, 109).

The two passages that come closest to presenting a cosmology occur in *Thus Spoke Zarathustra*. In the section entitled "The Convalescent" (*Z*, III, 13), Zarathustra finally manages to face what is there described as his "abysmal thought," an idea whose connection to the recurrence must be made clear as we proceed. This thought is so horrible that, having faced it, he lies impassive and insensible for seven whole days. At the end of this period, his animals, which have been watching over him, address him and say:

> Everything goes, everything comes back; eternally rolls the wheel of being. Everything dies, everything blossoms again; eternally runs

the year of being. Everything breaks, everything is joined anew; eternally the same house is being built. Everything parts, everything greets every other thing again; eternally the ring of being remains faithful to itself. In every Now, being begins; round every Here rolls the sphere There. The center is everywhere. Bent is the path of eternity. (Z, III, 13)

This, however, is once again nothing more than the Dionysian view of nature, which I have already discussed. The animals, though, go on to hail Zarathustra as "the teacher of the eternal recurrence" and tell him that he is the one who "must first teach this doctrine." They then claim to "know what you teach: that all things recur eternally, and we ourselves too; and we have already existed an eternal number of times, and all things with us" (Z, III, 13). There is irony in the fact that the animals claim that Zarathustra must be the *first* to teach a doctrine which, if true, has already been taught an infinite number of times. There is even greater irony in that it is *they* and not Zarathustra who become the first to present this doctrine. But what is even more important is that Zarathustra himself, who affectionately yet condescendingly calls his animals "buffoons and barrel-organs" and accuses them of turning his thoughts into "a hurdy-gurdy song," remains totally silent and does not once acknowledge the idea his animals attribute to him. And even this idea need not be the strict version of the eternal recurrence as a cosmology. Consistent with the animals' Dionysianism, it could be the idea that what constitutes us has already existed an infinite number of times, in all sorts of different combinations, and will recur again. Such an idea is what Nietzsche may have in mind in writing: "The world exists; it is not something that becomes, not something that passes away. Or rather: it becomes, it passes away, but it has never ceased from passing away—its excrements are its food" (WP, 1066). In fact, in *Schopenhauer as Educator,* Nietzsche argues explicitly that the same human being cannot exist twice even by means of an accident of cosmic proportions: "In our heart we all know quite well that, being unique, we will be in the world only once and that no imaginable chance will for a second time gather together into a unity so strangely variegated an assortment as we are" (*UM*, III, 1).

Is, then, Zarathustra's "abysmal thought" the cosmology of the eternal recurrence? Though it is often claimed that it is, the text actually suggests that it is not: "The great disgust with man—*this* choked me and had crawled in my throat . . . my sighing and questioning croaked and gagged and gnawed and wailed by day and night: 'Alas, man recurs eternally! The small man recurs eternally!' " (Z, III, 13). This suggestion is supported by another passage, in which Nietzsche writes that "Zarathustra is . . . he that has had the hardest, most terrible insight into reality, that has thought the 'most abysmal idea,' and nevertheless does not consider it an objection to existence, not even to *its eternal recurrence*—but rather one reason more for being himself the eternal Yes to all things" (*EH*, III, on *Z*, 6; my italics). It would be impossible to interpret this statement if we took the "abysmal idea" to be the thought that the universe recurs eternally, for, since this idea is described as a possible *objection* to existence and to its eternal recurrence, Nietzsche would then be writing that the eternal recurrence constitutes an objection to itself. This passage, however, can be read smoothly and without difficulty if we identify this abysmal thought with the recurrence of the type of person represented by "the small man." Zarathustra is disgusted with the thought that this contemptible type, related to the "last man" of the Prologue, who asks " 'What is love? What is creation? What is longing? What is a star?' . . . and . . . blinks" (Z, Pref., 5), is ineliminable and will never cease to exist. We do not need to suppose that the world repeats itself infinitely in order to explain Zarathustra's disgust. All he needs to think is that if he were to exist again, then everything about the world, evil as well as good, the small man included, would also have to exist again. More horrible still is the idea that if he were to want to live his life again, which is the desire he is trying to make his own, then he must also want all evil, the small man included, to exist again as well. This is Zarathustra's abysmal thought, and it does not even presuppose the obscure cosmology with which the recurrence is often identified.

In "On the Vision and the Riddle" (Z, III, 2) Zarathustra confronts his "spirit of gravity," a lame dwarf whom he has been carrying on his shoulders while climbing a hill (cf. Z, IV, 12). It is this dwarf, and not Zarathustra, who claims that "all truth is crooked, time itself is a circle," just as a soothsayer had earlier cried, "All is empty, all is the same, all has been!" (Z, II, 19). To liberate himself from the dwarf, Zarathustra, standing by a gateway, says to him:

> Behold . . . this moment! From this gateway, Moment, a long, eternal lane leads *backward:* behind us lies an eternity. Must not what-

ever *can* walk have walked on this lane before? Must not whatever *can* happen have happened, have been done, have passed by before? And if everything has been there before—what do you think, dwarf, of this moment? Must not this gateway too have been before? And are not all things knotted together so firmly that this moment draws after it *all* that is to come? Therefore, itself too? For whatever *can* walk—in this long lane out *there* too, it *must* walk once more.

And this slow spider, which crawls in the moonlight, and this moonlight itself, and I and you in the gateway, whispering together, whispering of eternal things—must not all of us have been there before? And return and walk in that other lane, out there, before us, in this dreadful lane—must we not eternally return? (Z, III, 2)

Though this passage contains the clearest statement of the cosmological version of the recurrence among Nietzsche's published texts, there still are some peculiarities about it. Zarathustra tells all this to the dwarf in order to ward him off; and at the end of his narrative the dwarf does indeed suddenly disappear. He is as unconditionally frightened by this idea as Zarathustra's animals are later unquestioningly glad about it. Zarathustra, that is, has a clear purpose in telling this story. Does he himself believe it? If he does, why does Nietzsche write in "The Convalescent," which occurs considerably later in this work, that Zarathustra has not yet taught the recurrence? Could it be that Zarathustra tells the story only in order to frighten the dwarf, while the psychological implications Nietzsche wants to draw from it presuppose only a weaker hypothesis?

Such a hypothesis would be that in this and in every moment is implicit everything that has occurred in the past and everything that will occur in the future. In discussing the will to power, I showed that Nietzsche believes that every event in the world is inextricably connected with every other. He believes that if anything had occurred differently, everything would have had to occur differently; that if anything happened again, everything would have to happen again. He thinks that the history of the whole world, or, in more modest terms, the history of each person, is totally involved in every moment: "Don't you know that? In every action you perform the history of every event is repeated and abridged" (*Grossoktav*, XII, 726; cf. *WP*, 373). In this sense nothing that ever happens to us, even if it is the result of the most implausible accident and the wildest coincidence, is contingent—once it has occurred. This is a point of which Zarathustra becomes increasingly aware in the course of his development, as the following passage, to which we shall have to refer again, shows: "The time is gone when mere accidents could still happen to me; and what could still come to me now that was not mine already? What returns, what finally comes home to me, is my own self and what of myself has long been in strange lands and scattered among all things and accidents" (Z, III, 1). Such an essential connection between the world's temporal stages implies that if any one of them recurred at any time, all the others would also have to recur. And therefore every cheap and detestable part of the world, which is as necessary to what the world is as its very best aspects and moments, would also recur if anything at all recurred. This is, I have just argued, the abysmal thought Zarathustra has to accept in "The Convalescent." But at the earlier stage of the narrative at which "On the Vision and the Riddle" is found, this thought prompts him to have a vision. He sees a shepherd who is choking because a snake has crawled into his mouth and has there bitten itself fast. He yells to the shepherd to bite the snake's head off, and the shepherd, who follows Zarathustra's advice, is transformed, "no longer shepherd, no longer human—one changed, radiant, laughing!" (Z, III, 2). Zarathustra then asks, in a riddle, who that shepherd is. Nietzsche answers the riddle in terms of the very same imagery in "The Convalescent" ("The great disgust with man—*this* choked me and had crawled into my throat" Z, III, 13): the shepherd is Zarathustra himself, once he has finally become able to want to undergo again all that is cheap and detestable in the world for the sake of all that is not.

Perhaps Nietzsche realized that this "thought" (*Gedanke*), which is what he often calls the eternal recurrence, is independent of the cosmology he sometimes entertained; this would explain why he never worked out in detail his attempts to prove that hypothesis. Or perhaps he did not. The evidence, though it suggests that he did, is not absolutely telling. Philosophically, however, the use Nietzsche makes of the eternal recurrence does not require that this highly doubtful cosmology be true or even coherent. But the defects of this theory have unfortunately obscured the most serious and valuable aspects of Nietzsche's writing about these issues: the psychological consequences he draws from the recurrence and his application of these consequences to his own life. The eternal recurrence is not a theory of the world but a view of the self.[8]

A version of this view appears in Nietzsche's works as early as the fourth book of *The Gay Science,* which contains his first sustained treatment of the problems connected with the thought of the eternal recurrence:

> *The greatest weight.*—What, if some day or night a demon were to steal after you into your loneliest loneliness and say to you: "This life as you now live it and have lived it, you will have to live once more and innumerable times more; and there will be nothing new in it, but every pain and every joy and every thought and every sigh and everything unutterably small or great in your life will have to return to you, all in the same succession and sequence—even this spider and this moonlight between the trees, and even this moment and I myself. The eternal hourglass of existence is turned upside down again and again, and you with it, speck of dust!"
>
> Would you not throw yourself down and gnash your teeth and curse the demon who spoke thus? Or have you once experienced a tremendous moment when you would have answered him: "You are a god and never have I heard anything more divine." If this thought gained possession of you, it would change you as you are or perhaps crush you. The question in each and every thing, "Do you desire this once more and innumerable times more?" would lie upon your actions as the greatest weight. Or how well disposed would you have to become toward yourself and to life to crave nothing more fervently than this ultimate confirmation and seal? (*GS,* 341; cf. *KGW,* V2 394)

It is clear that this passage, in which the demon plays the role Zarathustra plays in "On the Vision and the Riddle," does not presuppose the truth of the view that the world, or even that one's own life, eternally repeats itself; it does not even presuppose that this idea is at all credible. Nietzsche is simply not interested in this question. What he is interested in is the attitude one must have toward oneself in order to react with joy and not despair to the possibility the demon raises, to the thought that one's life will occur, the very same in every single detail, again and again and again for all eternity.[9]

As one reads this passage, it is absolutely crucial to note that Nietzsche considers only two reactions to the demon's question, somewhat in line with the shepherd's alternate choking and dancing: total despair and complete exhilaration. He does not, in particular, consider that one might, quite reasonably, remain indifferent to this thought. Such indifference could be of two sorts. The first sort is indifference to the actual fact of recurrence, and it is well described by Arthur Danto, who has interpreted the recurrence as a purely cosmological theory: "It does not matter that we pass away and return and pass away again. What counts is what we eternally do, the joy of overcoming, whatever our task may be, and the meaning we give to our lives. And all of this for the sake of the thing itself, not for any consequences: for it leads to what it has led to and always will" (p. 212). The very same attitude is envisaged by Nikos Kazantzakis: "I subdue the last, the greatest temptation: hope. We fight because so it pleases us; we sing though there are no ears to hear us. Where are we going? Shall we ever win? What is this whole battle about? Don't ask! Fight!"[10] This reaction does involve an affirmation, but this cannot be the "ultimate confirmation and seal" of Nietzsche's text, despite his having written, in a passage which Kazantzakis' text clearly echoes, "Unlearn this 'for,' you creators! Your very virtue wants that you do nothing 'for' and 'in order' and 'because' " (Z, IV, 13). The affirmation Danto and Kazantzakis describe is based on a prior indifference to the fact that what we are doing now we have already done and shall inevitably do again.[11] Yet Nietzsche seems to want to avoid all such indifference. In fact, Zarathustra, through his notion of self-overcoming, wants his followers to accept wholeheartedly even the whole past, which seems to be totally beyond their control: "A new will I teach to human beings: to *will* this way which humanity has walked blindly and to affirm it" (Z, I, 3).

A second sort of indifference has been discussed by Ivan Soll, who is concerned with the psychological consequences of the possibility, and not the actuality, of the recurrence of one's life. It would seem that, given the suprahistorical character of the recurrence, I cannot possibly anticipate now my experiences in future recurrences or remember then what I am going through now. And since some psychological continuity of this sort is at least a necessary condition for my being concerned with my self's future, the possibility that I may live again in exactly the way I have lived already, Soll concludes, "should actually be a matter of complete indifference."[12] But though it seems to me true that if I were to have any future experiences that would be totally unrelated to my present life, these could not possibly be of concern to me now, the fact remains that Nietzsche fails to consider this alternative altogether.

Should we conclude from this that Nietzsche, who is convinced of the crucial immediacy of the recurrence and of its capacity to generate the greatest affirmation or denial of this life, has misunderstood the implications of one of his own most central ideas? Though this is not of course impossible, it seems to me much more likely that the reason why Nietzsche does not consider indifference as possible reaction to recurrence shows that he does not consider the recurrence a cosmological theory in any way; for both the reactions I have just discussed require that one remain indifferent to the recurrence in its cosmological aspect: the former to recurrence as an actual fact, the latter to its possibility.

There is, however, an interpretation of the recurrence that makes no appeal whatsoever to the physical structure of the world, and to which the two reactions Nietzsche exclusively envisages are perfectly appropriate. In fact, on this understanding of the recurrence no other reaction to it is possible. To simplify our discussion, let us begin by considering the single repetition of an individual life; we shall then be able to generalize this case to infinitely many repetitions of the history of the world.

The most common view of the eternal recurrence construes it as the unconditional assertion of a cosmology:

(A) My life *will* recur in exactly identical fashion.

This construction results in either a totally fatalistic resignation or a totally indifferent, unconcerned joy in effort that is known to be doomed.

The second view takes the eternal recurrence as the conditional assertion of a cosmology:

(B) My life *may* recur in exactly identical fashion.

But the psychological consequence of this interpretation too seems to be utter and unqualified indifference. Both versions fail to capture the reactions Nietzsche so graphically describes in *GS*, 341.

The view I am about to propose takes the eternal recurrence to be the assertion of a conditional:

(C) If my life were to recur, then it could recur only in identical fashion.

This interpretation is totally independent of physics. It does not presuppose the truth of the cosmology I have discussed, or indeed its coherence, since it does not assert that my life *could* ever recur at all. What it does depend on instead is Nietzsche's general conception of how things are constituted, the view discussed in Chapter 3. It concerns the relation of a subject to its experiences and actions, or, more generally, the relation of an object to its properties. Its psychological consequences are direct, serious, and anything but a matter of indifference.

Before we ask what these consequences are, however, we must first determine how the conditional is to be justified. Why, one can wonder, are we not offered the possibility of living again, but also the option of doing at least some things differently in this new life? There are many times, for example, when we wish that we had had at an earlier age the kind of knowledge that we came to have only later in life, and so to have followed a different path to the present—that is, a path to a different present. We have all sometimes wished that we had not acted as we did or that we had acted as we didn't. We all may, with good reason, want to change part of our past, our present, or what we foresee to be our future.

Why then does Nietzsche's demon not offer us this apparently reasonable alternative? Why does he speak only of the repetition of the very same life in its every detail and not also of the return of a life that is similar but not identical to the one we have already had? The answer to these questions, I have been insisting, is not to be found in Nietzsche's physics or in his theory of time, even if he himself may have on occasion thought so. The answer is to be found in his rejection of the idea of the substantial subject, of the view that a person is something more than the totality of its experiences and actions. This is in turn a special case of his rejection of the idea of the thing-in-itself, which he conceives as an object that underlies the total set of its features and properties. Therefore, Nietzsche's ultimate reason for thinking that if my life were to recur it would have to be in every way identical with the life I have already had is his view of the will to power, of which the rejection of the thing-in-itself is in turn one aspect.

We have already found this view in Nietzsche's texts: "There is no 'being' behind doing, effecting, becoming; 'the doer' is merely a fiction added to the deed [or doing: *Thun*]—the deed is everything . . . our entire science still lies under the misleading influence of language and has not disposed of that little changeling, the 'subject' (the atom, for example, is such a changeling, as is the Kantian 'thing-in-itself')"

(*GM*, I, 13).[13] Nietzsche often illustrates this idea through the image of lightning, to which he appeals in this same passage as well as elsewhere: "If I say 'lightning flashes,' I have posited the flash once as an activity and a second time as a subject, and thus added to the event a being that is not one with the event but is rather fixed, *is*, and does not 'become' " (*WP*, 531). He relies on this same image when he attacks "our bad habit of taking a mnemonic, an abbreviative formula, to be an entity, finally as a cause, e.g. to say of lightning 'it flashes.' Or the little word 'I' " (*WP*, 548). His reference to lightning in the following passage establishes a connection between the will to power and the eternal recurrence and thus supports the interpretation I have started to develop: "If only a moment of the world recurred—said the lightning—all would have to recur" (*KGW*, VII, 1, 503).

Nietzsche believes that nothing is left over beyond the sum total of the features and characteristics associated with each object and that no person remains beyond the totality of its experiences and actions. If any of these were different, then their subject, which is simply their sum total, would also have to be different. He seems to think that strictly speaking all properties are equally essential to their subjects and thus that there is ultimately no distinction to be drawn between essential and accidental properties at all: if any property were different, its subject would simply be a different subject. But he also accepts the stronger view that if *any* object in the world were at all different, then *every* object in the world would also be different. This is because, as we have seen, he thinks that the properties of each thing are nothing but its effects on other things, the properties of which are in turn nothing but still further such effects. Therefore, if a property of something, and so that thing itself, were different, some other things would necessarily be affected differently by it. They would thus also be different, and would therefore in turn affect still other things differently, the chain rounding back to its hypothetical first member and beginning anew. The view that "there is no thing without other things" (*WP*, 557) underlies Zarathustra's famous statement: "Have you ever said Yes to a single joy? O my friends, then you have said Yes too to all woe. All things are entangled, ensnared, enamored; if ever you wanted one thing twice, if ever you said, 'You please me, happiness! Abide, moment!' then you wanted *all* back. All anew, all eternally, all entangled, ensnared, enamored" (Z, IV, 19). This same view also constitutes the background against which Nietzsche writes, "If we affirm one single moment, we thus affirm not only ourselves but all existence" (*WP*, 1032), and it accounts for his view that "the concept 'reprehensible action' presents us with difficulties. Nothing that happened at all can be reprehensible in itself: for one should not want to eliminate it: for everything is so bound up with everything else, that to want to exclude something means to exclude everything. A reprehensible action means: a reprehended world" (*WP*, 293).

It is therefore the will to power that explains why the demon offers us only the very same life, which we can either accept or reject entirely; a life that was different in any way would simply not be our life: it would be the life of a different person. To want to be different in any way is for Nietzsche to want to be different in every way; it is to want, impossible as that is, to be somebody else. This is precisely the ascetic attitude as Nietzsche describes it in the third essay of the *Genealogy* (*III*, 14): to want anything about oneself to change is for one to want to cease to be who one is.

Since Nietzsche thinks that everything in the world is interrelated, to want oneself to be different is also to want the whole world to be different. This fact now explains why he describes only two reactions to the demon's offer. If I accept any part of myself and my life, then I accept everything about it, and everything about the whole world as well; but if I reject any part, however small and insignificant, then I reject my entire life and all the world with it. There is no middle ground.

This version of the eternal recurrence can now be generalized and made to apply to everything in the world. Our earlier view (C) now becomes:

(C′) If anything in the world recurred, including an individual life or even a single moment within it, then everything in the world would recur in exactly identical fashion.

In *The Gay Science*, Nietzsche had probably not yet thought of his view in just these terms, and he had not expressly connected it with his view of the will to power, which he was at that time, as Kaufmann shows (pp. 188–189), in the process of developing. In this work his question is simply how would one react to the possibility of living one's life over again. But the foundation was set. What he then came to see in August 1881, "6000 feet beyond people and time" (*EH*, III, on Z, 1), what constitutes without doubt the fundamental conception of

Zarathustra, is the idea, whose implications are present and striking throughout this text, that if we were to have another life it would necessarily have to be, if it were to be *our* life at all, the very same life we have already had. And it could not be the very same life without being part of the very same world in which we have already lived, and which therefore would have to recur exactly as it has already occurred down to its most minute, its most detestable and most horrible details.[14]

Zarathustra "the godless," who bids his listeners "remain faithful to the earth, and . . . not believe those who speak . . . of otherworldly hopes" (Z, Pref., 3), discovers in the eternal recurrence that this life and this world are the only life and the only world there are: "This life—your eternal life" (*KGW,* VI, 513). Even if we were to live again, even if we were given that possibility infinitely many times, we would only be given the same life we have already had. If our life, then, is ever to be redeemed, it is to be redeemed now, and not in a distinct afterlife. The "other" world constitutes for Nietzsche a conceptual impossibility as well as a deceptive falsehood.

Nietzsche believes that a second, different life is impossible because of his view that every single one of my actions is equally essential to what I am. But why should we accept this view? Insignificantly different actions—for example, my having worn slightly different clothes on an immaterial occasion—should constitute only insignificant differences in my person. Should not Nietzsche allow for such variations in weight and importance?

Strictly speaking, Nietzsche's position is that every one of a person's actions is without qualification equally a part of that person's identity: no variations are possible. On a psychological level, however, the eternal recurrence can give a more complicated answer to this question; for, though the occurrence of an action is in some sense given and unalterable, its significance, and thus ultimately for him its very nature, can still be variable.

The first thing to note in this context is that it would be perverse of me to want to repeat my life exactly as it has occurred already with the sole exception of something—for example, once having worn an inappropriate tie—which I begin by considering insignificant. Why should I want that event to be different; why would I even notice it, single it out, and care about it, if it did not matter to me that it ever occurred in the first place? Insignificant events are precisely those that don't remain with us; they do not even form part of our own image of our life. Nietzsche cares about those aspects of our life about which we ourselves care: the aspects that are important to us, that give our life its character, and that determine in our own eyes the kind of person we are. Some people do in fact consider dress quite insignificant. And those for whom wearing the wrong tie constitutes a trifle will not be consumed by nausea and despair at the prospect of living through it again—that is, at the thought (if it occurs to them at all) that they have already done so. The same is true of anything anyone considers unimportant. To want only insignificantly different characteristics of our life to be different, provided we are even aware of them in the first place, is to want to be significantly like what we are. But just the fact that we are aware of some particular feature may suggest that it is more significant to us than we may want to admit.

What, then, is in general significant to the way we view ourselves? To this question there is, according to Nietzsche, no answer—for two reasons. The first is that there is no answer that applies uniformly to different individuals. Nietzsche's perspectivism dictates this approach: "They . . . have discovered themselves who say, 'This is *my* good and evil'; with that they have reduced to silence the mole and dwarf who say, 'Good for all, evil for all' . . . 'This is *my* way; where is yours?'—thus I answered those who asked me 'the way.' For *the* way—that does not exist" (Z, III, 11; cf. *KGW*, VI, 493). The second reason is that there is no fixed answer even to the question of what is significant for each particular individual over time. The relative importance of our experiences and actions is not determined once and for all; it is, rather, a characteristic over which we have serious control. Though Nietzsche believes that all our actions are equally important to our nature, he also thinks that how these actions are related to our nature, what nature they actually constitute, is always an open question. How we perceive the relationships among our actions, which patterns we take to be characteristic and determining of our conduct, which actions belong to them and have lasting implications and which do not and are only exceptions and accidents—all these he takes to be questions that are constantly receiving different answers. The character Nietzsche sometimes calls the *Übermensch* is essentially aware of the fluidity of the personality. And it is this fluidity that accounts for Nietzsche's emphasis on constant "self-overcoming" when he introduces the *Übermensch* in the Prologue and in the opening sections of *Zarathustra*.

The fluidity of character in turn explains why the eternal recurrence can function as the "highest formula of affirmation that is at all attainable" (*EH*, III, on Z, 1). The discussion in the section "On Redemption" (Z, II, 20) suggests that a life can be justified only if it comes to be accepted in its entirety. The mark of this is the desire to repeat this very life, and so everything else in the world as well, in all eternity. This means that we should want nothing in that life and the world to be in any way different. Let us then suppose that one comes to accept Zarathustra's thought, that one begins to try to be such as one would want to be again, that one tries to act as the *Übermensch* acts (cf. Z, I, 1, 16). Is this a project that could ever succeed?

Two grave difficulties would face this effort. First, our power to control the future does not seem to be as absolute as Zarathustra sometimes suggests, since what is possible at any given time is always limited by what has already occurred, by our past and present. Nietzsche's image of the "self-propelled wheel" (Z, I, 1) seems much too simple in this context. Second, from a naive but not easily assailable point of view, it would seem that our past is now given to us: it consists of events that have already occurred and over which we no longer have any control. Among them there are bound to be experiences and actions, character traits, and even whole phases of our personalities and parts of our lives which we would with good reason never want to repeat again, which we can't help regretting. These are fixed. How can we now accept these unacceptable parts of our past?

Such questions exercise Nietzsche in *Zarathustra:*

> To redeem those who lived in the past and to recreate all "it was" into "thus I willed it"—that alone I should call redemption . . . Willing liberates; but what is it that puts even this liberator in fetters? "It was"—that is the name of the will's gnashing of teeth and most secret melancholy. Powerless against what has been done, it is an angry spectator of all that is past. The will cannot will backwards; and that it cannot break time and time's covetousness, that is the will's loneliest melancholy. (Z, II, 20)[15]

Unless, by a stroke of unbelievable luck, we have never done anything we regret, or, by means of self-deception, we can convince ourselves we have not, the affirmation Nietzsche envisages seems to be impossible. The past forces us to repudiate whatever future it leads into. And since on Nietzsche's view every aspect of the personality is equally essential to it, it seems that if there is a single part of our life (or of the whole world, for that matter) that we cannot accept, then we cannot accept any other part of it. Partially to accept oneself presupposes that we can distinguish the self from at least some of its features. These are the features we can reject without rejecting ourselves, and therefore these features can only be accidental. Yet there are no accidental features.

Nietzsche, however, seems to be convinced that redemption is still possible, though of course he understands redemption in his own unusual way: "The deep instinct for how one must *live*, in order to feel oneself 'in heaven,' to feel 'eternal,' while in all other behavior one decidedly does *not* feel oneself 'in heaven'—this alone is the psychological reality of 'redemption.' A new way of life, *not* a new faith" (*A*, 33). Through a new way of life, he believes, even the past can be changed. In this new way of life the past itself becomes new: "The will is a creator. All 'it was' is a fragment, a riddle, a dreadful accident—until the creative will says to it, 'But thus I willed it.' Until the creative will says to it, 'But thus I will it; thus shall I will it' " (*Z*, II, 20). Such willing "backward" cannot literally undo the past. Yet it is not easy to say exactly what *the* past is in the first place. The events of the past are necessarily located through and within a narrative, and different narratives can generate quite different events. This is precisely Nietzsche's point. Once again, he is thinking of his view that every one of my past actions is a necessary condition for my being what I am today. How I see my present self affects crucially the very nature of my past. If I am even for a moment such as I would want to be again, then I would also accept all my past actions, which, essential to and constitutive of the self I want to repeat, are now newly redescribed. By creating, on the basis of the past, an acceptable future, we justify and redeem everything that made this future possible; and that is everything: "I taught them . . . to create and carry together into one what in human beings is fragment and riddle and dreadful accident; as creator, guesser of riddles, and redeemer of accidents, I taught them to work on the future and to redeem with their creation all that has been" (*Z*, III, 12).[16] To accept the present is then to accept all that has led to it. It is in this sense that one can now say of what has already happened, "Thus I willed it." The significance and nature of the past, like the significance and nature of everything else according to Nietzsche, lies in its relationships. In particular, the significance of the past lies in its relationship to the future. And since the future is yet to come, neither the significance of the past nor its nature is yet settled.

In one way, then, the past cannot be changed. This is implied in Nietzsche's view that if we were to live again, we would have to live through the very same life. He thinks that, taking the occurrence of the events of our past as given, we should try on their basis to achieve something that makes us willing to accept our whole self. At that point we accept all we have done, since every part of the past is by itself necessary and in combination sufficient for us to be what we are. But in this way the past is changed. The narrative that relates it to the present is altered, and even the accidents in our past can be turned into actions, into events for which we are willing to accept responsibility ("Thus I willed it"), and which we are therefore willing to repeat.

In the ideal case absolutely everything in the past is redeemed in this way. One is reconciled with time: "The time is gone when mere accidents could still happen to me" (Z, III, 1). This reconciliation cannot be accomplished without realizing that the significance of the past depends on its importance for the future. The inability to see this produces "the cheerfulness of the slave who has nothing of consequence to be responsible for, nothing great to strive for, and who does not value anything in the past or future higher than the present" (BT, 11). In its limiting case it distinguishes human beings from animals, creatures that "do not know what is meant by yesterday or today" (UM, II, 1). But it can also produce the exact opposite of such cheerfulness—a continual brooding over a past the significance of which one takes as completely given once and for all. This is what Zarathustra's "pale criminal" does. He "was equal to his deed when he did it; but he could not bear its image after it was done. Now he always saw himself as the doer of one deed . . . the exception now became the essence for him" (Z, I, 6). Such brooding is responsible for *ressentiment*, which, directed not only at others but also at onself (GM, III, 15), accounts for present unhappiness by locating it "in some guilt, in *a piece of the past*" (GM, III, 20). In *Zarathustra* (I, 18), Nietzsche writes that instead of seeking revenge for a wrong, it is better to show that an enemy has done one some good. Instead of resenting a harm, it is better to use it as material for further development and so to prevent it from constituting a harm at all. In the *Genealogy* the picture has become more complicated: "To be incapable of taking one's enemies, one's accidents, even one's misdeeds seriously for very long—that is the sign of strong, full natures in whom there is an excess of the power to form, to mold, to recuperate, and to forget" (*GM*, I, 10).[17]

We can take a past event seriously and try to incorporate it into a complex, harmonious, and unified pattern of which it can become an essential part. Or we can refuse to take it seriously and, through further action, turn it into an exception, into an event of no significance and of no lasting consequence for our life and character. If the event is insignificant, resentment is out of place. If it is not, and if, as James might have put it, we succeed in assimilating it into our personality, if we manage to see it and the other things of the past fall together and change themselves, undergo that relegation that transforms melancholy and misery, passion, pain, and effort into experience and knowledge, into the material of the future, resentment is again out of place; for no place remains for thinking that the consequences of the past on the self, and therefore that this self as well, need remain unchanged. No reason remains for thinking that any action or any accident is in itself harmful or beneficial. The character of each event depends on its eventual implications for the whole of one's constantly changing self.

The justification of a life, then, lies for Nietzsche in those moments when, in accepting the present, one also accepts all that is past; for though perhaps one did not will something in the past, one would not now have it any other way. In this ideal case everything about one would be, and would be seen to be, equally part of oneself and would be manifested in every action: "Oh, my friends, that your self be in your deed as the mother is in her child—let that be *your* word concerning virtue" (Z, II, 5). This seems to me to be a limiting case, in which a person would be different in every way if it were different in any, and in which a life would be so organized that if anything in it were changed, everything in it would fall apart. The eternal recurrence would then indeed constitute "the highest formula of affirmation," for such a person would actively want what would happen in any case if it happened at all: the eternal repetition of every single part of its life, which would appear to follow inevitably from every other. And, to generalize, such a person would also want what, in turn, would in any case happen: the eternal repetition of everything else in the world, past and present, accidental and intentional, good and evil.

A particularly serious problem for this project is created by self-deception, which may convince us that we are approaching this relationship to life and to the world when in fact we are not. I might be willing, for example, to repeat my life only because I do not let myself see it for what it is, because I do not allow myself to see in the proper light, or to see at all, large and objectionable parts of it. This is a grave difficulty because Nietzsche allows great freedom in determining what does and what does not in fact constitute part of a life. I might then be exhilarated at the prospect of repeating my life, at being who I am, just because I am attending to a very small part of it and refusing to see myself in my entirety.

Nietzsche is not at all unaware of these difficulties. This is why, for example, he describes the occasion for the demon's question as one's "loneliest loneliness": this is the time when one would be most likely to be honest with oneself. This is also why he emphasizes the great difficulty with which Zarathustra finally accepts the idea of the recurrence. In both cases Nietzsche tries to suggest how intense and painful a self-examination is necessary before one can even begin to answer the demon's question affirmatively. But it still is the case that the desire for *nothing* to be different presupposes that *everything* has been faced, and there is no independent way of ever establishing that this has been done. This problem is even more urgent because there seems to be no clear sense in which the totality of our actions can ever be faced: is it even possible to speak of "the totality" of a person's actions? The process of self-examination, as we shall see in detail in the next chapter, may have no end.

Nietzsche, however, might well consider the endlessness of this examination (or reinterpretation) as a perfectly acceptable consequence of his view. This would be especially true if, as I now would like to suggest, he once again models his ideal case, in which if anything is different everything is different, on his conception of the perfect narrative, the perfect story. In such a story no detail is inconsequential, nothing is out of place, capricious, haphazard, or accidental. Every "Why?" has an answer better than "Why not?"—which is not an answer at all. As William Labov has written: "Pointless stories are met with the withering rejoinder, 'So what?' Every good narrator is continually warding off this question; when his narrative is over it should be unthinkable for a by-stander to say, 'So what?' "[18] A story is not pointless when it lacks a moral that can be independently stated. A narrative is not successful because it allows one to provide such a short answer to the question of its point. A successful narrative does not allow the question to be raised at all. The narrative has already supplied the answer before the question is asked. The narrative itself is the answer. Similarly, a perfect life provides, and is, its own justification. Nietzsche himself suggests some of these ideas and hints at the connections between literature and life when, in a discussion of authors who find their best moments in their own works, he concludes:

> And if we consider that every human action, not only a book, is in some way or other the cause of other actions, decisions, and thoughts; that everything that happens is inseparably connected with everything that is going to happen, we recognize the real *immortality*, that of movement—that which has once moved is enclosed and immortalized in the general union of all existence [*in dem Gesammtverbande alles Seienden*], like an insect within a piece of amber. (*HH*, I, 208)

This model connects the eternal recurrence with Nietzsche's overarching metaphor of the world as a text that is to be interpreted. And since interpretation is a process without end, since there can be no complete or total interpretation of even a single text, the model accounts for the fact that the examination of a life with the purpose of putting all of it in the proper perspective—even if we assume that such a single perspective can ever exist—will have to go on forever.

More important, however, this analogy brings into the foreground two central features of Nietzsche's view even as it highlights two of its serious difficulties. We have seen that Nietzsche believes that as a matter of logical fact a person's life cannot be in any way different and still be the life of the same person. I have discussed his view that every property is equally essential to its subject, that a subject is nothing more than its properties, and that these properties are nothing more than a thing's effects on other things. This view implies that there can be no true counterfactual statements of the form "If I had done . . . instead of . . . , then I would have been . . . instead of . . ." Any change in my features would, by means of the chain reaction described earlier, altogether eliminate the person I have been as well as the world I have lived in. The ideal life, therefore, consists in the realization that it is not possible to think of oneself in this way and in the effort to become the sort of person who would not ever *want* any such counterfactual statement to be true.

By focusing attention on literary characters instead of actual individuals, this literary model provides an intuitive illustration of

Nietzsche's peculiar view. Literary characters are exhausted by the statements that concern them in the narratives in which they occur: they are in fact nothing more than what is said of them, just as they are also nothing less. Every detail concerning a character has, at least in principle, a point; it is to that extent essential to that character. In the ideal case, to change even one action on the part of a character is to cause both that character and the story to which it belongs to fall apart. In order to maintain the coherence of the story (and assuming that this idea is itself coherent), we would have to make corresponding changes throughout, and we would thus produce an entirely different story; if anything were different, indeed everything would have to be different.

Could Anna Karenina, for example, not have fallen in love with Vronsky? Could she not have left her husband? Could she have loved her son less than she did? Could she have been ultimately less conventional than in fact she was? Could she not have been Oblonsky's sister? In regard to literary characters, such questions are at least very difficult, if not impossible, to answer. It is just this feature of the literary situation that underlies and motivates Nietzsche's view of the ideal person and the perfect life.

But precisely this fact may also constitute one of the serious problems with Nietzsche's attitude; for even if it is true that literature cannot support counterfactuals of the sort I have been discussing, it may still be that Nietzsche is not justified in generalizing from the literary case to life itself. He himself was notoriously unwilling to accept any straightforward distinction between fact and fiction. But one might object that the fundamental difference between them is precisely that reality is capable of supporting counterfactuals of the sort that Nietzsche, having concentrated too heavily on literature, considers to be universally false.

The first central characteristic of Nietzsche's view, then, is that it assimilates the ideal person to an ideal literary character and the ideal life to an ideal story.[19] Just this, it may be argued, is also its first serious weakness. In the next chapter, however, we shall see that Nietzsche's emphasis on the aesthetic, organizational features of people's lives and characters may not constitute an overriding objection to his view. And in the last chapter we shall see that the peculiar use to which he puts this view may disarm this objection completely.

This aesthetic model brings out a second feature of Nietzsche's approach, and perhaps also another difficulty that attends it. This involves what one may feel compelled to consider a *moral* dimension. A literary character, as we shall see again in the next chapter, may be a perfect character but (represent) a dreadful person. If we assume that Nietzsche looks at people as if they were literary characters and at life as if it were a literary work, we may be able to explain why he is so willing and even eager to leave the content of his ideal life unspecified. Nietzsche is clearly much more concerned with the question of how one's actions are to fit together into a coherent, self-sustaining, well-motivated whole than he is with the quality of those actions themselves. Any particular action, whatever its character, can be made to fit well into a whole, provided that whole consists of actions to which the one singled out is appropriately related. This consideration, and not the moral quality of their actions, is central to the understanding and evaluation of literary characters. Even Nietzsche's view that individual actions and all events in general do not possess a character in themselves is accounted for by this model. We have seen that he believes that the significance of an action is not exhaustible and that it depends on the relation of that action to the whole of one's life. In this way a feature or an action of a literary character can be justified, and its significance perceived, only in relation to the rest of the features of that character and of the narrative to which it belongs.

We may now be able to account for Nietzsche's view that one should not take one's misdeeds seriously for long, that virtue does not depend on what one does but on whether what one does is an expression of one's whole self, of one's "own will" (Z, I, 1). These are again exactly the considerations that are relevant to the evaluation of literary characters. Their virtue as characters depends on just that coherence which Nietzsche insists is essential for people as well. Authors are not blamed for creating morally repugnant characters so long as these are believable and essential to the rest of the events that constitute the narrative to which they belong. A perfect case in point, drawn from an author Nietzsche himself greatly admired (cf. *TI,* IX, 45; *A,* 31), is the narrator of *Notes from the Underground,* magnificent as a character and unspeakable as a man. And though it is sometimes true that we react in what seems a direct moral manner to literary figures, the considerations that underlie our reaction are once again aesthetic. An immoral character constitutes a blemish when it is pointless, badly organized, or when its viciousness is gratuitous in that it does not function essentially in the story: when there is no reason for its being as it is and the answer to the question "Why?" is just "Why not?"

But precisely this fact may now appear as the second problem with Nietzsche's approach. The totally integrated person he so admires may well be morally repulsive. As we shall see, Nietzsche's "immoralism" is not the crude praise of selfishness and cruelty with which it is often confused (cf. *D*, 103). Nevertheless, the uncomfortable feeling persists that someone might achieve Nietzsche's ideal life and still be nothing short of repugnant.[20] This may not matter much for literary characters, who cannot affect us directly; but it does, one might think, matter for people, who can. Perhaps the proper approach to Nietzsche's view is to think of his ideal life, the life of the *Übermensch*, as a framework within which many particular lives, each one of which exhibits the unity and coherence he finds so important, can fit.[21] We could then try to develop independent reasons for excluding some of these lives, particularly those that are vicious or objectionable in some other way, as inappropriate. I do not know how we might accomplish this, and Nietzsche is not at all interested in providing the necessary guidelines. I think he realizes that his framework is compatible with more types of life than he would himself be willing to praise. This is a risk inherent in his "immoralism," and it is a risk he is willing to take. At the same time, however, we must keep in mind that the test involved in the thought of the eternal recurrence is not at all easy to pass. Constructing a self and a life that meet its requirements is an extremely difficult task: it is not as if every vicious person would satisfy it, or as if Nietzsche could not condemn many such lives. But his attention is not focused on excluding certain types from his perfect framework. He is concerned, as we shall see in the chapters that follow, with the formidable problem of constructing a single type that falls within it.

The model for the eternal recurrence is therefore not to be found in Nietzsche's superficial reflections on thermodynamics but in his deep immersion in writing. In thinking of his ideal life on the model of a story, we would do well to think of it in the specific terms supplied by Proust's *Remembrance of Things Past*. In this fictional autobiography the narrator relates in enormous, painstaking detail all the silly, insignificant, pointless, accidental, sometimes horrible things he did in his rambling efforts to become an author. He writes about the time he wasted, the acquaintances he made, the views and values he ac-

cepted at different times, his changes of heart and mind, his friendships, the ways in which he treated his family, his lovers, and his servants, his attempts to enter society, the disjointed and often base motives out of which he acted, and much else besides. Yet it is just these
unconnected, chance events that somehow finally enable him to become an author, to see them after all as parts of a unified pattern, the
result of which is his determination to begin at last his first book. This
book, he tells us, will relate in detail all the silly, insignificant, pointless, accidental, sometimes horrible things he did in his rambling efforts to become an author. It will concern the time he wasted, the acquaintances he made, the views and values he accepted at different
times, his changes of heart and mind, his friendships, the ways in
which he treated his family, his lovers, and his servants, his attempts
to enter society, the disjointed and often base motives out of which he
acted, and much else besides. It will also show how these unconnected
chance events somehow finally enabled him to become an author, to
see them after all as parts of a unified pattern, the result of which is his
determination at last to begin his first book, which will relate all the
pointless, accidental . . . —a book he has not yet begun to write but
which his readers have just finished reading.

The life of Proust's narrator need not have been, and never was,
Nietzsche's own specific ideal. But the framework supplied by this
perfect novel which relates what, despite and even through its very
imperfections, becomes and is seen to be a perfect life, and which
keeps turning endlessly back upon itself, is the best possible model for
the eternal recurrence.

To achieve or to create such a perfect life involves action as well as
the constant reinterpretation of what is in a sense already there, since
the whole self is implicit in its every action. Nietzsche seems to think
that to lead a perfect life is to come to know what the self is that is already there and to live according to that knowledge. But to live according to that knowledge will inevitably include new actions that
must be integrated with what has already occurred and the reinterpretation of which will result in the creation or discovery of a self that
could not have been there already. This paradoxical interplay between creation and discovery, knowledge and action, literature and
life is at the center of Nietzsche's conception of the self. This tension
now sets for us the task of understanding one of Zarathustra's most
puzzling self-descriptions: "For *that* is what I am through and

through: reeling, reeling in, raising up, raising, a raiser, cultivator, and disciplinarian, who once counseled himself, not for nothing: Become who you are!" (Z, IV, 1).

Nietzsche himself heeds Zarathustra's counsel. Characteristically, he follows it by making it the object of his writing as well as the goal of his life; consistently, he tries to reach it in a way that makes it, and makes it appear to be, essentially *his* way and that of no one else.

6 | How One Becomes What One Is

People are always shouting they want to create a
better future. It's not true. The future is an apathetic
void, of no interest to anyone. The past is full of life,
eager to irritate us, provoke and insult us, tempt us
to destroy or repaint it. The only reason people
want to be masters of the future is to change the
past.

Milan Kundera, *The Book of Laughter and
Forgetting*

Being and becoming, according to Nietzsche, are not
at all related as we commonly suppose. "Becoming," he writes, "must
be explained without recourse to final intentions . . . Becoming does
not aim at a final state, does not flow into 'being'" (*WP*, 708). One of
his many criticisms of philosophers ("humans have always been philosophers") is that they have turned away from what changes and concentrated instead on what is: "But since nothing *is*, all that was left to
the philosophers as their 'world' was the imaginary" (*WP*, 570). His
thinking is informed by his opposition to the very idea of a distinction between appearance and reality: "The true world—we have abolished. What world has remained? The apparent one perhaps? But no!
With the true world we have also abolished the apparent one" (*TI*, IV, 6).
"The 'true world' and the 'apparent world'—that means: the menda-
ciously invented world and reality" (*EH*, Pref., 2).[1] He denies that the
contrast itself is sensible: "The apparent world and the world invented by a lie—this is the antithesis." And he concludes that the pointless-

ness of this antithesis implies that "no shadow of a right remains to speak here of appearance" (*WP,* 461; cf. 567).

Nietzsche does not simply attack the distinction between appearance and reality. He also offers, as we have seen, a psychological account of its origin. He claims that the distinction is simply a projection onto the external world of our belief that the self is a substance, somehow set over and above its thoughts, desires, and actions. Language, he writes, "everywhere . . . sees a doer and doing; it believes in will as *the* cause; it believes in the ego, in the ego as being, in the ego as substance, and it projects this faith in the ego-substance upon all things—only thereby does it first *create* the concept of a 'thing' . . . the concept of being follows, and is a derivative of, the concept of ego" (*TI,* III, 5).

I have already discussed the difficulties of Nietzsche's "psychological derivation of the belief in things" (*WP,* 473). What we must now take up is the close analogy he finds to hold between things in general and the self in particular. He believes that both concepts are improper in the same way; the idea that "becoming . . . does not flow into 'being' " applies to the self as well as to the world at large. But if this is so, how are we to account for the phrase that stands at the head of this chapter? How are we to interpret that most haunting of his many haunting philosophical aphorisms, the phrase "How one becomes what one is" (*Wie man wird, was man ist*), which constitutes the subtitle of *Ecce Homo,* Nietzsche's intellectual autobiography and, with ironic appropriateness, the last book he ever was to write?[2]

It could be, of course, that this phrase was simply a very clever piece of language that happened to catch (as well it might have) Nietzsche's passing fancy. But this would be too simple, and not true. The idea behind the phrase and the phrase itself occur elsewhere in *Ecce Homo* (II, 9, and III, on *UM,* 3) and can actually be found throughout his writing. Nietzsche first uses a related expression as early as 1874, in *Schopenhauer as Educator,* the third of his *Untimely Meditations:* "Those who do not wish to belong to the mass need only to cease taking themselves easily; let them follow their conscience, which calls to them: 'Be your self [*sei du selbst*]! All that you are now doing, thinking, desiring, is not you yourself' " (*UM,* III, 1).[3] The formulation is simplified in *The Gay Science:* "What does your conscience say?—You must become who you are [*du sollst der werden, der du bist*]" (*GS,* 270). Later on in this same work Nietzsche writes that, in contrast to those who worry about "the moral value" of their actions, he and the type of people to which he belongs "want to become those we are" (GS, 335). And, in the late writings, we have already found Zarathustra saying that he "once counseled himself, not for nothing: Become who you are!" (Z, IV, 1). In short, this phrase leads, if not to the center, at least through the bulk of Nietzsche's thought.

The phrase "Become who you are" is problematic, and not only because Nietzsche denies the distinction between becoming and being. Its interpretation is made even more difficult because he is convinced that the very idea of the self as a subject in its own right, from which he claims this distinction is derived, is itself an unjustified invention: "There is no such substratum; there is no 'being' behind doing, effecting, becoming; 'the doer' is merely a fiction added to the deed—the deed is everything" (GM, I, 13). But if there is no such thing as the self, there seems to be nothing that one can in any way become.

In reducing the agent self to the totality of its actions ("doings"), Nietzsche is once again applying his doctrine of the will to power, part of which consists in the identification of every object in the world with the sum of its effects on every other thing. This view, as we have seen, does away altogether with things as they have traditionally been conceived. And this immediately raises in regard to the self a problem that has already confronted us in general terms: how can we determine which actions to group together as actions of one agent; who is it whose deed is supposed to be "everything"? But even before we can seriously raise this question, the following passage, which goes yet one step further, puts another obstacle in our way: "The 'spirit,' something that thinks—this conception is a second derivative of that false introspection which believes in 'thinking': first an act is imagined which simply does not occur, 'thinking,' and secondly a subject-substratum in which every act of thinking, and nothing else, has its origin: that is to say, *both the deed and the doer are fictions*" (WP, 477).[4] We must postpone for the moment the discussion of this twist, which seems to leave us with no objects whatsoever. Instead, we must begin by placing Nietzsche's reduction of each subject to a set of actions within the context of his denial of the distinction between appearance and underlying reality: "What is appearance to me now?" he asks in *The Gay Science*. "Certainly not the opposite of some essence: what could I say about any essence except to name the attributes of its appearance!" (GS, 54). The connection between these two views immediately blocks what might otherwise seem an obvious interpretation of the phrase that concerns us.

Such an interpretation would proceed along what we might call Freudian lines. It would be an effort to identify the self that one both is and must become with that group of thoughts and desires which, for whatever reason, are repressed, remain hidden, and constitute the reality of which one's current, conscious self is the appearance. This approach naturally allows for the reinterpretation of one's conscious thoughts and desires as a means of realizing who one really is and determining the underlying thoughts and desires of which these are merely signs. To that extent, I think, it would be congenial to Nietzsche, who had once written: "There is no trick which enables us to turn a poor virtue into a rich and overflowing one; but we can reinterpret its poverty into a necessity so that it no longer offends us when we see it and we no longer sulk at fate on its account" (*GS*, 17). This passage raises crucial questions regarding self-deception, which we shall eventually have to face. But for the moment we must simply note that, despite its emphasis on reinterpretation, this view cannot account for Nietzsche's aphorism. The similarities and connections between Nietzsche and Freud are many and deep.[5] But the vulgar Freudian idea that the core of one's self is always there, formed to a great extent early on in life, and waiting for some sort of liberation is incompatible both with Nietzsche's view that the self is a fiction and with his general denial of the idea of a reality that underlies appearance.

In addition this interpretation depends centrally on the idea that one's fixed or true self is there to be found; it thus contradicts Nietzsche's ambiguous attitude toward the question whether truth is discovered or created: " 'Truth' is . . . not something there, that might be found or discovered—but something that must be created and that gives a name to a process, or rather to a will to overcome that has in itself no end—introducing truth as a *processus in infinitum*, an active determining—not a becoming conscious of something that is in itself firm and determined" (*WP*, 552).[6] Nietzsche actually thinks that there is a close connection between the belief that truth is an object of discovery and the belief that the self is a stable object. It is very important to social groups, he writes at one point, that their members not keep too many secrets from one another. The need for truthfulness, the obligation to show "by clear and constant signs" who one is, he continues, has arisen partly for that reason. But if this is to be a plausible demand at all, "you must consider yourself knowable, you may not be concealed from yourself, you may not believe that you change. Thus, the demand for truthfulness presupposes the knowability and stability of the person. In fact, it is the object of education to create in the herd member a definite faith concerning human nature: it first invents the faith and then demands 'truthfulness' " (*WP*, 277).

By contrast, Nietzsche writes, he wants to "transform the belief 'it *is* thus and thus' into the will 'it *shall become* thus and thus' " (*WP*, 593). In general he prefers to think of truth as the product of creation rather than as the object of discovery. His attitude toward the self is similar. The people who "want to become those they are" are precisely "human beings who are new, unique, incomparable, who give themselves laws, who *create themselves*" (*GS*, 335; my italics). *Thus Spoke Zarathustra* is constructed around the idea of creating one's own self or, what comes to the same thing, the *Übermensch*. Zarathustra and his disciples as well are constantly described as "creators." Nietzsche is paying Goethe, one of his few true heroes, his highest compliment when he writes of him that "he created himself" (*TI*, IX, 49).

Yet once again we must come to terms with the ambiguity which Nietzsche's attitude on this issue too inevitably exhibits. Despite his constant attacks on the notion that there are antecedently existing things and truths waiting to be discovered, despite his almost inordinate emphasis on the idea of creating, Zarathustra at one point enigmatically says, "Some souls one will never discover, unless one invents them first" (Z, I, 8). This same equivocal view comes into play later when he tells his disciples, "You still want to create the world before which you can kneel" (Z, II, 2; cf. III, 3). And even though Nietzsche writes that "the axioms of logic . . . are . . . a means for us to *create* reality" (*WP*, 516), he still believes that "rational thought is interpretation according to a scheme that we cannot throw off" (*WP*, 522). Making and finding, creating and discovering, imposing laws and being constrained by them are involved in a complicated, almost compromising relationship. Our creations eventually become our truths, and our truths circumscribe our creations.[7]

It seems, then, that the self, even if it is to be at some point discovered, must first be created. We are therefore faced with the difficult problem of seeing how that self can be what one is before it comes into being itself, before it is itself something that is. Conversely, if that self is something that is, if it is what one already is, how is it still possible for one to become that self? How could, and why should, *that* self be what one properly is and not some, or any, other? Why not, in particular, one's current self, which at least has over all others the significant advantage of existing?

Let us stop for a moment to note that, however equivocal, Nietzsche's emphasis on the creation of the self blocks another apparently obvious interpretation of the phrase "Become who you are." This interpretation holds that to become what one is is to actualize all the capacities for which one is inherently suited. It might be inaccurate but not positively misleading to say that such a view follows along Aristotelian lines. By appealing to the distinction between actuality and potentiality, this construction may account for some of the logical peculiarities of Nietzsche's phrase, since one may not (actually) be what one (potentially) is. But despite this advantage, such an interpretation faces two serious difficulties. The first is that, since one's capacities are in principle exhaustible, if one does actualize them, then one *has* in fact become what one is. But in that case becoming has ceased; it has "flowed into being" in the very sense in which we have seen Nietzsche deny that this is possible. The second difficulty is that to construe becoming as the realization of inherent capacities makes the creation of the self appear very much like the uncovering of something that is already there. Yet Nietzsche seems intent on undermining precisely the idea that there are antecedently existing possibilities grounded in the nature of things or of people, even though (as on the view we are considering) we may not know in advance what these are: this is a significant part of his scattered but systematic attack on the very notion of "the nature" of things.

We are therefore still faced with the problem of explaining how a self that truly must be created and that does not in any way appear to exist can be considered that which an individual is. In addition, Nietzsche's view, to which we keep returning, that becoming does not aim at a final state puts yet another obstacle in our way, for Nietzsche holds that constant change and the absence of stability characterize the world at large: "If the motion of the world aimed at a final state, that state would have been reached. The sole fundamental fact, however, is that it does not aim at a final state" (*WP,* 708).[8] He also holds that exactly the same is true of each individual. In *The Gay*

Science, for example, he praises "brief habits," which he characterizes as "an inestimable means for getting to know *many* things and states" (*GS,* 295). Later on in the same work he relies on a magnificent simile between the will and a wave in order to express his faith that continual change and renewal are both inevitable and inherently valuable:

> How greedily this wave approaches, as if it were after something! How it crawls with terrifying haste into the inmost nooks of this labyrinthine cliff! It seems that something of value, great value, must be hidden there.—And now it comes back, a little more slowly but still quite white with excitement; is it disappointed? Has it found what it looked for? Does it pretend to be disappointed?— But already another wave is approaching, still more greedily and savagely than the first, and its soul, too, seems to be full of secrets and the last to dig up treasures. Thus live waves—thus live we who will—more I shall not say. (*GS,* 310)

The idea of constant change is also one of the main conceptions around which *Zarathustra* revolves: "All the permanent—that is only a parable. And the poets lie too much . . . It is of time and becoming that the best parables should speak: let them be a praise and a justification of all impermanence . . . there must be much bitter dying in your life, you creators. Thus are you advocates and justifiers of all impermanence. To be the child who is newly born, the creator must also want to be the mother who gives birth" (*Z,* II, 2).

These passages suggest that Nietzsche is himself an advocate of all impermanence. But if this is so, he cannot think that there is any such thing as being at all: what relation, then, could possibly exist between becoming and being? To answer this question we must examine Nietzsche's own notion of being, which, like all such traditional notions, assumes a double aspect in his writing. Though he denies that being, construed as anything that is not subject to history and change, exists, he still constantly relies on this concept as he himself interprets it. Perhaps, then, his interpretation is unusual enough to escape the contradictions that have stopped us so far without lapsing at the same time into total eccentricity.

A first glimmer of the answer to the questions I have been raising may appear through the final obstacle that is still in our way. We have already seen that Nietzsche is convinced that the ego, construed as a metaphysically abiding subject, is a fiction. But also, as by now we may be prepared to expect, he does not even seem to believe in the most elementary unity of the person as an agent. Paradoxically, however, his shocking and obscure breakdown of what we have assumed to be the essential unity of the human individual may be the key to the solution of our problems. It may also be one of Nietzsche's great contributions to our understanding of the self as well as to our own self-understanding.

Consider the breakdown first. As early as the time when he was writing the second volume of *Human, All-Too-Human,* Nietzsche had written that students of history are "happy, unlike the metaphysicians, to have in themselves not one immortal soul but many mortal ones" (*MOM,* 17). In *The Gay Science* he had already denied that consciousness constitutes or underlies "the unity of the organism" (*GS,* 11). We might of course suppose that Nietzsche is here merely denying that we have any grounds for supposing that we know that the self abides over time. This would be a skeptical position common to a number of modern philosophers who wrote under the influence of Hume. But that this is not all that Nietzsche's view amounts to is shown by the following radical and, for our purposes, crucial passage from *Beyond Good and Evil:*

> The belief that regards the soul as something indestructible, eternal, indivisible, as a monad, as an *atomon:* this belief ought to be expelled from science! Between ourselves, it is not at all necessary to get rid of "the soul" at the same time . . . But the way is open for new versions and refinements of the soul-hypothesis; and such conceptions as "mortal soul," and "soul as subjective multiplicity," and "soul as social structure of the drives and affects" want henceforth to have citizens' rights in science. (*BGE,* 12)[9]

The idea of "the subject as multiplicity" constantly emerges in *The Will to Power,* where we find the following characteristic passage: "The assumption of one single subject is perhaps unnecessary; perhaps it is just as permissible to assume a multiplicity of subjects, whose interaction and struggle is the basis of our thought and our consciousness in general? A kind of aristocracy of 'cells' in which dominion resides? To be sure, an aristocracy of equals, used to ruling jointly and understanding how to command?" (*WP,* 490). In the same note Nietzsche includes "the subject as multiplicity" and "the continual transitoriness and fleetingness of the subject: 'Mortal soul' " in a list of his own "hypotheses." I have already discussed in detail his view that all "unity is unity only as organization and cooperation" and his opposition to the belief in the subject, which, he claims, "was only invented as a foundation of the various attributes" (*WP*, 561). As with all social and political entities, unity cannot be presupposed; it is achieved, if it is achieved at all, only when the elements of the system are directed toward a common end and goal.

This political metaphor for the self, which, despite Nietzsche's reputation, is at least more egalitarian than Plato's, can now set us, I think, in the right direction for understanding the phrase that concerns us. Nietzsche believes that we have no good grounds for assuming a priori that a living subject, or anything else for that matter, is already unified, that its unity is something it possesses in itself. He is deeply suspicious of the idea of unity in general: as Zarathustra says, "Evil I call it, and misanthropic—all this teaching of the One and the Plenum and the Unmoved and the Sated and the Permanent" (Z, II, 2).[10] And yet, not at all surprisingly by now, it is also Zarathustra who claims that "this is all my creating and striving, that I create and carry together into One what is fragment and riddle and dreadful accident" (Z, II, 20; cf. III, 12).

Nietzsche's denial of the unity of the self follows from a view we have already seen in connection with the will to power. This is his view that the "mental acts" of thinking and desiring (to take these as representative of the rest) are indissolubly connected with their contents, which are in turn indissolubly connected with the contents of other thoughts, desires, and, of course, actions (cf. *WP*, 584, 672). He holds, first, that we are not justified in separating such an act from its content; to remove the "aim" from willing is, he writes, to eliminate willing altogether, since there can only be a "willing *something*" (*WP*, 668). And it is this view, as we have said, that allows him, despite his tremendous and ever-present emphasis on willing, to make the shockingly but only apparently incompatible statement that "there is no such as will" (*WP*, 488; cf. 671, 715, 692). His position on the nature of thinking is strictly parallel: " 'Thinking,' as epistemologists conceive it, simply does not occur: it is a quite arbitrary fiction, arrived at by selecting one element from the process and eliminating all the rest, an artificial arrangement for the purposes of intelligibility" (*WP*, 477; cf. 479).

The considerations that underlie Nietzsche's approach must be something like the following. We tend first to isolate the content of each thought and desire from that of all the others; we suppose that each mental act intends a distinct mental content, whose nature is independent of the content of all other mental acts. My thought that such-and-such is the case is *there* and remains what it is whatever else I may come to think, want, and do in the future. Though my thought may turn out to have been false, its significance is given and determined once and for all. Having now isolated the contents of our mental acts from one another, we proceed to separate the content of each act from the act that intends it. My thinking is an episode which we take to be distinct from what it concerns (or "intends"). Having performed these two "abstractions," we are now confronted with a set of qualitatively identical entities—thoughts, or thinkings—that we can attribute to a subject which, since it performs all these identical and therefore perfectly compatible and harmonious acts, we can safely assume to be unified.

It seems to me that it is this view that underwrites Nietzsche's conviction that the deed itself is a fiction and the doer "a second derivative." He appears to think that we tend to take the self without further thought as one because when we try to form a conception of the self in the first place, we commonly fail to take the contents of our mental acts into account. The strategy of abstracting from these contents and concentrating on the qualities of the mental states themselves with the purpose of finding out what the true self is can be traced back to Descartes' *Meditations.* Can doubt, understanding, affirming, desiring, being averse, imagining, or perceiving, Descartes asks, "be distinguished from my thought"? Can any of them "be said to be separated from myself?" By these "attributes" Descartes clearly understands only the mental acts themselves, and nothing besides. In particular, he excludes their content: even if what I imagine is false, he argues, "nevertheless this power of imagining does not cease to be really in use, and it forms part of my thought"; even if I am perceiving nothing real, he insists, "still it is at least quite certain that it seems to me that I see light, that I hear noise, and that I feel heat. That cannot be false."[11]

But for Nietzsche each "thing" is nothing more, and nothing less, than the sum of all its effects and features. Since it is nothing *more* than that sum, it is not at all clear that conflicting sets of features are capable of generating a single subject: conflicting features, unless we already have an independent subject whose features we can show them to be, generate distinct things. But since a thing is also nothing *less* than the sum of its features, when we come to the case of the self, what we must attribute to each subject, what we must use in order to generate it, cannot be simply the sum of its mental acts considered in isolation from their content: " 'The subject' is the fiction that many similar states in us are the effect of one substratum: but it is we who first created the 'similarity' of these states; our adjusting them and making them similar is the fact, not their similarity (—which ought rather to be denied—)" (*WP*, 485). What we must therefore attribute to the self is the sum of its acts along with their contents: each subject is constituted not simply by the fact *that* it thinks, wants, and acts but also by precisely *what* it thinks, wants, and does. And once we admit contents, we admit conflicts. What we think, want, and do is seldom if ever a coherent collection. Our thoughts contradict one another and contrast with our desires, which are themselves inconsistent and are in turn belied by our actions. The unity of the self, which Nietzsche identifies with this collection, is thus seriously undermined. This unity, he seems to believe, is to be found, if it is to be found at all, in the very organization and coherence of the many acts that each organism performs. It is the unity of these acts that gives rise to the unity of the self, and not, as we often think, the fact of a single self that unifies our conflicting tendencies.

An immediate difficulty for Nietzsche's view seems to be caused by his apparent failure to distinguish clearly between unity as coherence on the one hand and unity as "numerical identity" on the other. Numerical identity is singleness. And one might argue that even if the self is not organized and coherent in an appropriate manner, this still need not prevent it from being a single thing. In fact, this argument continues, it is only because the self is a single thing in the first place that it is at all sensible to be concerned with its coherence: whose coherence would even be in question otherwise? The idea that we are faced with conflicting groups of thoughts and desires itself depends on the assumption that these are the thoughts and desires of a single person: why else would they be conflicting rather than merely disparate?

We might try to reply that Nietzsche is concerned only with the problems of the coherence of selves that are already unified and not with the grounds of these selves' identity and unity. But in fact his own view that everything is a set of effects results precisely in blurring this distinction and prevents us from giving this easy and uninteresting answer. Since there is nothing above or behind such sets of effects, it is not clear that Nietzsche can consistently hold that there is anything to the identity of each object above the unity of a set of effects established from some particular point of view; it is not clear, that is, that Nietzsche can even envisage the distinction between coherence and numerical identity. But the question, then, is pressing: what is it that enables us to group some multiplicities together so as to form a single self and to distinguish them from others, which belong to distinct subjects?

At this point we can appeal once again to our political metaphor for the self. On a very basic level the unity of the body provides for the identity that is necessary, but not at all sufficient, for the unity of the self. Nietzsche, quite consistently, holds that the unity of the body, like all unity, is itself not an absolute fact: "The evidence of the body reveals a tremendous multiplicity" (*WP*, 518); the title of note 660 of *The Will to Power* is "The Body as a Political Structure." But in most cases, this multiplicity is, from our own point of view, organized coherently; the needs and goals of the body are usually not in conflict with one another: "The body and physiology the starting point: why?—we gain the correct idea of the nature of our subject-unity, namely as regents at the head of a communality (not as 'souls' or 'life forces'), also of the dependence of these regents upon the ruled and of an order of rank and division of labor as the conditions that make possible the whole and its parts" (*WP*, 492). This too is the point Zarathustra makes when he says that the body is "a plurality with one sense, a war and a peace, a herd and a shepherd" (Z, I, 4).

Because it is organized coherently, the body provides the common ground that allows conflicting thoughts, desires, and actions to be grouped together as features of a single subject. Particular thoughts, desires, or actions move the body in different directions, they place it in different situations and contexts, and can even be said to fight for its control. Exactly the same is true of their patterns—that is, of our character traits. Dominant habits and traits, as long as they are dominant, assume the role of the subject; in terms of our metaphor, they assume the role of the leader. It is such traits that speak with the voice of the self when they are manifested in action. Their own coherence and unity allow them to become the subject that, at least for a while, says "I." In the situation I am discussing, however, the leadership is not stable. Different and even incompatible habits and character traits coexist in the same body, and so different patterns assume the role of "regent" at different times. Thus we identify our-selves differently over time. And though, as is often the case with the voice of the state, the "I" always seems to refer to the same thing, the content to which it refers and the interests for which it speaks do not remain the same. It is constantly in the process of changing. This pro-cess may sometimes tend in the direction of greater unity.

Such unity, however, which is at best something to be hoped for, certainly cannot be presupposed. Phenomena like *akrasia,* or weak-ness of will, and self-deception, not to mention everyday inconsis-tency, are constantly posing a threat to it. Wittgenstein once wrote that "our language can be seen as an ancient city: a maze of little streets and squares, of old and new houses, and of houses with addi-tions from various periods; and this surrounded by a multitude of new boroughs with straight regular streets and uniform houses."[12] In a recent discussion of *akrasia* and self-deception, Amélie Rorty has used this same metaphor for the self. She urges that we think of the self not as a contemporary city built on a regular grid but more as a city of the Middle Ages, with many semi-independent neighbor-hoods, indirect ways of access from one point to another, and without a strong central municipal administration. She writes, "We can regard the agent self as a loose configuration of habits, habits of thought and perception and motivation and action, acquired at different stages, in the service of different ends."[13]

The unity of the self, which therefore also constitutes its identity, is not something given but something achieved, not a beginning but a goal. And of such unity, which is at best a matter of degree and which comes close to representing a regulative principle, Nietzsche is not at all suspicious. It lies behind his earlier positive comments on "the One," and he actively wants to promote it. It is precisely its absence that he laments when, addressing his contemporaries, he writes, "With the characters of the past written all over you, and these char-acters in turn painted over with new characters: thus have you con-cealed yourselves perfectly from all interpreters of characters" (Z, II, 14).[14]

Nietzsche's view, it may now appear, is surprisingly similar to Plato's analysis of the soul in the *Republic.* Both divide the subject, both depend on a political metaphor for the self, and both are faced with the problem of relocating the agent once they have accom-plished their division. But within the terms provided by this comparison, the differences between the two views are still striking. Nietzsche's breakdown of the individual is much more complicated and much less systematic than Plato's. He rejects Plato's belief that there are only three sources of human motivation. And he fights vehemently against Plato's conviction that reason should be the one that dominates. Having identified a large number of independent motives and character traits, Nietzsche, in contrast to Plato, considers that the question which should govern the self requires a different answer in each particular case. And he insists that this answer cannot be constrained by moral considerations.

The particular traits that dominate on one occasion can sometimes simply disregard their competitors and even refuse to acknowledge their existence: this is the case of self-deception. Or they may acknowledge them, try to bring them into line with their own evaluations, and fail: this is the case of *akrasia*. Or again they can try, and manage, to incorporate them, changing both themselves and their opponents in the process: this is to take a step toward the integration of the self which, in the ideal case, constitutes the unity which we too are pursuing:

> No subject "atoms." The sphere of a subject constantly growing or decreasing, the center of the system constantly shifting: in cases where it cannot organize the appropriate mass, it breaks into two parts. On the other hand, it can transform a weaker subject into its functionary without destroying it, and to a certain extent form a new unity with it. No "substance," rather something that in itself strives after greater strength, and that wants to preserve itself only indirectly (it wants to *surpass* itself—). (*WP*, 488; cf. 617)

This passage makes it clear that at least in some of the cases in which Nietzsche speaks of mastery and power, he is concerned with mastery and power over oneself, envisaging different habits and character traits competing for the domination of a single person. This is one of the reasons why I think that a primary, though by no means the only, object of the will to power is one's own self.[15] But more important, we find in this passage the suggestion that, as our metaphor has already led us to expect, what says "I" is not the same at all times. And we can also see that the process of dominating, and thus creating, the individual, the unity that concerns us, is a matter of incorporating more and more character traits under a constantly expanding and evolving rubric. This may now suggest that, on Nietzsche's own understanding of these notions, the distinction between becoming and being is not absolute, and that his concept of "being" may indeed avoid the difficulties that earlier appeared to face it. But this suggestion must be elaborated in some detail before we can take it seriously.

Nietzsche often criticizes the educational practices of his time. One of his central objections to education in late nineteenth-century Germany is that it encouraged people to want to develop in all directions instead of showing them how they could fashion themselves into true individuals, sometimes even at the cost of eliminating certain beliefs and desires which they previously valued (*TI*, IX, 41). In *The Will to Power*, for example, he writes, "So far, the Germans . . . are nothing: that means they are all sorts of things. They will become something: that means, they will stop some day being all sorts of things" (*WP*, 108; cf. *UM*, II, 4, 10). But the project of "becoming an individual" and of unifying one's own features requires hardness (a favorite term with him) toward oneself. Its opposite, which he finds everywhere around him, is "tolerance toward oneself"; this is an attitude that "permits several convictions, and they all get along with each other: they are careful, like all the rest of the world, not to compromise themselves. How does one compromise oneself today? If one is consistent. If one proceeds in a straight line. If one is not ambiguous enough to permit five conflicting interpretations. If one is genuine" (*TI*, IX, 18). This crucial passage suggests that Nietzsche is not as unqualified a friend of polysemy as it is sometimes claimed today. But the main point on which one must insist in this context is that though he clearly believes that certain character traits may have to be eliminated if unity is to be achieved, he does not in any way consider that such eliminated features are to be disowned.

It is, as we saw in the last chapter, one of Nietzsche's most central views that everything one does is equally essential to who one is. Everything that I have ever done has been instrumental to my being who I am today. And even if today there are actions I would never do again and character traits I am grateful to have left behind forever, I would not have my current preferences had I not had those other preferences earlier on. My thoughts and actions are so intimately involved with one another and with my whole history that it is very difficult to say where one ends and another begins: "The most recent history of an action relates to this action: but further back lies a prehistory which covers a wider field: the individual action is at the same time a part of a much more extensive, later fact. The briefer and the more extensive processes are not separated" (*WP,* 672).

It begins to seem, then, that Nietzsche does not think of unity as a state of being that follows and replaces an earlier process of becoming. Rather, he seems to think of it as a continual process of integrating one's character traits, habits, and patterns of action with one another. This process can also, in a sense, reach backward and integrate even a discarded characteristic into the personality by showing that it was necessary for one's subsequent development. When one shows this, of course, that trait's "nature" is itself altered through a highly complex process:

> *One thing is needful.*—To "give style" to one's character—a great and rare art! It is practiced by those who survey all the strengths and weaknesses of their nature and then fit them into an artistic plan un- til every one of them appears as art and reason and even weaknesses delight the eye. Here a large mass of second nature has been added; there a piece of original nature has been removed—both times through long practice and daily work at it. Here the ugly that could not be removed is concealed; there it has been reinterpreted and made sublime. Much that is vague and resisted shaping has been saved and exploited for distant views . . . In the end, when the work is finished, it becomes evident how the constraint of a single taste governed and formed everything large and small. Whether this taste was good or bad is less important than one might suppose, if only it was a single taste! (*GS,* 290)

This process is as gradual as it is difficult; as Zarathustra says: "Verily, I too have learned to wait—thoroughly—but only to wait for *myself.* And above all I learned to stand and walk and run and jump and climb and dance. This, however, is my doctrine: whoever would learn to fly one day must first learn to stand and walk and run and climb and dance: one cannot fly into flying" (*Z,* III, 11). The unity Nietzsche has in mind can become apparent and truly exist only over time. Though if it is ever achieved, it is achieved at some time, what is achieved at that time is the unification of one's past with one's present. The future is, therefore, always a danger to it: any new event may prove impossi- ble to unify, at least without further effort, with the self into which one has developed.

But apart from this problem, the unity Nietzsche is after is also in danger from the constant possibility of self-deception, for one may "give style" to one's character and constrain it by "a single taste" simply by denying the existence, force, or significance of antithetical styles and tastes and by considering only part of oneself as the whole. Nietzsche seems aware of this difficulty. This is shown by his distinction between two sorts of people who have faith in themselves. Some, he writes, have faith because they refuse to look at all: "What would they behold if they could see to the bottom of themselves!" Others must acquire it slowly and are faced with it as a problem themselves: "Everything good, fine, or great they do is first of all an argument against the skeptic inside them" (GS, 284; cf. Z, II, 21). The possibility that we are deceiving ourselves cannot ever be eliminated; unity can always be achieved by refusing to acknowledge an existing multiplicity.

It would be more accurate to say, however, that only the feeling of unity, and not unity itself, can be secured in this way. One can think that the difficult task described in the passages we are considering has been completed when in fact one has not succeeded at all. The distinction can be made because the notions of style and character are essentially public. Nietzsche, of course, constantly emphasizes the importance of evaluating oneself only by one's own standards. Nevertheless, especially since he does not believe that we have any special access to knowledge of ourselves, such questions are finally decided from the outside. This outside, which includes looking at one's own past, may consist of a very select public, of an audience that perhaps does not yet exist. Still, the distinction between the fact and the feeling of unity must be pressed and maintained. Zarathustra taunts the sun when he asks what its happiness would be were it not for those for whom it shines (Z, Pref., 1; cf. GM, II, 7, 23). Similarly, it takes spectators for unity to be made manifest and therefore for it to be there. To an extent, one is at the mercy of one's audience. Nietzsche in particular, as we shall see at the end of this chapter, may be totally at the mercy of his readers.[16]

Akrasia, the inability to act according to our preferred judgment, is a clear sign that unity is absent. It indicates that competing habits, patterns of valuation, and modes of perception are at work within the same individual—if we can use the term at all at this stage. Nietzsche is a great enemy of the notion of the freedom of will; naturally, however, he is no less opposed to the notion of the compelled or unfree will. Both ideas, he writes, are "mythology": in real life "it is only a matter of strong and weak wills" (BGE, 21; cf. 19, 36; TI, VI, 7). But strength and weakness are themselves notions that he interprets in his own way, connecting them with the very kind of organization and integration that I have been discussing:

> *Weakness of the will:* that is a metaphor that can prove misleading. For there is no will, and consequently neither a strong nor a weak will. The multitude and disgregation of impulses and the lack of any systematic order among them result in a "weak will"; their coordination under a single predominant impulse results in a "strong will": in the first case it is the oscillation and the lack of gravity; in the latter, the precision and clarity of the direction. (*WP*, 46; cf. 45).

But despite denying that both freedom and necessity exist, Nietzsche can also have Zarathustra praise those occasions "where necessity was freedom itself" (*Z*, III, 12). Similarly, he takes "peace of soul" to signify either a mind becalmed, an empty self-satisfaction, or, on the contrary, "the expression of maturity and mastery in the midst of doing, creating, working, and willing—calm breathing, *attained* 'freedom of the will' " (*TI*, V, 3; cf. *GM*, II, 2). Once again, Nietzsche appropriates traditional concepts for his own idiosyncratic, but not totally eccentric or unrelated, purposes.

Freedom of the will so construed is not the absence of causal determination but a harmony among all of a person's preference schemes. It is a state in which desire follows thought, and action follows desire, without tension or struggle, and in which the distinction between choice and constraint may well be thought to disappear. Nietzsche thinks of this state as a limiting case, to be reached, if at all, only with the greatest difficulty. In this we once again see his complex relation to Socrates, who in Plato's early dialogues argues that everyone already is in that condition and that only ignorance of the good prevents us from actually doing it.

Nietzsche is very clear about the extraordinary difficulty with which this state of harmony of thought and action can be reached. Success can in this case too be expressed through his political metaphor: "*L'effet c'est moi:* what happens here is what happens in every well-constructed and happy commonwealth; namely, the governing class identifies itself with the success of the commonwealth" (*BGE*, 19). In more literal terms, success consists in having the minimum level of discord among the maximum possible number of diverse tendencies. This view, which is anticipated by section 290 of *The Gay Science,* is explicit in the following passage: "The highest human being would have the highest multiplicity of drives, in the relatively greatest strength that can be endured. Indeed, where the plant 'human being' shows itself strongest one finds instincts that conflict powerfully (e.g., in Shakespeare) but are controlled" (*WP*, 966; cf. 259, 928). It is just because of his ability to control this multiplicity that Goethe, who tried "to form a totality out of himself, in the faith that only in the totality everything redeems itself and appears justified" (*WP*, 95), and who according to Nietzsche bore all the conflicting tendencies of his age within him, became his great hero: "What he wanted was totality... he disciplined himself to wholeness, he *created* himself" (*TI*, IX, 49; cf. *WP*, 1014).[17]

An even better example, though unavailable to Nietzsche, is once again Proust's narrator, who creates himself, out of everything that has happened to him, in his own writing—as in what follows we shall see that Nietzsche himself tries to do. In addition, Proust's narrator believes "that in fashioning a work of art we are by no means free, that we do not choose how we shall make it but that it pre-exists and therefore we are obliged, since it is both necessary and hidden, to do what we should have to do if it were a law of nature, that is to say to discover it."[18] Yet this discovery, which he explicitly describes as "the discovery of our true life," can be made only in the very process of creating the work of art which describes and constitutes it. And the ambiguous relation between discovery and creation, which matches exactly Nietzsche's own view, also captures perfectly the tension in the very idea of being able to become who one actually is.

The creation of the self therefore appears to be the creation, or imposition, of a higher-order accord among our lower-level thoughts, desires, and actions. It is the development of the ability, or the willingness, to accept responsibility for everything that we have done and to admit what is in any case true: that everything that we have done actually constitutes who each one of us is.

From one point of view this willingness is a new character trait, a new state of development that is reached at some time and replaces a previous state. From another point of view, however, to reach such a state is not at all like having one specific character trait replace another, as when courage, for example, replaces cowardice, or munificence miserliness. The self-creation Nietzsche has in mind involves accepting everything that we have done and, in the ideal case, blending it into a perfectly coherent whole. Becoming brave is becoming able to avoid all the cowardly actions in which I may have previously engaged and to pursue a new kind of action instead. But I need not alter my behavior just because I realize that all my actions are my own. What, if anything, will change depends on the patterns that have characterized my behavior so far and on the new sorts of actions, if any, in which I may now want to engage.

But Nietzsche's conception of the unified self is still compatible with continued change, and this provides a sharp contrast between his view and a realization many of us make at some point in our life, when we see or decide that our character has developed enough and that we neither need nor want to change any more. Becoming who one is, in Nietzsche's terms, excludes such complacency altogether: "All those who are 'in the process of becoming' must be furious when they perceive some satisfaction in this area, an impertinent 'retiring on one's laurels' or 'self-congratulation' " (*WP*, 108). The creation of the self is not a static episode, a final goal which, once attained, forecloses the possibility of continuing to change and to develop.

For one thing, it is not at all clear that such an "episode" can actually occur, that it does not constitute, as I have said, a regulative principle. If there were a good sense in which we could count our mental states, then perhaps we might succeed in fitting "all" of them together. Yet how they fit with one another clearly has a bearing on how they are counted—whether, for example, two thoughts separated by time may not after all be parts of one single longer thought. Nietzsche's view that the contents of our acts are indissolubly connected with one another argues for the same point, for to be able to reinterpret a thought or an action and thus to construe it as only part of a longer, "more extensive" process, as only a part of a single mental act, has exactly the same consequence: there is no such thing as the number of our experiences and actions.

More important, however, is the fact that so long as we are alive, we are always finding ourselves in new and unforeseen situations; we constantly have new thoughts and desires, we continue to perform new actions. In their light we may at any point come to face the need to reinterpret, to reorganize, or even to abandon earlier ones. And Nietzsche's exhortation "to revolve around oneself; no desire to become 'better' or in any way other" (*WP*, 425; cf. *Z*, IV, 19) is quite compatible with this continual development. To desire to remain who I am in this context is not so much to want any specific character traits to remain constant: the very same passage speaks of "multiplicity of character considered and exploited as an advantage" (cf. *GS*, 371). Rather, it is to desire to appropriate and to organize as my own all that I have done, or at least that I know I have done, into a coherent whole. It is simply to become able to accept all such things, good and evil, as things I have done. It is not to cultivate stable character traits that make my reactions predictable and unsurprising. It is not simply to age, though aging is certainly connected with it: the young still have "the worst of tastes, the taste for the unconditional" and have not yet learned "to put a little art in their feelings and rather to risk trying even what is artificial—as the real artists of life do" (*BGE*, 31). Rather, it is to become flexible enough to use whatever I have done, do, or will do as elements within a constantly changing, never finally completed whole.

Because they are continually being reinterpreted, none of the elements of this whole need remain constant. Zarathustra's mistrust of unity—his desire to avoid goals of stability—is his aversion to the permanence of specific character traits, parallel to Nietzsche's praise of "brief habits" in section 295 of *The Gay Science*. By contrast, when he proudly describes his own teaching as "carrying into One" fragments, riddles, and accidents, he refers to the never-ending integration and reinterpretation of such brief habits.

The final mark of this integration, its limiting case, is provided by nothing other than the test involved in the thought of the eternal recurrence. This is the desire to do again what I have already done in this life if I were to live again: " 'Was *that* life?' I want to say to death," Zarathustra exclaims, " 'Well then! Once more!' " (Z, IV, 19). We have seen that the opportunity to live again would necessarily involve the exact repetition of the very same events that constitute my present life. The question therefore is not whether I would or would not do the same things again; in this matter there is no room for choice. The question is only whether I would *want* to do the same things all over again. This is simply the question whether I am glad to have done whatever I have done already, and therefore the question whether I would be willing to acknowledge all my doings as my own.

Becoming and being are therefore related in a way that does not make nonsense of Nietzsche's imperative to "become who you are." To be who one is, we can now see, is to be engaged in a constantly continuing and continually broadening process of appropriation of one's experiences and actions, of enlarging the capacity for assuming responsibility for oneself which Nietzsche calls "freedom" (*TI,* IX, 38). He writes: "To impose upon becoming the character of being: that is the supreme will to power" (*WP,* 617). But the character of being is not stability and permanence. On the contrary, as this interpretation implies, "that *everything recurs* is the closest *approximation of a world of becoming to a world of being*" (*WP,* 617).

The eternal recurrence signifies my ability to want my life and the whole world to be repeated just as they are. This is the ability to make "a Dionysian affirmation of the world as it is, without subtraction, exception, or selection—it wants the eternal circulation:—the same things, the same logic and illogic of entanglements. The highest state a philosopher can attain: to stand in a Dionysian relationship to existence—my formula for this is *amor fati*" (*WP,* 1041; cf. *EH,* II, 10, and III, on *CW,* 4; *NCW,* Epi., 1). In the limiting case this desire presupposes that I have assembled all that I have done and all that has led to it into a whole so unified that nothing can be removed without that whole crumbling down. Being, for Nietzsche, is that which one does not *want* to be otherwise.

What one is, then, is just what one becomes. In counseling himself to become who he is, Zarathustra becomes able to want to become what in fact he does become and not to want anything about it, about himself, to be different. To become what one is, we can see, is not to reach a specific new state and to stop becoming—it is not to reach a state at all. It is to identify oneself with all of one's actions, to see that everything one does (what one becomes) is what one is. In the ideal case it is also to fit all this into a coherent whole and to want to be everything that one is: it is to give style to one's character; to be, we might say, becoming.

The idea of giving style to one's character brings us back to Nietzsche's view that to have a single character or "taste" is more important than the quality of that taste itself (*GS,* 290). And this idea, in turn, raises the notorious problem of his immoralism, his virulent contempt for traditional moral virtue, and his alleged praise of cruelty and the exploitation of the "weak" by the "strong."

Nietzsche certainly glorifies selfishness, but he is, once again, equally serious in denying a sharp distinction between egoism and altruism. He speaks of "some future, when, owing to continual adaptation, egoism will at the same time be altruism," when love and respect for others will just be love and respect for oneself: "Finally, one grasps that altruistic actions are only a species of egoistic actions—and that the degree to which one loves, spends oneself, proves the degree of individual power and personality" (*WP*, 786; cf. 964). And though he also believes that mindless cruelty has certainly been practiced by people on one another in the past and that it will continue to be practiced by us in the future, this is not the cruelty he praises. In fact he thinks that its net effect is the opposite of its intent:

> Every living thing reaches out as far from itself with its force as it can, and overwhelms what is weaker: thus it takes pleasure in itself. The increasing "humanizing" of this tendency consists in this, that there is an ever subtler sense of how hard it is really to incorporate another: while a crude injury done others certainly demonstrates our power over them, it at the same time estranges their will from us even more—and thus makes them less easy to subjugate. (*WP*, 769)

We have already seen that such "subjugation" can result in a new alliance, a new unity, even a new self (*WP*, 488; cf. 636). Since the self is not an abiding substance, it too changes as it incorporates other objects "without destroying" them. In the final analysis, Nietzsche's ominous physical metaphors can be applied even to the behavior of a powerful and influential teacher.

In any case, Nietzsche's view that character is important independently of its moral quality should not be dismissed out of hand. I am not certain of the proper word in this context, and I use this one with misgivings, but I think that there is something admirable in the very fact of having character or style. This does not mean that merely having character overrides all other considerations and justifies any sort of behavior. This is not true, nor does it represent Nietzsche's attitude, which is only that "whether this taste was good or bad is *less important* than one might suppose" (*GS*, 290; my italics). But Nietzsche believes that the evaluation of people and lives must appeal to a formal factor in addition to the content of our actions, the nature of which itself depends, as Aristotle also argued, on character: "An action is perfectly devoid of value: it all depends on *who* performs it" (*WP*, 292). He wants to introduce, at least as a major consideration, the question whether a person's actions, whatever their moral quality, together constitute a personality. This is not merely a sensible consideration; it is in fact one on which we often rely in our everyday dealings with one another.

It is not clear to me whether a consistently and irredeemably vicious person does actually have a character; the sort of agent Aristotle describes as "bestial" probably does not.[19] In some way there is something inherently praiseworthy in having character or style that prevents extreme cases of vice from being praised even in Nietzsche's formal sense. Perhaps the viciousness of such people overwhelms whatever praise we might otherwise be disposed to give them. Probably, however, the matter is more complicated. The existence of character is not quite as independent of the quality of the actions of which it constitutes the pattern: consistency may not in itself be sufficient for its presence. Being *too* consistent, after all, often suggests the absence of character and a mechanical way of acting. Perhaps, to appeal to another Aristotelian idea, some sort of moderation in action may in the long run be necessary for having character. Nietzsche would not, of course, accept Aristotle's view that moderation in every specific area of behavior consists in a mean between excess and defect: these are for him the materials through which a higher synthesis, which he sometimes calls "the grand style," may emerge. In any case, he would attribute character to more types of agent than Aristotle would and would praise them on account of that character even if their actions were, from a moral point of view, seriously objectionable.

Even when we admire immoral people of character, our admiration is bound to be most often mixed. Yet there are many cases in which we feel absolutely free to admire characters who are (or who, in the nature of the case, would be if they existed) dreadful people: we do so constantly in the case of literature. The best argument for Nietzsche's view of the importance of character is provided by the great literary villains, figures like Richard III (in Shakespeare's version), Fagin, Don Giovanni, Fyodor Karamazov, Charlus. In their case we freely place our moral scruples in the background. What concerns us about them is the overall manner of their behavior, the very structure of their minds, and not primarily the content of their actions. Here we can admire without reservations or misgivings.

Once again, literature emerges as the model behind Nietzsche's view of the importance of character and the nature of the self. Because organization is the most crucial feature of literary characters, the quality of their actions is secondary: the significance and nature of a character's action is inseparable from its place in that organization. Ideally, absolutely everything a character does is equally essential to it; characters are supposed to be constructed so that their every feature supports and is supported by every other. These are the features I discussed in connection with the eternal recurrence in the last chapter. Nietzsche came to see perfect self-sufficiency as a proper test for the perfect life at least partly because his thinking so often concerned literary models.

It might be objected to this view that our admiration for villainous or even inconsistent characters (who are consistently depicted) is directed not at those characters themselves but at the authors who create them. Therefore, this argument concludes, Nietzsche's generalization from literature to life is once again shown to be illegitimate. But we should note that when it comes to life, the "character" and the "author" are one and the same, and admiring the one cannot be distinguished from admiring the other. This is also the reason, I suspect, that though inconsistent characters can be admired in literature, they cannot be admired in life: in life an inconsistent character constitutes a poor author; there is no room for the distinction between creature and creator. The parallel between life and literature may not be perfect, but it is not flawed in the manner this objection envisages.[20]

Nietzsche always depended on literary and artistic models for understanding the world. This accounts for some of his most peculiar thoughts, and it underlies some of his most original ideas. As early as *The Birth of Tragedy* he saw Dionysus reborn in the person of Wagner and in the artwork of the future by means of a process that was the symmetrical opposite of what he took to be the process of the dissolution of classical antiquity (*BT*, 19). But, as Paul de Man has written, "passages of this kind are valueless as arguments, since they assume that the actual events in history are founded in formal symmetries easy enough to achieve in pictorial, musical, or poetic fictions, but that can never predict the occurrence of a historical event" (p. 84). We know that Nietzsche, who was a compulsive letter writer, preferred what in his time still was a literary genre in its own right to conversation and personal contact as a means of communication even with his close friends.[21] Often enough he urges that we fashion our lives in the way artists fashion their works: "We should learn from artists while being wiser than they are in other matters. For with them this subtle power [of arranging, of making things beautiful] usually comes to an end where art ends and life begins; but we want to be the poets of our life—first of all in the smallest, most everyday matters" (*GS*, 299; cf. 301). Nietzsche writes that freedom is "facility in self-direction. Every artist will understand me" (*WP*, 705). And it is primarily in artists that he finds the peace of soul we have already seen him call "attained freedom of the will." As he writes, it is artists who "seem to have more sensitive noses in these matters, knowing only too well that precisely when they no longer do something 'voluntarily' but do everything of necessity, the feeling of freedom, subtlety, full power, of creative placing, disposing, and forming reaches its peak—in short, that necessity and 'freedom of will' then become one in them" (*BGE*, 213).

How, then, can one achieve the perfect unity and freedom that are primarily possessed by perfect literary characters? How does one become both a literary character who, unlike either the base Charlus or the noble Brutus, really exists and also that character's very author?

One way of achieving this perhaps impossible goal might be to write a great number of very good books that exhibit great apparent inconsistencies among them but that can be seen to be deeply continuous with one another when they are read carefully and well. Toward the end of this enterprise one can even write a book about these books that shows how they fit together, how a single figure emerges through them, how even the most damaging contradictions may have been necessary for that figure or character or author or person (the word hardly matters here) to emerge fully from them: "*Natura non facit saltum.*—However strongly one may develop upwards and appear to leap from one contradiction to another, a close observation will reveal the dovetails where the new building grows out of the old. This is the biographers' task: they must reflect upon their subject on the principle that nature takes no jumps" (*WS*, 198).

Zarathustra had said, "What returns, what finally comes home to me, is my own self" (*Z*, III, 1). Now Nietzsche can write of his *Untimely Meditations*, three of which concern important historical figures and one history itself: "At bottom they speak only of me . . . *Wagner in Bayreuth* is a vision of my future, while in *Schopenhauer as Educator* my innermost history, my *becoming*, is inscribed" (*EH*, III, on *UM*, 3; cf. III, *BT*, 4; III, *HH*, 1). Earlier Nietzsche had written: "Now something that you formerly loved . . . strikes you as an error . . . But perhaps this error was as necessary for you then, when you were still a different person—you are always a different person—as all your present 'truth' " (*GS*, 307). Now he can look back at *Schopenhauer as Educator* and claim:

> Considering that in those days I practiced the scholar's craft, and perhaps *knew* something about this craft, the harsh psychology of the scholar that suddenly emerges in this essay is of some significance: it expresses the *feeling of distance,* the profound assurance about what could be my task and what could only be means, *entr'acte* and minor works. It shows my prudence that I was many things and in many places in order to be able to become one thing— to be able to attain one thing. I *had* to be a scholar, too, for some time. (*EH*, III, on *UM*, 3)

One way, then, to become one thing, one's own character, what one is, is, after having written all these other books, to write *Ecce Homo* and even to give it the subtitle "How One Becomes What One Is." It is to write this self-referential book in which Nietzsche can be said with equal justice to invent or to discover himself, and in which the character who speaks to us is the author who has created him and who is in turn a character created by or implicit in all the books that were written by the author who is writing this one.

But the fact that this character emerges out of many works may seem to present a serious difficulty for this interpretation of unity and, in particular, for the literary model on which I have claimed it depends. Literary characters often appear in numerous works; Odysseus and Oedipus keep reemerging in Western literature. And though there is a popular view that behind each character there is a "myth" or "legend" that dictates that some of that character's features must remain invariant across different treatments, this view is simply popular—and nothing else. The "myth" consists of those features which, as a matter of fact, have remained the same so far in a character's treatment. It is an abstraction from such particular treatments and has no prescriptive powers of its own. No noncircular argument can show that an Odysseus who did not participate in the siege of Troy, or an Odysseus who returned to Ithaca immediately after the war, or even an Odysseus who was slow witted and clumsy could not be the "real" Odysseus. Euripides, after all, has given us a Helen who never went to Troy. But if no such myth dictates the essential features of each character, then different treatments can attribute, without contradiction, inconsistent properties to any particular character. This may imply that there can be no single literary character called "Odysseus," or that literary characters in general cannot be unified in the manner that I have presupposed: perhaps Odysseus is a single character who is nevertheless, as all characters can be, deeply inconsistent. If this is so, then it may seem that Nietzsche had too naive an understanding of literary characters or that it was wrong to attribute this model to him. Conversely, it may seem that even if Nietzsche intended to create a literary character out of himself, he still need not have aimed at unity and coherence: literariness and unity, according to this argument, do not go with one another.

Now it is absolutely true that literary characters have no essence and can well be inconsistent across different works.[22] But who are the characters who, like Odysseus, have offered themselves for the greatest number of different treatments and versions? They are precisely those who, at least at some point in their history, were given a highly unified, coherent, and consistent presentation. It is just this feature, I think, that provokes other authors into creating variants of these characters with the aim of seeing whether they will still be recognizable. Inconsistency can therefore easily arise across different works; it may even be considered a desirable feature for a character in the long run: the most interesting characters are often those who keep reappearing in fiction. But this does not imply that each particular version of a character is itself inconsistent. On the contrary, the great characters are those who receive many treatments which, though perhaps inconsistent with one another, are still internally coherent and highly organized. Since Nietzsche, therefore, is developing only a single treatment of this character, nothing prevents him from aiming at coherence on the basis of the literary model which, we can insist, he accepts.

This misplaced objection, however, inadvertently reveals a new dimension in Nietzsche's project. Apart from creating a unified and coherent version of a character, his project has also given rise to a large number of different interpretations, or versions, of that character. Each one of those versions, the present one included, aims at unity and coherence in its own right. Even interpretations that attribute to Nietzsche inconsistent or polysemous views do so for a reason; the Nietzsche such interpretations produce is still, at least in principle, consistent and seriously motivated. But there are by now many different versions of Nietzsche, many of which (like the different versions of some literary characters) are inconsistent with one another. And this, as I think Nietzsche actually hoped, may make the questions "Who is the real Nietzsche? Which is the correct interpretation of his views?" as easy or as difficult to answer, and perhaps as pointless to pose, as the questions "Who is the real Odysseus? Which is the correct version of his story?" But even though such questions may be pointless, we can still ask and decide whether some specific interpretation of Nietzsche is better than another, just as we can decide that Tennyson's version of Odysseus is a trifle compared to Homer's. We must keep resisting, in this context too, the assumption that Nietzsche's perspectivism itself tries to undermine: even if there is no "ultimate" truth, it does not follow that every view is as good as every other.

Nietzsche's enterprise, however, may still appear to many of his readers to be doomed from its beginning. No one has managed to bring life closer to literature than he did, and yet the two may finally refuse to become one, making his ideal of unity impossible to approach. *Ecce Homo,* one might argue, leaves great parts of Nietzsche's life undiscussed, and, unfortunately for him, his life did not end with it but twelve miserable years later. To make a perfectly unified character out of all that one has done, as Nietzsche wants, may involve us in a vicious effort: we may have to be writing our autobiography as we are living our life, and we would also have to be writing about writing that autobiography, and to be writing in turn about that, and so on, and so on without end. But as Nietzsche had written long before his own end: "Not every end is a goal. A melody's end is not its goal; nevertheless, so long as the melody has not reached its end, it also has not reached its goal. A parable" (*WS,* 204). This parable explicates the phrase that has occupied us and expresses Nietzsche's attitude toward the relationship between the world and art as well as anything he ever wrote. But for some the doubt remains whether any melody, however complicated, could ever be a model that a life (which is not to say a biography) can imitate.

Nietzsche, though, writes: "One does best to separate artists from their work, not taking them as seriously as their work. They are, after all, only the precondition of their work, the womb, the soil, sometimes the dung and manure on which, out of which, it grows—and therefore in most cases something one must forget if one is to enjoy

the work itself" (*GM*, III, 4). What, then, if the work itself, in its totality, results in the construction of a character whose "biography" it
turns out to be? In that case the doubt that was lingering just above
may be counterbalanced by the suspicion that only the "biography"
that emerges through Nietzsche's works, and not the "life" out of
which they grow, is of any importance. In his eyes, at least, it is only
such a character who can influence history and thought and who, like
the Socrates who emerges out of Plato's dialogues, can manifest the
will to power in fashioning values and modes of life. We have seen
that characters are usually evaluated without regard for their morality, for the specific content of their actions; they are in this sense situated "beyond good and evil." But what mode of evaluation is appropriate for the character who emerges out of Nietzsche's writing and
who is beyond good and evil not only in this generalized sense but
also because, in the manner which by now we have found to be essential to him, the very content of his actions is an effort to base all evaluation beyond good and evil, beyond regard for the specific content of
our actions?

7 | *Beyond Good and Evil*

> A man who is born falls into a dream like a man who falls into the sea. If he tries to climb out into the air as inexperienced people endeavour to do, he drowns—*nicht wahr?* . . . No! I tell you! The way is to the destructive element submit yourself, and with the exertions of your hands and feet in the water make the deep, deep sea keep you up.
>
> Joseph Conrad, *Lord Jim*

In order to convince the citizens of his model state to love their land, sacrifice their lives to it, and be content with their position in its hierarchical structure, Plato in the *Republic* invents the myth of the metals. According to this myth, which they will be taught to accept as the actual truth, the citizens are all born and raised within the earth itself, and are therefore literally its children. The myth also says that the citizens are born with varying proportions of different metals, more or less precious, in their bodies, and that the different mixtures account for the different roles each one will eventually have in the state. Though it is necessary in order to support his new moral and political scheme, Plato knows that this story is completely false. In his own uncompromising words, it is "a noble lie" (*Rep.* 414b).[1]

This lie is a small but significant part of what Nietzsche has in mind when he writes: "That the lie is permitted as a means to pious ends is part of the theory of every priesthood . . . But philosophers, too, as soon as, with priestly ulterior motives, they form the intention of taking in hand the direction of humanity, at once also arrogate to themselves the right to tell lies: Plato before all" (*WP,* 141). The theme of this passage is in turn a small but significant part of what Nietzsche at one point describes as his "campaign against morality" (*EH,* III, on *D,* 1), a cluster of views that constitutes one of the most central as well as most obscure and disquieting features of his thought.

A quick reading of Nietzsche's text might give the impression that he accuses morality of being essentially hypocritical, since he claims that no moral system can be established without relying on the very practices which, once it has become dominant, it absolutely excludes. This impression might be reinforced by the fact that Nietzsche uses the very same example in order to make a related but more general point:

> We may proclaim it as the supreme principle that, to *make* morality, one must have the unconditional will to its opposite . . . A small, and at bottom modest, fact—that of the so-called *pia fraus*—offered me the first approach to this problem: the *pia fraus,* the heirloom of all philosophers and priests who "improved" humanity. Neither Manu nor Plato nor Confucius nor the Jewish and Christian teachers have ever doubted their *right* to lie . . . Expressed in a formula, one might say: *all* the means by which one has so far attempted to make humanity moral were through and through *immoral.* (*TI,* VII, 5)

Though the distinction is far from absolute, Nietzsche generally tries to keep morality, a system of rules and values according to which life is lived, apart from moral philosophy, which he sees as the attempt to codify and justify some particular system of such values (*BGE,* 210). It is in regard to the former that he rather reasonably writes, "The history of a moral ideal is achieved by the same 'immoral' means as every victory: force, lies, slander, injustice" (*WP,* 306). This view, in turn, underwrites his notorious claim that "morality is a special case of immorality" (*WP,* 308; cf. 401, 461).

Yet it would be wrong to think that Nietzsche considers that this fact constitutes in itself an objection to morality. To object to morality simply because it relies on immoral means would be, for him, to make yet another moral judgment and thus to perpetuate moral valuation, which is just what his "campaign" is directed against. On the contrary, Nietzsche seems to believe that immorality cannot be condemned because it cannot be avoided:

> Life itself is *essentially* appropriation, injury, overpowering of what is alien and weaker; suppression, hardness, imposition of one's own forms, incorporation and at least, at its mildest, exploitation—but why should one always use those words in which a slanderous intent has been imprinted for ages? . . . "Exploitation" . . . belongs to the essence of what lives, as a basic organic function; it is the consequence of the will to power, which is after all the will to life. (*BGE*, 259)

To show that something is immoral, even if that is morality itself, is therefore not at all to show that it must be rejected: "There are those who go looking for immorality. When they judge: 'This is wrong,' they believe one should abolish and change it. I, on the contrary, cannot rest as long as I am not yet clear about the immorality of a thing. When I unearth it I recover my equanimity" (*WP*, 309). Nietzsche's "deconstruction" of morality, his effort to show that its establishment and authority depend on the very same means which, after its establishment and through its authority, it excludes, is simply his effort to account for morality in a naturalistic manner. His aim is to explain its emergence and survival by showing that morality too, like everything else in the world, is a product of the will to power.

Nietzsche's attitudes toward these problems are complex and equivocal. His writing about them is often murky and passionate, and it has in turn provoked murky and passionate writing about him.[2] But if Nietzsche is not simply accusing morality of hypocrisy, what is the point of his effort to reveal its immoral presuppositions—assuming that such an effort can be even partially successful? And what, if anything, would he like to put in its place once it is realized, if it is realized, that despite its earlier utility morality is now "only a burden that has become a fatality" and that "morality itself, in the form of honesty, compels us to deny morality" (*WP*, 404; cf. *GM*, III, 27)?

A simple answer to these two questions would be that since Nietzsche believes that morality, like life itself, is immoral, he also believes that we can only act immorally, whether we like it or not. We must therefore give up the pretense of morality and live according to nature, as the will to power inclines us to do: we must become explicitly immoral. This common interpretation of Nietzsche's immoralism construes it as a view urging us to satisfy any desire that possesses us and aligns Nietzsche with Callicles as he is portrayed in Plato's *Gorgias*. But both the interpretation and the alignment are deeply wrong.[3] Nietzsche explicitly writes that the ideal of living according to nature is either impossible or inevitable. It is impossible if nature is understood as that part of the world that consists only of nonhuman or nonliving things; for living, he writes, is "precisely wanting to be other than that nature." And it is inevitable if nature includes life, since in that case we cannot but live according to nature and are doing so already: "How could you not do that? Why make a principle of what you yourselves are and must be?" (*BGE*, 9).

Nietzsche therefore does not advocate a type of life that consists only or even mostly of those actions which we now consider immoral. His "revaluation of all values" does not amount to this sort of straightforward reversal, even though he sometimes describes it as "a liberation from all moral values . . . saying Yes to and having confidence in all that has hitherto been forbidden, despised, and damned" (*EH*, III, on *D*, 1). His attitude is much more complicated, as we can see from the following early passage, which expresses a view which Nietzsche never abandoned:

> I deny morality as I deny alchemy, that is, I deny their premises: but I do *not* deny that there have been alchemists who believed in these premises and acted in accordance with them.—I also deny immorality: *not* that countless people *feel* themselves to be immoral, but that there is any *true* reason so to feel. It goes without saying that I do not deny—unless I am a fool—that many actions called immoral ought to be avoided and resisted, or that many called moral ought to be done and encouraged—but I think the one should be encouraged and the other avoided *for other reasons than hitherto*. (*D*, 103)

Though Nietzsche's attitude toward morality implies that if we accept his views our modes of action will not remain unchanged, his primary concern is not with the specific content of particular actions but with our reasons and motives for acting as we do. He locates both morality and immorality in the motives with which we act and, as we shall see, in the nature of the obligations morality tries to impose upon individual agents rather than in our actions themselves. These are the main targets of his campaign: "There are altogether no moral facts . . . Morality is merely an interpretation of certain phenomena—more precisely, a misinterpretation" (*TI*, VII, 1). And in a note in which this same passage had appeared years earlier, he adds, "This interpretation itself is of extra-moral origin" (*WP*, 258).

The view that Nietzsche wants to reinterpret, rather than directly attack, both morality and immorality is neither new nor surprising. But the problems it generates are still enormous, at least partly because he himself did not always construe moral motives in the same way.[4] In his earlier writings he holds that moral actions are those that are supposed to be performed, as Schopenhauer had argued, out of motives in which personal considerations play no part. But he claims that such motives cannot possibly exist and that therefore there simply are no moral actions: "When closely examined, the whole idea of 'unegoistic' actions vanishes into air. No one has ever done anything that was done solely for the sake of another and without a personal motive. How indeed *could* one do anything that had no relation to oneself, and therefore without an inner necessity (which simply must have its foundation in a personal need)? How could the *ego* act without *ego*?" (*HH*, I, 133). This view, however, was both logically and psychologically unsatisfactory, and Nietzsche gave it up by the time he came to write *Daybreak*. There he considers the following: "*the chief proposition:* morality is nothing other (therefore nothing more!) than obedience to customs, of whatever kind they may be . . . In things in which no tradition commands there is no morality . . . What is tradition? A higher authority which one obeys, not because it commands what is useful to us, but because it *commands*" (*D*, 9).

The "morality of mores," which Nietzsche had earlier placed at the origin of morality (cf. *HH*, I, 96, 99; *MOM*, 89), now becomes its very essence (*D*, 16, 18). The morality of mores actually instills its motives in its adherents, and Nietzsche no longer denies that moral motives and moral actions exist. More under Kant's influence, he still considers moral action unegoistic, since it is motivated by respect for tradition and authority and not by concern for utility, but he no longer conceives of it as particularly other regarding. And though he believes that such motives exist and guide actions, he argues that they should not: their presuppositions, he claims, are false. The same passage from *Daybreak* continues: "What distinguishes this feeling in the presence of tradition from the feeling of fear in general? It is fear in the presence of a higher intellect which here commands, of an incomprehensible, indefinite power, of something more than personal—there is *superstition* in this fear" (*D*, 9).

In the late writings, Nietzsche's conception of morality becomes much more complicated. He claims that it presupposes the notion of free will, a notion that "has been invented essentially for the purpose of punishment, that is, because one wanted to impute guilt" (*TI*, VII, 7). Responsibility, guilt, and punishment, which he discusses in detail in the *Genealogy*, now become central to his view of the moral interpretation of action. He includes as elements in this interpretation the conception of an everlasting world in which guilt is punished through eternal torture (*A*, 24) and the metaphysics of Christianity and Platonism ("Christianity is Platonism for the people," *BGE*, Pref.), which provide reasons or at least presuppositions for that faith. His views become increasingly complex and his elaborations progressively more intricate and intertwined.

This topic is very large, if indeed it is one topic at all, and we can single out only one of its many strands. We have already asked what the point is of Nietzsche's claim that morality is based on immoral presuppositions as well as whether he aims to present a positive alternative of his own. These are the questions, themselves anything but simple, which we must press. In order to give an answer to them I will approach them obliquely, by way of an interpretation of the sign under which Nietzsche waged his campaign against morality, the phrase that provides the title of *Beyond Good and Evil*, a phrase that appears throughout that book and everywhere in Nietzsche's late writings (*GM*, I, passim; *Z*, IV, 6; *WP*, 132; *TI*, VII, 1).

The main problem with the interpretation of the phrase "Beyond good and evil" is that it is not often read against the many contexts in which it is found in Nietzsche's writings. Instead it is most often discussed in connection with the first essay of the *Genealogy*, where, as we have seen, Nietzsche argues that moral valuation or "slave morality," expressed in the opposition good-evil *(böse)*, is the reversal of an earlier nonmoral, "noble" mode of valuation, expressed in the opposition good-bad *(schlecht)*.[5]

Nietzsche writes that the nobles he discusses in this essay are in many circumstances "not much better than uncaged beasts of prey . . . they perhaps emerge from a disgusting procession of murder, arson, rape, and torture, exhilarated and undisturbed of soul, as if it were no more than a student's prank, convinced that they have provided the poets with much more material for song and praise" (*GM*, I, 11).[6] In order to resist the view that Nietzsche's immoralism consists simply in praising barbarism and cruelty, Walter Kaufmann has insisted that "despite the polemical tone, it does not follow from Nietzsche's 'vivisection' of slave-morality that he identifies his own position with that of the masters" (p. 297). And indeed logically it does not. But Nietzsche's attitude toward the noble mode of valuation is much more positive than Kaufmann was ever willing to allow: "Must not the ancient fire not some day flare up much more terribly, after much longer preparation? More: must not one desire it with all one's might? even will it? even promote it?" (*GM*, I, 17). Kaufmann continues, "Nietzsche's own ethic is beyond both master and slave morality" (p. 297).[7] But his very wording, I think, is contradicted by the concluding lines of this same section of Nietzsche's text: "It has long been abundantly clear what my *aim* is, what the aim of that dangerous slogan is that is inscribed at the head of my last book *Beyond Good and Evil.*—At least this does *not* mean 'Beyond Good and Bad.' "[8] To be beyond good and evil cannot therefore be to leave behind the mode of valuation that characterizes the barbarian nobles.

We can escape this problem, which has disturbed and unsettled so many of Nietzsche's readers, if we can show that, though Nietzsche accepts the mode of valuation that characterizes the nobles of *On the Genealogy of Morals*, these nobles still do not constitute a particular type of person he wants directly to praise. Rather, we can take them as one manifestation, under specific historical circumstances, of a general personality type which Nietzsche outlines and of which they are an example.[9] But we cannot show this unless we first give an interpretation of the slogan "Beyond good and evil," the aim of which, despite Nietzsche's statement, is still far from clear. If we concentrate solely on the *Genealogy*, we may easily be forced to the conclusion that to situate oneself beyond good and evil is to abandon Christian morality and accept instead the specific mode of behavior of the barbarous nobles this text so graphically describes and glorifies. But when Nietzsche mentions this phrase, he explicitly refers his readers to the work of which it is the title. And this work, together with the many other texts to which it is related, shows that the situation Nietzsche has in mind is much more complicated. To be beyond good and evil is not simply to discard these terms of valuation and the system to which they belong. Since it is not even necessary to abandon all the qualities that this system commends, to be beyond good and evil is to see how good and evil qualities have been thought to be related so far, to realize how, according to Nietzsche, they are related in fact, and to reconsider that relationship and all that it implies.

When Nietzsche writes, "Have not all gods so far been . . . devils who have become holy and been rebaptized?" (*BGE*, 227), he is asking a complex question: history, he claims, shows that actions and qualities that are considered immoral and evil are necessary in order to secure the possibility of other actions and qualities that are considered moral and good. Is it then correct to believe, as he thinks we do, that such actions and qualities belong to two distinct sorts, that they are essentially opposed to one another? Does each set possess its own character in itself, independently of what it is used to accomplish and of who it is who uses it? Are some features and actions simply and in all contexts to be commended while others are simply and in all contexts to be fought against?

Nietzsche gives an early intimation of his eventual answer to these questions when he writes that "between good and evil actions there is no difference in species, but at most of degree. Good actions are sublimated evil ones; evil actions are vulgarized and stupefied good ones" (*HH*, I, 107). But it is only in his later works that his view emerges in its full complexity. Consider, for example, Nietzsche's discussion of the phenomenon of the saint. The saint has been such a fascinating phenomenon for so long because of

> the air of the miraculous that goes with it—namely, the immediate *succession of opposites*, of states of the soul that are judged morally in opposite ways. It seemed palpable that a "bad human being" [*ein schlechter Mensch*] was suddenly transformed into a "saint," a good human being [*ein guter Mensch*]. The psychology we have had so far suffered shipwreck at this point: wasn't this chiefly because it had placed itself under the dominion of morals, because it, too, *believed* in opposite moral values and saw, read, *interpreted* those opposites into the text of the facts?
>
> What? The "miracle" merely a matter of interpretation? A lack of philology? (*BGE*, 47)

The conversion of sinner to saint represents a deep psychological paradox because all of a sudden immoral features like lust, ambition, and cruelty disappear and are replaced by their opposites—chastity, self-denial, and kindness. But how is this conversion possible? If there is no such thing as divine intervention, capable of changing everything about a person but that person itself (and the faith in which therefore is connected to the belief that the subject is a substance), what mechanism can possibly account for such a transformation? How can *anyone* change in this way?

It is crucial to note that Nietzsche does not deny that sinners can become saints. But he claims that the fact that this transformation is possible shows that we have misunderstood its nature. It constitutes a paradox because the conversion of sinner to saint seems to consist in the transformation of a set of qualities into others to which they are inherently opposed in value and in nature. But if this opposition were only apparent, then no paradox would be generated. The contradiction would disappear if these qualities were not contrary but essentially related to one another: "It might even be possible that what constitutes the value of these good and revered things is precisely that they are insidiously related, tied to, and involved with these wicked, seemingly opposite things—maybe even one with them is essence. Maybe!" (*BGE*, 2). Zarathustra makes a related, if weaker point when he tells his disciples, "Once you suffered your passions and called them evil. But now you have only your virtues left: they grew out of your passions" (*Z*, I, 5). The moral character of qualities, which seems to separate them so radically from one another, is actually, Nietzsche believes, the result of an interpretation: "The same drive evolves into the painful feeling of *cowardice* under the impress of the reproach custom has imposed upon this drive: or into the pleasant feeling of *humility* if it happens that a custom such as the Christian has taken it to its heart and called it *good* . . . In itself it has, *like every drive*, neither this moral character nor any moral character at all" (*D*, 38).

All value in general, Nietzsche seems to believe, is produced by interpretation. But since he thinks that life itself would be impossible without values (*Z*, II, 13; *BGE*, 9), he must have a specific reason in mind for thinking that moral value in particular is the product of a misinterpretation. Where, then, does the interpretation that generates moral values go wrong?

This question, in one form or another, had occupied Nietzsche ever since *The Birth of Tragedy:* "It was against *morality* that my instinct turned with this questionable book," he writes in section 5 of his 1886 preface to that work. He eventually answers it with another slogan, the notorious phrase "Morality denies life." He bases this vague and sweeping charge, which itself needs to be carefully interpreted, on his view that moral asceticism is a falsification of life on the part of those who cannot face the life they are bound to live. And this, he writes, "*explains everything.* Who alone has good reason to lie one's way out of reality? One who suffers from it. But to suffer from reality is to be a piece of reality that has come to grief" (*A*, 15).

But Nietzsche's most serious reason for thinking that morality denies life, the most crucial flaw he finds in the interpretation that produces moral values, is the fact that moral valuation is essentially absolutist. He thinks of this absolutism in two ways. First, as the paradox of the saint shows, the moral interpretation of phenomena attaches positive or negative value to actions or character traits in themselves; it presupposes that their worth is fixed once and for all and in all contexts. Second, as we shall see, this interpretation requires that, since value is determined in this manner, everyone should live according to a single code of conduct.

This is not to say that Nietzsche believes simply that moral value varies with different social groups. We have already seen that cultural moral relativism is a position he finds as "childish" as the absolutism against which it has been designed (*GS*, 345). The moral absolutism Nietzsche attacks can grant that different cultures can have different values; but it still insists that, wherever the distinction is made, good and evil belong to two clearly distinct categories, the boundaries of which cannot be crossed. It takes, that is, the difference between good and evil within each culture (if differences among cultures can be found) to be absolute and objective. It is precisely this last view that Nietzsche denies and of which he writes that it in turn denies life. Morality, according to Nietzsche, "takes good and evil for realities that contradict one another (not as complementary value concepts, which would be the truth), it advises taking the side of the good, it desires that the good should renounce and oppose the evil down to its ultimate roots—it therewith denies life which has in all its instincts both Yes and No" (*WP*, 351).

The essential unity of what we commonly distinguish as good and evil is one of the most central themes in Nietzsche's writing. He often discusses it in connection with a metaphor drawn from trees: "It is with people as it is with the trees. The more they aspire to the height and light, the more strongly do their roots strive earthward, downward, into the dark, the deep—into evil" (*Z*, I, 8; cf. III, 1; *GS*, 371; *GM*, I, 8). But both this theme and the metaphor that illustrates it are difficult to interpret. Their weakest interpretation would suppose that Nietzsche simply believes that good and evil are equally parts of life and that evil can never be finally eliminated. Chekhov once expressed such an idea: "A writer must be as objective as a chemist; he must abandon the subjective line; he must know that dungheaps play a very respectable part in a landscape and that evil passions are as inherent in life as good ones."[10] But though Nietzsche certainly believes this, his attitude has nothing of Chekhov's dispassionateness and objectivity. On the contrary, he consistently urges that "evil" tendencies should be further developed: "Human beings need what is most evil in them for what is best in them . . . whatever is most evil is their best power and the hardest stone for the highest creator. . . human beings must become better and more evil" (Z, III, 13; cf. IV, 13).

A stronger version of Nietzsche's view, taking account of this statement, would hold that evil features are not simply ineliminable but actually necessary if any good features are to be possessed at all. This would be a radical denial of the traditional thesis of the unity of virtue. Philippa Foot has recently raised the possibility that contrary to the view of Aristotle and St. Thomas (among others), according to whom having one virtue entails having the rest of them as well, a person

> can only become good in one way by being bad in another, as if, e.g., he could only rein in his ruthless desires at the cost of a deep malice against himself and the world; or as if a kind of dull rigidity were the price of refusing to do what he himself wanted at whatever cost to others . . . Nietzsche found thoughts about the possibility that hatred, envy, covetousness and the lust to rule must be present in the "general economy of Life," and must be "further enhanced if life is further to be enhanced," terrible thoughts; but with his extraordinary and characteristic courage he did not decide that therefore they must be false.[11]

The passage cited in this elegant statement (BGE, 23), along with other similar texts (see, for example, WP, 464), makes exactly this point. But Nietzsche often gives his view one further unsettling dimension.

The passages we have just been considering envisage a distinction between good and evil even as they urge that one enhances the other. But sometimes Nietzsche writes that the passions we call evil are themselves the very passions that result in the best, greatest, and most admirable achievements. In a text that brings to the fore the connections between this issue and the interpretation of the phrase with which we are concerned, he writes: "My demand upon philosphers is known, that they take their stand *beyond* good and evil and leave the illusion of moral judgment *beneath* themselves. This demand follows from an insight which I was the first to formulate: that *there are altogether no moral facts*" (*TI*, VII, 1). If there are no moral facts at all, nothing is in any way good or evil: "*My purpose:* to demonstrate the absolute homogeneity of all events and the application of moral distinctions as conditioned by perspective; to demonstrate how everything praised as moral is identical in essence with everything immoral" (*WP*, 272). This thesis is the stongest of the three I have mentioned. It does not simply include evil among the necessary aspects of the world. It does not simply claim that in order to possess any good qualities one must possess evil qualities as well. It actually denies that the distinction between good and evil can be made at all, and suggests that the very same quality that is considered evil from one perspective may at least as accurately be characterized as good from another.

But since everything is conditioned by perspective, the crucial question once again concerns the particular perspective that results in moral valuations. Nietzsche's answer to this question informs his writing and appeals to sociological considerations. The perspective from which moral valuations are made, he notoriously claims, is just the perspective dictated by "the utility of the herd . . . the preservation of the community" (*BGE*, 201; cf. *GM*, I, 2).

This idea finally connects this discussion with Nietzsche's view of the immoral presuppositions of morality. How, he asks, are new states and societies, with their own laws and values, established? He believes that history answers this question unequivocally: in all cases, they are established by revolting against former masters, by eliminating external dangers, by overpowering internal opposition, by war and injustice in the name of justice and peace, in short by what he calls "fear of the neighbor." Only by means of such activities and the passions, drives, motives, and values that make them possible can a new society establish and safeguard itself. But once that is accomplished, these same passions and activities become great dangers; their exercise, which overturned some earlier group, now threatens the new group's stability:

> Certain strong and dangerous drives, like an enterprising spirit, foolhardiness, vengefulness, craftiness, rapacity, and the lust to rule, which had so far not merely been honored insofar as they were socially useful—under different names, to be sure, from those chosen

here—but had to be trained and cultivated to make them great (because one constantly needed them in view of the dangers to the whole community, against the enemies of the community), are now experienced as doubly dangerous, since the channels to divert them are lacking and, step upon step, they are branded as immoral and abandoned to slander. (*BGE*, 201)

Nietzsche makes the converse point, which he also accepts, when he writes that "everything good is the evil of former days made serviceable" (*WP*, 1025). The very same drive that produces peacefulness and cooperation within a stable society results in submissiveness and collaboration in a society that should be fighting for its survival. In itself the drive has no moral character. This, I think, is what Nietzsche has in mind when he claims that there are no moral facts: the activity produced by a particular drive, if we abstract from the context within which it is performed, is always the same. But once we supply a context, once we introduce a point of view, both the drive and the activity come to possess a specific value. Once again the complex relation between Nietzsche and Plato becomes apparent: Nietzsche argues in a manner very close to the manner of Socrates that what we commonly consider good depends essentially on the context that we implicitly introduce into our evaluation, and that it is not therefore good in itself (cf., for example, *Rep.* 331c-d); but unlike both Socrates and Plato he refuses to believe that something that is good in itself, independently of all context or perspective, must exist after all.

Nietzsche has nothing but contempt for the morality of the "herd," which locates virtue in the "striving for *English* happiness—I mean for comfort and fashion (and at best a seat in Parliament)" (*BGE*, 228). He attacks Christian morality precisely because of its "leveling" effect, its successful effort to prolong the life of a society composed of mediocrities: "We can see nothing today that wants to grow greater, we suspect that things will continue to go down, to become thinner, more good-natured, more prudent, more comfortable, more mediocre, more indifferent, more Chinese, more Christian—there is no doubt that human beings are getting 'better' all the time" (*GM*, I, 12; cf. I, 11; III, 14). Recent history shows that Nietzsche's view is most certainly false. Sometimes, however, I think we can account for it by taking it as his interpretation of our current self-image rather than of the facts of the situation. It is true that, even though we may be wrong to do so, we generally think of our own era and society as better and more humane than others. But, despite Nietzsche's insistence to the contrary, I find it difficult to believe (and even more difficult to substantiate) that other societies and eras have been different from ours in that respect and have seen themselves as more dangerous and more evil than those they fought or replaced.

Apart from such historical difficulties, however, Nietzsche's attitude generates a more serious philosophical problem. To see this problem, we may suppose for the moment that he is correct in deriving moral distinctions from the tendency of every social group to maintain itself in existence for as long as possible. We may also agree with him that the drives and activities that are most dangerous to a stable society are exactly those that brought it into being in the first place, since they are inherently disruptive and destructive. Now such tendencies are also necessarily elitist, in the following sense. They presuppose that "we," the new social order or subgroup within that order, are better and more valuable than those we want to abolish and eradicate. They also presuppose that "we" are justified in employing means that in the abstract (that is to say, in other hands) we would deem disastrous. The desire to maintain a social group as it has existed so far will therefore involve a serious effort to diminish and even to eliminate altogether elitist tendencies of this sort; for such tendencies always pit one group against another and, considered from society's point of view, are inherently destabilizing: "What has been *deified*? The value instincts in the community (that which has made possible its continued existence). What has been *slandered*? That which *set apart* the higher human beings from the lower, the desires that create clefts" (*WP*, 32).

To eliminate such tendencies it is necessary to have a system of behavior to which everyone will conform. In this way no individual or group can feel justified in adopting the practices that, though they once brought their society into existence, now constitute a threat to its survival. But this absolutism of conduct can be secured only by means of an absolutism of doctrine, by means of the doctrine that good and evil traits and actions are inherently distinct from one another and that their character does not depend on the character of those who manifest and engage in them on each particular occasion.[12] Some actions, therefore, are always to be performed by everyone, and others are always to be unconditionally avoided. Absolutism of doctrine, according to Nietzsche, conceals the fact that one group within a society is legislating the values by which all are required to live. That is, it masks its own will to power: "This state is actually encountered in Europe today: I call it the moral hypocrisy of those commanding. They know no other way to protect themselves against their bad conscience than to pose as the executors of more ancient or higher commands (of ancestors, the constitution, of right, the laws, or even of God)" (*BGE*, 199).[13] The final mechanism by which this absolutism of doctrine is accomplished is directly connected with the absolutism of conduct for which it is the means. In order to eliminate all differences between people and to treat them all equally, it separates each action from its agent, considers it an entity in its own right, and makes the action itself the primary object of evaluation. Following on the "abstractions" discussed in the last chapter, this approach creates the view that "there are actions that are good or bad in themselves," whereas in reality, according to Nietzsche, "an action in itself is perfectly devoid of value: it all depends on *who* performs it," for what reason and with what effect (*WP*, 292).

Nietzsche's greatest objection to the doctrinal absolutism he considers central to morality is precisely that it requires everyone to follow the same principles of action. This is in fact the very feature that distinguishes moral approaches to conduct, among which he places Christianity, from approaches which, like the noble mode of valuation, are explicitly perspectivist, nonabsolutist, and therefore nonmoral. Morality aims at a code of conduct to which everyone must conform. This must therefore also be a code that everyone *can* follow, and morality thus necessarily addresses itself to the lowest common denominator among the people whose conduct it guides. This is its "leveling" effect, which Nietzsche so despises. The only actions it allows aim at the interest of each group as a whole and therefore at the interest of its weakest members. But the rules that prescribe such actions may not at all be in the interest of the (not very helpfully so described) strong members of that group. They actually prevent them from exploiting qualities that may be dangerous to the group as a whole and by means of which they can distinguish themselves from their community and accomplish the deeds Nietzsche sometimes, equally unhelpfully, describes as unique, high, or great.

These deeds need not themselves be dangerous to a society as a whole, nor need the qualities and abilities that bring them about when exercised by the proper individuals create such dangers. The problems, he thinks, are generated when these qualities are encouraged in general within a society. But morality, according to Nietzsche, recognizes only two alternatives: a feature is acceptable either in every case or in none. Morality, he repeatedly insists, refuses to recognize an "order of rank" and does not want to run the risk of encouraging some qualities in some people while denying them to others.

And it is exactly at this point that the most serious objection against Nietzsche's view arises. It is precisely here that the specter of Nietzsche's "immoralism" comes to haunt many of his readers. One wants to ask, who are the people who are exempt from the morality of the herd? What would they do to that herd once they were liberated from its morality? And what would they accomplish through their liberation?

"Egoism," Nietzsche writes, "belongs to the nature of a noble soul—I mean that to a being such as 'we are' other beings must be subordinate by nature and have to sacrifice themselves" (*BGE*, 265). But who are the beings such as "we are"? Once again this question is often answered only by citing some of the most extreme formulations of the *Genealogy*. This effectively closes, for many of Nietzsche's readers, the further question whether his answer deserves any serious attention: "One may be quite justified in continuing to fear the blond beast at the core of all noble races and in being on one's guard against it: but who would not a hundred times sooner fear where one can also admire than *not* fear but be permanently condemned to the repellent sight of the ill-constituted, dwarfed, atrophied, and poisoned?" (*GM*, I, 11).

To stop with this formulation, however, would be a serious mistake. To begin with, we should realize that this obnoxious statement does not differ all that much from a view once expressed by Socrates himself: "Oh, Crito, if only the many were capable of accomplishing the greatest evils! Then they would also be able to achieve the greatest goods—that would be fine. But as it is now, they are capable of neither" (*Cr.* 44d). But more important, though it is quite true that Nietzsche admires the barbarian nobles, he does not, I think, admire them *because* they are cruel (though neither, to be fair, does he criticize them on that account). He admires them primarily for their lack of absolutism, for their attitude that it is impossible for everyone to be bound by the same rules of conduct, for their "pathos of distance" (*GM*, I, 2). The nobles cannot even conceive that "the base" ever should, or even that they ever could, act in the way they themselves act as a matter of course. Nietzsche also admires them for not thinking that their enemies are evil just because they are their enemies (*GM*, I, 10)—an attitude he had already discussed in *Human, All-too-Human:* "In Homer, the Trojan and the Greek are both good" (*HH*, I, 45). And he admires them because, unlike the group that replaced the nobles' pluralistic values with its own single set, they refuse to disown any of their features.

To be unwilling to disown a tendency is not to be eager to indulge it at any opportunity. The nobles are indeed horrible enemies, but they are also "resourceful in consideration, self-control, delicacy, loyalty, pride, and friendship" with one another (*GM*, I, 11). In *Beyond Good and Evil* Nietzsche writes that among people of equal rank it is "good manners" to refrain from mutual injury and to respect one another's will. But, he continues, if this principle is adopted generally as "the fundamental principle of society," it immediately becomes "a principle of disintegration and decay" (*BGE*, 259). But this does not in turn imply that one is allowed or expected to do violence indiscriminately to those "below": "When exceptional human beings treat the mediocre more tenderly than themselves and their peers, this is not mere politeness of the heart—it is simply their duty" (*A*, 57). Nietzsche is willing to countenance and even to condone the constant possibility of violence; this is in itself a position that is seriously dangerous and difficult to accept. But it must not be confused with the silly view according to which he advocates the continuous actual cruel treatment of the "weak" by the "noble" or the "strong."

When, in *Beyond Good and Evil,* Nietzsche writes of "injury, violence, and exploitation" (259), does he have in mind the cruelty, heartlessness, and torture he discusses in the *Genealogy?* The answer, I think, is that he does not. The nobles are one specific instance of a more general type whom Nietzsche admires at least partly for the reasons I have just outlined.[14] The central feature of this type of person is the realization that good and evil qualities are essentially related and not inherently opposed: "Love and hate, gratitude and revenge, good nature and anger, affirmative acts and negative acts, belong together. One is good on condition one also knows how to be evil; one is evil because otherwise one would not understand how to be good" (*WP*, 351). Nietzsche's texts are full of praise for this type of character; but this is a type that can be manifested in a number of different ways, and

Nietzsche does not advocate a return to the specific instance which the nobles constitute. Such a return would be in principle impossible on sound historical grounds in any case: the nobles belong to an era that has passed once and for all. In addition, Nietzsche explicitly writes, "One recognizes the superiority of the Greeks and of the people of the Renaissance—but one would like to have them without the causes and conditions that made them possible" (*WP*, 882). The cruelty, for example, that characterizes the nobles need not be manifested in the same manner in different historical circumstances.

How, then, would such cruelty be manifested today? How would the type Nietzsche admires appear in our present condition? The answer to these questions is given in some remarkable passages in *Beyond Good and Evil*. Startlingly, but in consonance with the general interpretation proposed here, Nietzsche describes his ideal characters as *philosophers*. These, he writes, are "the bad conscience of their time," and their enemy is always "the ideal of today." When the degenerate Athenian conservatives were behaving in a manner that was as vulgar as their mode of talking was noble, Socrates, according to Nietzsche's idiosyncratic interpretation, looked both into his own soul and into theirs and saw that they were quite as decadent as he knew himself to be. Nietzsche has him say to them: "Don't dissemble in front of me. Here—we are equal" (*BGE*, 212; cf. *TI*, II, 9). Today, by contrast, Nietzsche considers that equality is the prevalent ideal. Accordingly, in the present state of things

> the concept of greatness entails being noble, wanting to be by oneself, being able to be different, standing alone and having to live independently. And philosophers will betray something of their own ideal when they posit: "They shall be greatest who can be loneliest, most concealed, most deviant, human beings beyond good and evil, masters of their virtues, they that are overrich in will. Precisely this shall be called *greatness*: being capable of being as manifold as whole, as ample as full." (*BGE*, 212)

No character traits, desires, drives, or passions are to be disowned because, even under their most superficial description, all of them are essential to who one is. But apart from this general philosophical point, Nietzsche also believes that they are necessary because of the double aspect he finds all such features to have. Once again his physical imagery must not be taken literally. When he writes that hardness and cruelty are essential to life, he does not mean that it would be good if people repeated the actual behavior of earlier barbarians in the world of today. Rather, he is concerned with the drive that produced the nobles' cruel behavior in their particular circumstances. This drive can result in behavior that is specifically different from, though perhaps generically the same as, the viciousness it has already produced: "Almost everything we call 'higher culture' is based on the spiritualization of *cruelty*, on its becoming more profound . . . The 'savage animal' has not really been 'mortified'; it lives and flourishes, it has merely become—divine" (*BGE*, 229; cf. *HH*, I, 43). The physical cruelty of the nobles results from a drive that should not be eliminated in itself; on the contrary, the drive is to be maintained and its expression refined into

> that sublime inclination of the seeker after knowledge who insists on profundity, multiplicity, and thoroughness, with a will which is a kind of cruelty of the intellectual conscience and taste. All courageous thinkers will recognize this in themselves . . . They will say: "There is something cruel in the inclination of my spirit"; let the virtuous and kindly try to talk them out of that! Indeed, it would sound nicer if we were said, whispered, reputed to be distinguished not by cruelty but by "extravagant honesty," we free, very free spirits—and perhaps that will actually be our posthumous reputation. (*BGE*, 230)

Nietzsche's psychological hypothesis is that honesty is sublimated cruelty. It is not easy to decide whether this hypothesis is correct. And the behavior for which it accounts is compatible both with the view that evil features are necessary if good features are to be possessed and with the idea that evil features are the very same as good features, under different circumstances. But one argument in favor of Nietzsche's general approach is that however much progress is made toward controlling and humanizing aggressive tendencies, there are not many cases in which these have been successfully eliminated. Under what is often minimal provocation, cruelty and hardness appear in their crudest form where they are least expected, destroying not only other people and the world but also our complacent feeling that we had succeeded in leaving them behind, and leaving us, in turn, speechless with horror. Nietzsche's view suggests that the more honesty is cultivated, the more cruelty too increases in principle. Honesty can always, under specific conditions, manifest itself as physical cruelty of the worst sort.

Nietzsche does not in any way think that this is desirable. But it is a risk he is perfectly willing to take, and he finds that this risk is itself desirable. This is one of the main reasons his attitudes toward behavior are so deeply unsettling. Such risks are terrible, but, as Philippa Foot writes, he does not for this reason shy away from them. On the contrary, he puts his message in the mouth of Dionysus, whom he admires because he is the god of both generation and corruption, life and death, good and evil, the god in whom both are glorified: "Human beings are to my mind agreeable, courageous, inventive animals with no equals on earth; they find their way in any labyrinth. I am well disposed toward them: I often reflect how I might yet advance them and make them stronger, more evil, and more profound than they are . . . also more beautiful" (*BGE*, 295).

Nietzsche's "new philosophers" are clearly aware of the essential connections between good and evil, engaged as they are in "a mode of thought that prescribes laws for the future, that for the sake of the future is harsh and tyrannical toward itself and all things of the present; a reckless, 'immoral' mode of thought, which wants to develop both the good and the bad qualities in human beings to their fullest extent, because it feels it has the strength to put both in their right place—in the place where each needs the other" (*WP*, 464). The price of fruitfulness, Nietzsche writes, "is to be rich in internal oppositions" (*TI*, V, 3). Such oppositions can always get out of control and result in behavior that is nothing short of criminal. Nietzsche recognizes this, and claims that "in almost all crimes some qualities also find expression which ought not to be lacking in a human being" (*WP*, 740). But this is not to say that he glorifies crime. "Criminals," he writes, making the very dubious assumption that they constitute a distinct type, are "strong human beings made sick" (*TI*, IX, 45).

Nietzsche's exact conception of the relationship between good and evil features remains ultimately unsettled. Are these simply necessary for one another, or are they literally the same? His texts do not answer this question unequivocally. But even though this is a serious difficulty with his view, he can still claim that with either alternative the idea of a purely good agent is a fiction. He thinks that the appearance of perfect goodness is created by stunting *all* of one's features and abilities so that one no longer represents, even potentially, a danger to others and to the community as a whole (see *GM*, I, 14). Such an agent, who is incapable of greatness as well as of harm, constitutes for him the goal of morality: "We want that some day there should be nothing any more to be afraid of!" (*BGE*, 201). But in fact, Nietzsche insists, great accomplishments involve exploiting all available means, perhaps evil by the standards of the previous order, but seen in a different light once those accomplishments become parts of the life of others: "In great human beings, the specific qualities of life—injustice, falsehood, exploitation—are at their greatest. But insofar as they have had an *overwhelming* effect, their essence has been most misunderstood and interpreted as goodness. Type: Carlyle as interpreter" (*WP*, 969).

But Nietzsche's negative attitude toward this Whiggish interpretation of history does not imply that "self-realization and self-becoming," by whatever means and whatever their goals and effects, have "unconditioned value."[15] The jester who jumps over the tight-rope walker and causes him to fall to his death in the Prologue to *Zarathustra* does not thereby show himself to be better or stronger than his victim (Z, Pref., 6). "There are many ways of overcoming: see to that yourself!" Zarathustra later says, in a clear allusion to this incident; "but only a jester thinks: 'Man can also be skipped over' " (Z, III, 14). Nietzsche consistently rejects the Calliclean view that we must give our impulses, whatever they are, free rein: "Blind indulgence of an affect, totally regardless of whether it be a generous and compassionate or hostile affect, is the cause of the greatest evils. Greatness of character does not consist in not possessing them to the highest degree—but in having them under control" (*WP*, 928). The affects must be overcome; but instead of weakening or extirpating them we must master and direct them (*WP*, 384; cf. 870, 871). One of his central criticisms of Christian morality is that it fights the passions with excision, that "its practice, its 'cure,' is *castratism*." And though he agrees that unbridled passion is "stupid," he argues that to destroy it as a preventive measure is itself "merely another form of stupidity" (*TI*, V, 1). He claims that this is the practice of those who are afraid of the two-sided consequences of strong impulses: "Castration, extirpation . . . [are] instinctively chosen by those who are too weak-willed, too degenerate, to be able to impose moderation upon themselves" (*TI*, V, 2). We have seen that Nietzsche construes freedom of the will as the internalization of rules and constraints by means of which one can do with automatic and instinctive ease what used to be most difficult (cf. *A*, 14). So now he interprets moderation as the developed and cultivated ability to direct one's desires in such a way that resistance to them is no longer necessary (cf. *Z*, I, 5; *WP*, 933). His ideal character is a master of such moderation: "The greatest human beings perhaps also possess great virtues, but in that case also their opposites. I believe that it is precisely through the presence of opposites and the feelings they occasion that the great person, *the bow with the great tension*, develops" (*WP*, 967; cf. *TI*, IX, 38).

Nietzsche connects this Heraclitean idea with his own version of "classicism": to be classical in his sense one must possess "*all* the strong, seemingly contradictory gifts and desires—but in such a way that they go together under a yoke" (*WP*, 847). And he in turn relates classicism so conceived to "the grand style," which he had earlier characterized as the victory of the beautiful over the monstrous (*WS*, 96), and which, as Heidegger was first to note, is most closely approximated by the rigorous classical style.[16] Nietzsche's classicism, however, is profoundly different from the classicism praised as a form of naturalism by the German Enlightenment (cf. *BT*, 9; *WP*, 849).[17] For Nietzsche, both classicism and "the grand style" are not pure expressions of nature but victories over it: they are efforts to "become master of the chaos one is; to compel one's chaos to become form: to become logical, simple, unambiguous, mathematics, *law*" (*WP*, 842).

These, then, are some of the main elements of Nietzsche's campaign against morality. But what is the aim of this campaign? What if Nietzsche were victorious? This is the central question his writing on these issues inevitably generates. Nietzsche's "negative" views about morality, his dissection of the motives and goals of Christianity, his attack on the radical distinction between good and evil, his effort to undermine traditional moral psychology are all complex views and, whether right or wrong, worth arguing with, for or against. But the moment Nietzsche begins to try to draw explicit consequences from these views, and the moment his readers try to articulate these consequences, the promise implicit in them disappears. These consequences have little if any of the apocalyptic significance that is often claimed for them, by Nietzsche himself as well as by some of his commentators. Nietzsche's "positive" morality, if that is what it is, seems to be appallingly disappointing. In particular, it faces four grave problems.

First, as it may already have become unfortunately apparent from this discussion, Nietzsche's views are, to put it bluntly but not inaccurately, simply *banal*. Arthur Danto characterizes them well when he writes: "A sultry heart plus a cool head, minus the human-all-too-human . . . Here is an ancient, vaguely pagan ideal, the passions disciplined but not denied, in contrast with the life and attitude of guilty celibacy which has been an official moral recommendation until rather recent times" (p. 199). Walter Kaufmann's approving description of Nietzsche's view of self-mastery shows that Nietzsche's attitude is also excruciatingly *vague*: "To become powerful, to gain freedom, to master his impulses and perfect himself, man must first develop the feeling that his impulses are evil . . . At that point, man is divided against himself . . . Self-overcoming is not accomplished by a man's saying to himself: I would rather sublimate my impulses. First . . . he must brand his own impulses with contempt and become aware of the contradiction between good and evil" (p. 253). Leaving other difficulties with this passage aside, it is obvious that if this is Nietzsche's view, then it is almost impossible to see how this perfection and self-mastery can ever be achieved. How are we even to start on the process? How can we develop contempt for ourselves? What is the end product of this process, the new philosopher or the *Übermensch*, actually like? Why has it been so persistently difficult to describe this character in even minimally informative terms? Many of the descriptions we have rely so heavily on Nietzsche's own unexplicated metaphors that it is hard to avoid the suspicion that little indeed can be said of it.[18] For the same reason, it is hard to avoid the suspicion that Nietzsche has little of positive value to say. For some this has been an objection against taking Nietzsche seriously. For others it has been an objection against thinking that a philosopher should have positive views at all.

But the difficulties do not end here. If Nietzsche wants to propose a new code of conduct, however vague and unoriginal, then his general position may be deeply *inconsistent*. How can such a code fit with his perspectivism, which seems to be a refusal to develop a general position on any subject? How can Nietzsche want to present us with general guidelines for life if he objects to Christianity precisely on the grounds that it tries to offer such guidelines and that it tries to hide its partial and interested nature from its followers?

Finally, if Nietzsche, as he claims, rejects or denies morality and all that it has ever been, isn't his approach *incoherent*? Such a charge has recently been made by Hilary Putnam against all efforts to place oneself completely beyond one's tradition at the same time that one also offers to improve upon it. "Many thinkers," Putnam writes, "have fallen into Nietzsche's error of telling us that they had a 'better' morality than the entire tradition; in each case they only produced a monstrosity, for all they *could* do was *arbitrarily* wrench certain values out of their context while ignoring others."[19] If morality is to be rejected in its entirety, then it seems that nothing that formerly belonged to it can be salvaged and used to construct a better system instead; any selection is bound to be arbitrary. If absolutely nothing is retained, then why is one's new proposal, if it is at all possible to make such a proposal under these conditions, a new morality? If, by contrast, some aspects, some motives, or some values of the old morality are kept for a reason and hence not arbitrarily, then the new code cannot be so radically new after all; it will inevitably be a stage in the development of the old tradition.

Nietzsche's own moral view, then, is banal, vague, inconsistent with his view on knowledge, and perhaps even internally incoherent. None of this would be true, however, if Nietzsche did not propose to replace what has passed for morality so far with a positive code of conduct of his own. And in fact he does not. Nietzsche does not describe a positive morality, though this does not mean that he remains totally silent on the question of how to act and live. His ambitious aim is to undermine the moral tradition. But he is afraid that if he offers a direct attack and a direct alternative to that tradition, he will only succeed in perpetuating it. Yet he cannot ignore it completely, for in that case he will not have provided an attack against it at all. We must now examine his original and deeply characteristic effort to avoid this dilemma.

Nietzsche, as we have already seen, does not directly object to actions that have been considered moral so far. His main objection to morality is its absolutism, the fact that it exhibits what he calls elsewhere "the worst of tastes, the taste for the unconditional" (*BGE*, 31). "The slave," he writes, "wants the unconditional and understands only what is tyrannical, in morals, too" (*BGE*, 46). One of the most important features of "the herd" is that its need for obedience has been cultivated for so long that "it may fairly be assumed that . . . it is now innate in the average person, as a kind of *formal conscience* that commands: 'thou shalt unconditionally do something, unconditionally not do something else,' in short, 'thou shalt'" (*BGE*, 199). Nietzsche rejects morality at least partly on account of a characteristic that it shares with many other codes of conduct that may not be moral in the specific sense discussed in the *Genealogy*. This characteristic is its avowed aim to be unconditional and universal and to apply equally to all human beings on the basis of reasons provided by some features in which we all essentially share. This makes his position even more radical than it may sometimes appear to be, for it shows that it is directed not only against a morality that is in one way or another based upon belief in God but also against any system of conduct that demands unqualified loyalty and obedience of its adherents.

Yet Nietzsche accompanies his rejection of moral and other universalistic codes with a strange idea that has not yet received, so far as I know, the attention it deserves. Exemplifying the very attitude that prompts him to reject unconditional codes, Nietzsche does not reject them unconditionally. His demand is only that philosophers, and not all people, "take their stand *beyond* good and evil and leave the illusion of moral judgment *beneath* them" (*TI*, VII, 1). And, with a twist that gives his view a double irony, he writes, "Beyond good and evil—but we demand that herd morality should be held sacred unconditionally" (*WP*, 132). He claims explicitly: "I have declared war on the anemic Christian ideal (together with what is closely related to it), not with the aim of destroying it but only of putting an end to its tyranny and clearing the way for new ideals, for *more robust* ideals" (*WP*, 361). In this sense at least it is clear that Nietzsche does not want to eliminate the codes of conduct he rejects and replace them with another, which, though perhaps "better" in some vague way, will be equally binding (cf. *A*, 57). He does not even reject codes of conduct as such; as he writes, "The ideals of the herd should rule in the herd" (*WP*, 287). But he also expects his nobles to obey rules and principles, for example the "principle that one has duties only to one's peers" (*BGE*, 260). He rejects only unconditional codes, that is, codes that are imposed not only on those for whom they are suited but on everyone else as well: "Decadence itself is nothing *to be fought:* it is absolutely necessary and belongs to every age and every people. What should be fought rigorously is the contagion of the healthy parts of the organism. Is this being done? The *opposite* is being done" (*WP*, 41). He actually thinks that from one point of view traditional morality is not only necessary but desirable: it produces exactly what it fights:

> We others, we immoralists . . . make it a point of honor to be *affirmers*. More and more our eyes have opened to that economy which needs and knows how to utilize all that the holy witlessness

of the priest, of the *diseased* reason of the priest, rejects—that economy in the law of life which finds an advantage even in the disgusting species of the prigs, the priests, the virtuous. *What* advantage? But we ourselves, we immoralists, are the answer. (*TI*, V, 6)

Nietzsche, therefore, does not advocate and does not even foresee a radical change in the lives of most people. The last thing he is is a social reformer or revolutionary.

But perhaps, one might suggest, a time could come when some select people will realize that they need not be bound by the same rules that govern the rest of the world. Perhaps these are the people for whom Nietzsche is writing and for whom he is setting out the principles they will then need to follow. After all, as early as the second of his *Untimely Meditations* Nietzsche had written that "the *goal of humanity* cannot lie in its end but only *in its highest exemplars*," by which he meant the great individual figures of history (*UM*, II, 9). Later he writes, "Today the individual still has to be made possible" (*TI*, IX, 41), while in *The Will to Power* he notes, "My idea: goals are lacking and these must be individuals" (*WP*, 269). Perhaps, then, Nietzsche's positive morality is not addressed to everyone. Perhaps it consists only in a code of conduct by which a select few can become, and come to be recognized as, "higher" human beings, creators of their own values, true individuals.

But the moment we describe Nietzsche's project in these terms, it becomes obvious that this interpretation cannot possibly be correct. To try to follow rules and principles in order to become able to create one's own values is to find oneself in Wotan's predicament, when he exclaims in the second act of Wagner's *Die Walküre*, "What good is my own will to me? I cannot will a being that is free." A true individual is precisely one who is different from the rest of the world, and there is no formula, no set of rules, no code of conduct that can possibly capture in informative terms what it is to be like that. There are no principles that we can follow in order to become, as Nietzsche wants us to become, unique. On the contrary, it is by breaking rules that such a goal, if it is indeed a goal at all, can ever be reached. And it is as impossible to specify in advance the rules that must be broken for the process to succeed as it is, say, to specify in advance the conventions that must be violated for a new and innovative genre in music or literature to be established. The very notion of the individual makes it impossible to say in informative terms how one can ever become that.

The best that can be expected in this regard is a set of vague and banal guidelines, statements like, "Use all your abilities and deny none, for any denial will be guided by the values that rule your world, whether you want to or not, and so you will fail to be different after all"—statements of which Nietzsche's writing is full (though in more elegant versions). We can also, of course, expect examples of such successful characters; these too we can find throughout his work. But again such examples are singularly unhelpful: they are seldom detailed, and they can never be generalized. It is of little use, for instance, to be told that Cesare Borgia, to whom Nietzsche refers without supplying many details, can show us what it is to be "the beast of prey and the man of prey" (*BGE*, 197), or that Napoleon is a "synthesis of the *inhuman* and *superhuman*" (*GM*, I, 16). None of Nietzsche's examples shows how one can become like the individuals he admires, and it is not even clear that this is their intent.

Consider now a passage from *Daybreak*, entitled "To deploy one's weaknesses as an artist." Nietzsche writes here that no one can ever be without some shortcomings. What is important, he continues, is to have sufficient "artistic power" to set such shortcomings off against one's strengths and virtues and make each need the other. This, he writes by way of an example, is "the power possessed in so exceptional a degree by the great composers." In Beethoven's music, he notes, there often is "a coarse, obstinate, impatient tone," in Mozart's "a joviality of humble fellows who have to be content with little," in Wagner's "a convulsive and importunate recklessness." But just at the point where these features are about to overwhelm the music, the virtues of these composers reassert themselves: "By means of their weaknesses they have all produced in us a ravenous hunger for their virtues and a ten times more sensitive palate for every drop of musical spirit, musical beauty, musical goodness" (*D*, 218).

In each of these cases a different weakness ("evil") is combined with a different strength ("good"), and their combination accounts for the music's greatness. This passage embodies the second of the three interpretations of Nietzsche's attitude toward the unity of good and evil already discussed: it sees each as necessary for the other. But its main importance consists in the fact that its point is general and unrestricted. Nietzsche uses music as an example and as the basis for generalizing his view to all of life. He still persists in drawing his models from art and not from nature.

The characters Nietzsche admires and the achievements he honors, as we have already noted more than once, are overwhelmingly literary and artistic. At one point he praises the "great Europeans" of his century. Surprisingly, in view of the fact that he takes their achievement to have been the paving of the way toward a unified Europe, these are not politicians or statesmen but figures like Goethe, Beethoven, Stendhal, Heine, Schopenhauer, Wagner, Balzac—and of course Napoleon, who seems to be the only obvious choice, until we read that like all the others, he too was "steeped in world literature"! Nietzsche insists that their literary dimension was the sole reason why these figures became "great discoverers in the realm of the sublime, also of the ugly and the gruesome" (*BGE*, 256). Elsewhere, Nietzsche quotes approvingly Taine's description of Napoleon as an artist, as "the posthumous brother of Dante and Michelangelo," and underscores that connection himself (*WP,* 1018). When he writes that in the greatest human beings we find the most powerfully conflicting instincts under control, his example is none other than Shakespeare—that is to say, Shakespeare's plays (*WP,* 966). Even when he praises Julius Caesar as the "most beautiful type" of the character that contains "inexorable and fearful instincts that provoke the maximum of authority and discipline among themselves" (*TI,* IX, 39), we must not assume without question that he is thinking of Caesar as a historical figure. Rather, we must recall that he writes, "When I seek my ultimate formula for *Shakespeare,* I only find this: he conceived of the type of Caesar" (*EH,* II, 4), who therefore turns out to be himself a literary character.

To be beyond good and evil is to combine all of one's features and qualities, whatever their traditional moral value, into a controlled and coherent whole. Nietzsche's conception is as always modeled on his view of literature and the arts. He is so taken by this model that he even turns historical figures into literary characters so that he can attribute to them the unity that he finds essential for greatness. And he is perfectly aware of his dependence: "The phenomenon 'artist' is the most transparent:—to see through it to the basic instincts of power, nature, etc.! Also those of religion and morality!" (*WP,* 797). "An anti-metaphysical view of the world—yes, but an artistic one" (*WP,* 1048). Nietzsche also knows which particular features of his model he wants to project onto life in general. Among them is the fact that great artworks, though they always have great effects and influence, are not justified through them; in some way they provide their own justification—or at least so it is often thought. Similarly, Nietzsche's choice individuals have this characteristic in an even more extreme form: "One misunderstands great human beings if one views them from the miserable perspective of some public use. That one cannot put them to any use, that in itself may belong to greatness" (*TI*, IX, 50). In fact the relationship between greatness and influence is much more complicated than Nietzsche seems to think in this context. Though greatness and influence do not come to the same thing, there is a much closer connection between great artworks, and great individuals, and their far-ranging effects than Nietzsche's statement suggests. Still, the central idea on which this parallel depends is suggestive and important, and so is the question of complexity, which is another feature of his model Nietzsche projects onto life. Artists, he writes, are combinations of drives that are conflicting and controlled; they are also "buffoon and god side by side; saint and *canaille*" (*WP*, 816). This is also true of the composers he discusses in section 218 of *Daybreak*, and it constitutes the tension that underlies some of the greatest artworks. This tension, I think, provides the basis for Nietzsche's admiration of his chosen figures. And it is no accident that he finds this combination in philosophers as well: "To live alone one must be a beast or a god, says Aristotle. Leaving out the third case: one must be both—a philosopher" (*TI*, I, 3).

We can now see that the reason that Nietzsche's positive ethical views, when stated explicitly, are bound to be banal and vague is provided precisely by his artistic model: "The most powerful people, the creators, would have to be the most evil, inasmuch as they carry their ideal against the ideals of other people and remake them in their own image. Evil here means: hard, painful, enforced" (*WP*, 1026). Just as there is no general characterization of what constitutes a great artist or a great work of art, so there can be no general and informative account of how such "hardness" is to be manifested. The pain and force that each particular case involves depend on the constantly changing ideals and values they are used to combat, and on the necessarily provisional ideals they establish instead.

If we interpret Nietzsche's demand to take our position beyond good and evil in connection with his desire that we become "the poets of our life" (*GS*, 299), we can explain why we can associate no substantive ethical views with his slogan. Recalling our earlier discussion of literary characters, we can see that weaknesses must be combined with strengths in such a way that neither can be what it is without the other. No feature, no character trait, is a weakness, a liability, or an evil in itself; none is in itself a strength, a virtue, or a good. Given his general view that the character of everything is given only through its constantly changing interrelations, Nietzsche can now argue that traits of character and actions can be evaluated only in light of their contribution to a complete person, a complete life, or, as he would doubtless prefer to put it himself, a complete *work* (cf. Z, IV, 1, 20). But just as there is no single type of great artist or artwork, there also is no type of life that is in itself to be commended or damned. Nietzsche cannot therefore have a general view of conduct that can apply to everyone and also be specific and interesting.

In a famous passage of *Remembrance of Things Past* the author Bergotte goes to see one of his favorite paintings, Vermeer's *View of Delft*. In the painting, Proust writes, there was "a little patch of yellow wall . . . which was so well painted that it was, if one looked at it by itself, like some priceless specimen of Chinese art, of a beauty that was sufficient in itself . . . 'precious in itself.' " Nietzsche, I think, would deny that this is possible; he would argue that nothing, either within an artwork or in any other context, could ever be precious in itself. He would doubtless prefer the view of the narrator, who at one point writes of "those finished works of art in which there is not one touch that is isolated, in which every part in turn receives from the rest a jus-tification which it confers on them in turn."[20] The yellow patch of wall, radiant within Vermeer's controlled and understated palette, would be hardly noticeable in a field of wheat painted by Van Gogh and positively garish in one of Morandi's overwhelmingly muted compositions. The "joviality of humble fellows that have to be con-tent with little," which is a weakness in the music of Mozart, can be a strength in a composer of somber, serious, and controlled music.

There is no general set of considerations that can determine in ad-vance what can and cannot, what must and must not be part of a great artwork or, according to Nietzsche, part of a life of value and impor-tance. New art movements are often successful precisely because they show that what the tradition, explicitly or implicitly, had excluded from art can become the source and matter of a new genre.[21] The same design, the same theme, the same narrative mode, the same sort of transition can account for the greatness of one work and also justify the rejection of another. Nietzsche generalizes the relatively uncontroversial point that no artistic feature is in itself either beautiful or ugly to the radical view that no actions and character traits, unless they are described in a question-begging way, can be in themselves good or evil. He insists that their quality is the product of interpretation. It depends on the contribution they are taken to make to a whole that consists of more such features that are equally devoid of value in themselves but that are construed as parts of a single complex on account of which one can be grateful, or horrified—or both.

What, then, apart form this controversial but vague message does Nietzsche have to offer? Does he make any effort to fill out his general framework and to give some detail to the very abstract type of character he consistently, but unhelpfully, praises? Is it because he is unable to present positive views of his own, or is it because he holds some particular principle against such views in general that he does not supply a single carefully drawn description of the type of person he admires and commends?

The answer is that it is because of neither. The fault has been ours. We have been looking for Nietzsche's positive views in the wrong place, or, more correctly, in the wrong dimension. Nietzsche does not describe his ideal character, but he still does produce a perfect instance of it. The immensely specific detail in which this character is presented answers the charge of vagueness, constitutes in itself an implicit commendation of that character, and at the same time constitutes an obstacle to its being a general model that should, or that even could, be followed by others.

Nietzsche's presentation of this character is perfectly consistent with his perspectivism, which does not forbid that views be developed and accepted but which dictates that they always be presented as views of one's own. His manner of remaining perspectivist on this issue is a special case of his general solution to the problem of perspectivism, which I discussed in this book's first chapter. We have now come full circle. Nietzsche's highly specific, very novel, and perfectly coherent portrait is, in two senses, inherently his own. It thus avoids all four problems his views generate under more traditional interpretations.

Who, then, is this character? Where and how does Nietzsche present him? It is, to begin with, a character with a number of weaknesses, physical and intellectual, many of which have already been discussed before and on whose basis he has been severely criticized. But though physically infirm, "in the midst of the torments that go with an uninterrupted three-day migraine, accompanied by laborious vomiting of phlegm," he still possessed "a dialectician's clarity *par excellence* and thought through with very cold blood matters for which under healthier circumstances" he would not have been "mountainclimber. . . subtle . . . *cold* enough" (*EH,* I, 1). And just like the characters Nietzsche praises, this one too "exploits bad accidents to his advantage; what does not kill him makes him stronger. Instinctively he collects from everything he sees, hears, lives through, *his* sum . . . he honors by *choosing,* by *admitting,* by *trusting*" (*EH,* I, 2).

Intellectually unable to engage in long, sustained argument, he makes up for this shortcoming by returning to the same issues again and again in his writings. Aware that none of his single, short discussions could ever resolve the problems that concern him, he prefers to approach these problems from as many points of view as possible, and he even constructs a "theory of knowledge" that underwrites his practice. He thus creates one of his greatest strengths out of one of his central weaknesses: "I approach deep problems like cold baths: quick into them and quickly out again. That one does not get to the depths that way, not deep enough down, is the superstition of those afraid of the water, the enemies of cold water; they speak without experience. The freezing water makes one swift" (*GS,* 381).

Trained in philology but having become deeply dissatisfied with it, he abandons that field but continues to apply its interpretive methods to the new questions that now come to occupy him. In this way he exploits and redeems what might otherwise have been simply a wrong and regrettable choice. Cruel and heartless, neither protective nor respectful of the sensibilities of others, he can still truthfully say of himself, "I never attack persons; I merely avail myself of a person as a strong magnifying glass that allows us to make visible a general but creeping calamity" (*EH,* I, 7). Disdainful and contemptuous of the values and lives of most people, he can nevertheless insist with no self-deception, "To this day, I still have the same affability for everyone; I even treat with special respect those who are lowliest" (*EH,* I, 6). He has offended and hurt many and will doubtless continue to do so in the future. But he never, or at least no more than most of us, hurt his family and friends, or any other individual. He himself attacks and savages as he urges it be done by others: not by fighting but by writing.

He believes in general terms, though he also justifies his belief by means of his view that everything is interrelated with everything else, that people must exploit absolutely everything that happens to them in order to accomplish something that is truly their own. And he writes that "given the way I am, strong enough to turn even what is most questionable and dangerous to my advantage and thus to become stronger, I call Wagner the great benefactor of my life" (*EH*, II, 6). From the obscure and overwritten language of *The Birth of Tragedy* he moves to the spare and clear prose of *Beyond Good and Evil* and knows that the latter was made possible only through the former. Envious of Socrates and of his position in the history of thought, he attacks him throughout his writings, though he knows that in doing so he is endowing his enemy with yet another dimension, and that he is therefore giving Socrates his greatest gift, which is to make him still more important and influential than he has already been, and the subject of even more writing than before. In the process he also succeeds, working out the consequences of his own will to power, in becoming the subject of more writing himself.

Having claimed that there is no objective truth about the world, and having argued that this world is the joint product of external causes and human interpretation, neither thing-in-itself nor invention, he devotes himself to fashioning a way of life that is part of such a world and acknowledges it for what it is (*WP*, 585A). He develops the idea of the eternal recurrence and praises those rare people who accept the world just as it is and who would want it to return just as it has been, if it ever could return:

> The first question is by no means whether we are content with ourselves, but whether we are content with anything at all. If we affirm one single moment, we thus affirm not only ourselves but all existence. For nothing is self-sufficient, neither in us ourselves nor in things; and if our soul has trembled with happiness and sounded like a harpstring just once, all eternity was needed to produce this one event—and in this single moment of affirmation all eternity was called good, redeemed, justified, and affirmed. (*WP*, 1032)

And now, despite the misery, the poverty, the sickness, the ridicule, and the lack of recognition that have accompanied him throughout, he can ask, "How could I fail to be grateful to my whole life?" (*EH*, Epigraph).

Nietzsche's texts therefore do not describe but, in exquisitely elaborate detail, *exemplify* the perfect instance of his ideal character.

And this character is none other than the character these very texts constitute: Nietzsche himself. He writes that the will to power, the tendency to rearrange everything with which one is confronted and to stamp one's own impress upon what is to come, is the fundamental drive in life. Perhaps he was wrong about this, or perhaps, as is more likely, this may simply have been his own most insistent ambition. But whether he was right or wrong, by writing this he succeeded in re-interpreting much of the history of his world and in securing his own place within it.

None of this is to say that Nietzsche avoids or escapes from theo-retical or philosophical thought, that he has no positive views of his own, that we should read him as an "artist" rather than as a "philos-opher," or that he has accomplished something that, as he himself may sometimes have thought, had never been accomplished before. But along with figures like Plato's Socrates and Kierkegaard, he both engaged in philosophical thought and, for his own reasons, mistrusted it. His texts yield not only philosophical views but also a view of what it is to be engaged in giving philosophical views. This one view among many possible others is deeply ambivalent and gives Nietzsche him-self a deeply equivocal position in the history of this tradition.

The character exemplified in Nietzsche's writing is so specific and idiosyncratic that all attempts to imitate it have so far produced only caricatures. His explicit ethical views permit much that is objection-able, obnoxious, and even dangerous, at least partly because they are vague, general, and schematic. Like a handbook for producing great literature, his advice can be followed to the letter and result not sim-ply in a mediocrity but in an actual monstrosity. Unlike all other handbooks, however, his own is itself a magnificent literary and philosophical work. If we accept his view about actions and turn our attention not only to what is said in his texts but also to who it is who says it, the picture he draws becomes specific, original, and, though perhaps not always acceptable, deeply admirable.

The final consequence of the reading this book has attempted is that it is not only Nietzsche's model that is literary. In a serious sense his product is literary as well. Nietzsche created a character out of himself. "Fortunately," he writes, "for the great majority books are mere literature" (*A*, 44); for him they are life itself.[22] As he thought Goethe had done, he too created himself. His great innovation was to accomplish this end by saying that to create oneself is the most important goal in life, by saying in effect that this was just what he was doing. His passion for self-reference combines with his urge for self-fashioning to make him the first modernist at the same time that he is the last romantic. The content of his works, however, remains a set of philosophical views: the literary character who is their product is still a philosopher who has made of these views a way of life and who urges others to make a way of life out of views of their own—views which, consistently with his persectivism, he cannot and will not supply for them.

Nietzsche wanted to be, and was, the Plato of his own Socrates. In praising people and deeds who are beyond good and evil he has managed to situate himself beyond moral evaluation as well, in that the question of his importance has become more pressing than the question of his goodness. His own cruelty, his attacks on many of our ideas and values, on our habits and sensibilities, are not reasons why we should turn away from him. On the contrary, they are reasons why we should continue to read him and why we should admire him even as we disagree with him. In engaging with his works, we are not engaging with the miserable little man who wrote them but with the philosopher who emerges through them, the magnificent character these texts constitute and manifest, the agent who, as the will to power holds, is nothing but his effects—that is, his writings. Always his own best reader as well as his own author, Nietzsche knew this, too: "The 'work,' whether of the artist or of the philosopher, invents the person who has created it, who is supposed to have created it: 'the great,' as they are venerated, are subsequent pieces of wretched minor fiction" (*BGE*, 269).

Nature has therefore not turned against itself; Nietzsche has succeeded in writing himself into history. But as he also knew, this is not a task one can ever accomplish alone: every text is at the mercy of its readers. And just as Nietzsche's texts are ever at their readers' mercy, so too is this one. The reading suggested here has aimed to show that Nietzsche was right to take this risk. And of course in so doing it has taken the same risk, though on a lesser scale, itself. But if this reading even provokes a refutation, then Nietzsche will have acquired one more reader, and one more reading. And, so long as Nietzsche's writing is being read, the question whether truth is created or discovered will continue to receive the essentially equivocal answer presupposed, as I have argued here, by his very effort to turn his life into literature.

NOTES

INDEX

A NOTE ON
TEXTS AND
TRANSLATIONS

For Nietzsche's texts I have relied on *Werke: Kritische Gesamtausgabe* (KGW), ed. Giorgio Colli and Mazzino Montinari, 30 vols. (Berlin: de Gruyter, 1967–1978). In a few instances I have made use of the earlier *Gesamtausgabe in Grossoktav* (to which I refer by volume number), edited by various editors under the general direction of Elizabeth Förster-Nietzsche, 2nd ed., 20 vols. (Leipzig: Naumann, later Kröner, 1901–1926). Other texts of Nietzsche to which I refer in detail, along with the translations on which I generally depend but which I have occasionally emended, follow.

The Antichrist (*A*), trans. Walter Kaufmann, in *The Portable Nietzsche*, ed. Walter Kaufmann (New York: Viking Press, 1954)

Beyond Good and Evil (*BGE*), trans. Walter Kaufmann (New York: Vintage Press, 1966)

The Birth of Tragedy (*BT*), trans. Walter Kaufmann (New York: Vintage Press, 1966)

The Case of Wagner (*CW*), trans. Walter Kaufmann (New York: Vintage Press, 1966)

Daybreak (*D*), trans. R. J. Hollingdale (Cambridge: Cambridge University Press, 1982)

Ecce Homo (*EH*), trans. Walter Kaufmann (New York: Vintage Press, 1968)

The Gay Science (*GS*), trans. Walter Kaufmann (New York: Vintage Press, 1974)

On the Genealogy of Morals (*GM*), trans. Walter Kaufmann and R. J. Hollingdale (New York: Vintage Press, 1968)

Human, All-Too-Human (*HH*) trans. Helen Zimmern and Paul V. Kohn, in *The Complete Works of Friedrich Nietzsche,* ed. Oscar Levy, 18 vols. (New York: Macmillan, 1909–1911); I have provided my own versions

Mixed Opinions and Maxims (*MOM*), in *HH,* vol. 2, trans. Paul V. Kohn; I have provided my own versions

Nietzsche Contra Wagner (*NCW*), trans. Walter Kaufmann, in *The Portable Nietzsche*

Philosophy in the Tragic Age of the Greeks (*PTG*), trans. Marianne Cowan (Chicago: Henry Regnery, 1962)

Thus Spoke Zarathustra (*Z*), trans. Walter Kaufmann, in *The Portable Nietzsche*

Twilight of the Idols (*TI*), trans. Walter Kaufmann, in *The Portable Nietzsche*

Untimely Meditations (*UM*), trans. R. J. Hollingdale (Cambridge: Cambridge University Press, 1983)

The Wanderer and His Shadow (*WS*), in *HH,* vol. 2, trans. Paul V. Kohn; I have provided my own versions

The Will to Power (*WP*), trans. Walter Kaufmann and R. J. Hollingdale (New York: Vintage Press, 1968)

I have also relied on the text of *On Truth and Lies in a Nonmoral Sense,* trans. Daniel Brazeale, in *Philosophy and Truth: Selections from Nietzsche's Notebooks of the Early 1870s* (Atlantic Highlands, N.J.: Humanities Press, 1979), which is not explicitly cited.

NOTES

1. The Most Multifarious Art of Style

1. Amélie Oksenberg Rorty has discussed the importance of style in the classification of some writings as philosophical and in the exclusion of others from the genre in "Experiments in Philosophic Genre: Descartes' *Meditations,*" *Critical Inquiry,* 9 (1983), 545–564.

2. Stefan George, "Nietzsche," which is included in Walter Kaufmann, *Twenty German Poets: A Bilingual Edition* (New York: Random House, 1963). George's verse can be traced directly to Nietzsche's "Attempt at a Self-Criticism," his preface to the second edition of *The Birth of Tragedy* (1886). A history of Nietzsche's reception as a poet in England and America can be found in Patrick Bridgwater, *Nietzsche in Anglosaxony* (Leicester: Leicester University Press, 1972).

3. T. S. Eliot, "Review of A. Wolf, *The Philosophy of Nietzsche,*" *International Journal of Ethics,* 26 (1915–16), 426–427. The quotation appears on p. 426.

4. An extensive discussion of Nietzsche's relation to the French moralists and of the function of the aphorism in his writing can be found in Brendan Donnellan, *Nietzsche and the French Moralists* (Bonn: Bouvier, 1982). Donnellan, quite appropriately, concentrates on Nietzsche's middle-period works.

5. Nietzsche himself discusses the aphorism in these terms in *GM,* Pref., 8, and in *GS,* 381. In the latter passage, however, his discussion is not confined specifically to that form; his interest is in his style in general.

6. Crane Brinton, *Nietzsche* (New York: Harper and Row, 1965), p. 167. Even John Burt Foster's recent *Heirs to Dionysus: A Nietzschean Current in Literary Modernism* (Princeton, N.J.: Princeton University Press, 1981), a book that is in many respects very sensitive to Nietzsche's writing, persists in referring to *all* sections of Nietzsche's works as "aphorisms"; see for example pp. xi, 438, n. 11.

7. Walter Kaufmann, *Nietzsche: Philosopher, Psychologist, Antichrist* (Princeton, N.J.: Princeton University Press, 1974), p. 72. All further references to this work in this chapter will be made parenthetically in the text.

8. Sarah Kofman, *Nietzsche et la métaphore* (Paris: Payot, 1972), pp. 163–164. Further references to this work in this chapter will be given parenthetically in the text.

9. Martin Heidegger, *Nietzsche,* trans. David Farrell Krell (New York: Harper and Row, 1979), I, 9.

10. Heidegger, *Nietzsche,* p. 7. Mazzino Montinari, in *Nietzsche Lesen* (Berlin: de Gruyter, 1982), pp. 92–120, has undermined the philological grounds of Heidegger's claim. *The Will to Power,* however, still remains an important source not only for Nietzsche's own thought but also for its reception in the first eighty years after his death. See also Heidegger, *Nietzsche,* trans. Frank A. Capuzzi (New York: Harper and Row, 1982), IV, 11–12.

11. Jacques Derrida, *Spurs: Nietzsche's Styles,* trans. Barbara Harlow (Chicago: University of Chicago Press, 1979), p. 125.

12. Derrida, *Spurs,* p. 133. For a related view see Maurice Blanchot, "Nietzsche et l'écriture fragmentaire," in his book *L'Entretien infini* (Paris: Gallimard, 1969), pp. 227–255.

13. Derrida may, however, be imposing unusually strict conditions on what is to count as an acceptable interpretation. He writes, for example, that there is no "infallible" way of knowing on what occasion Nietzsche's sentence was composed, and continues, "We will never know *for sure* what Nietzsche wanted to say or do when he noted these words" (*Spurs,* p. 123; his emphasis). He does not defend his assumption that infallibility and certainty are necessary if interpretation is to be possible.

14. Arthur C. Danto, *Nietzsche as Philosopher* (New York: Macmillan, 1965), p. 19.

15. For a discussion of this feature of *The Birth of Tragedy,* see Paul de Man, *Allegories of Reading* (New Haven: Yale University Press, 1979), pp. 85–87. Even more traditional in form than *The Birth of Tragedy* is Nietzsche's *Philosophy in the Tragic Age of the Greeks,* written at about the same time, but never finished and published posthumously.

16. Gary Shapiro, "The Rhetoric of Nietzsche's *Zarathustra,*" in Berel Lang, ed., *Philosophical Style* (Chicago: Nelson Hall, 1980), pp. 347–385, offers a reading of this work that is organized along the rhetorical lines suggested in Hayden White's *Metahistory* (Baltimore: Johns Hopkins University Press, 1973). Though Shapiro's argument is not finally convincing, it suggests that the investigation of the complex structure of *Zarathustra* can still yield important results.

17. Walter Kaufmann (*Nietzsche,* p. 92) argues that *On the Genealogy of Morals* is Nietzsche's most highly organized work; see also his introduction to his translation of the work. However, a much more complicated, tight, and articulate structure has been proposed by Maudemarie Clark in her dissertation "Nietzsche's Attack on Morality" (University of Wisconsin, 1977).

18. Karl Jaspers, *Nietzsche: An Introduction to the Understanding of His Philosophical Activity* (Tucson: University of Arizona Press, 1965), p. 10.

19. That an artist exhausts a particular genre, incidentally, need in no way be taken as a negative feature; this suggests that the paraphrase I have given does not constitute the "literal" content of Nietzsche's hyperbolic statement about Euripides. Consider, for example, Shaw's "Mozart's Finality": "Many Mozart worshippers cannot bear to be told that their hero was not the founder of a dynasty. But in art the highest success is to be the last of your race, not the first. Anybody, almost, can make a beginning: the difficulty is to make an end—to do what cannot be bettered." The essay is reprinted in Dan H. Laurence, ed., *Shaw's Music* (New York: Dodd, Mead and Co., 1981), II, 478–484. The quotation comes from pp. 479–480.

20. Werner J. Dannhauser, *Nietzsche's View of Socrates* (Ithaca, N.Y.: Cornell University Press, 1974), p. 272. Dannhauser, however, qualifies his view in regard to Nietzsche's middle works, in which, as he points out, Socrates is given a much more sympathetic treatment. An extensive chronological and systematic treatment of Nietzsche's relation to Socrates can be found in Hermann Josef Schmidt, *Nietzsche und Sokrates* (Meisenheim: Anton Hain, 1969).

21. It may be objected to this claim that, in fact, if the same idea is presented in a variety of styles, it may well appear that this idea can be presented in any style, that it is thus independent of style, and that it is therefore absolutely true. But it seems to me that we cannot easily describe Nietzsche's various writings as each presenting the same idea in a different mode. Though there are naturally connections and repetitions, each work makes it own contribution to Nietzsche's literary and philosophical production. If a single object does emerge out of Nietzsche's writings, this is the figure of their author, which emerges from all these texts together.

22. Arthur C. Danto, *The Transfiguration of the Commonplace* (Cambridge, Mass.: Harvard University Press, 1981), pp. 197, 207.

23. Brigid Brophy, *Mozart the Dramatist* (New York: Harcourt, Brace and World, 1964), p. 22.

2. Untruth as a Condition of Life

1. Eventually this process may have exactly the opposite result. The Christian emphasis on the virtue of truthfulness, for example, essential as it was to Christian morality, has finally enabled people to see the falsehood that is involved, according to Nietzsche, in the belief in God. The same morality has now turned on itself and been forced to recognize, through the very means it has itself cultivated, its own deceptiveness: it is in the process, as Nietzsche puts it, of overcoming itself. This is discussed in, among other places, *GS*, 357 and *GM*, III, 27; and it forms part of the concerns of Chapter 4.

2. It could, of course, be objected that Nietzsche thinks that such judgments are false only if truth is construed as correspondence to reality. This is the essential step in the pragmatist effort to reconcile Nietzsche's attack on truth (construed as correspondence) with his emphasis on it (construed as utility). But, as we shall see, grave difficulties face this effort to attribute to Nietzsche a positive account of the nature of truth.

3. This view appears much more often than one might expect in Nietzsche and is in fact essential to his approach; cf. *WP*, 144, and also Nietzsche's discussion of the "morality of mores" in his middle works, particularly *D*, 9, 13, 14, 16, 18; *HH*, I, 96; *MOM*, 89. In *GM*, II, 2, Nietzsche makes this point explicitly and himself refers to all but one of the passages just cited; cf. also *GM*, III, 9.

4. Nietzsche makes similar comments about Christianity in relation to art, philosophy, and science in *WP*, 464, 469. In *GM*, III, 12, he claims that the sustained effort of Christianity to depreciate the world, the senses, and the body has actually been very valuable because it has taught people how perspectives can be reversed. In this way, he writes, it has "prepared the intellect for its future 'objectivity,' " which he construes as the ability to employ "a *variety* of perspectives and affective interpretations in the service of knowledge."

5. Nietzsche seems to have reached his view by radicalizing a metaphor first introduced into modern epistemology from the domain of painting by Leibniz. Leibniz had argued that just as a city appears different to different observers situated at different points of view, so the universe as a whole appears different to each monad. But he also believed that both the city and the universe possess their characteristics in themselves, independently of all observation; though distinct from one another, the objects the different monads perceive are but "perspectives on a single universe" (*Monadology*, sec. 57; cf. sec. 58, and *Theodicy*, secs. 147, 357). The real nature of the world, which is beyond all perspective, could be described neutrally if we knew our position and the laws, as it were, of metaphysical projection. Nietzsche extended the metaphor in serious ways. He adopted the term *perspectivism* from *Die wirkliche und die scheinbare Welt* (1882), a work by his one-time colleague at Basel, Gustav Teichmüller, for whose chair in philosophy Nietzsche unsuccessfully applied when Teichmüller resigned (see Ronald Hayman, *Nietzsche: A Critical Life*, New York: Oxford University Press, 1980, p. 137). Nietzsche then used the term to refer to the view that there is nothing apart from such perspectives and that the idea of the world as it is in itself is a fiction: "As if a world would still remain after one had deducted the perspective!" (*WP*, 567). I have discussed a number of issues connected with the epistemology of perspectivism in "Immanent and Transcendent Perspectivism in Nietzsche," *Nietzsche-Studien*, 12 (1983), 473–490.

6. See Richard Rorty, "The World Well Lost," in *Consequences of Pragmatism* (Minneapolis: University of Minnesota Press, 1982), pp. 3–18; Nelson Goodman, "The Way the World Is," in *Problems and Projects* (Indianapolis: Bobbs-Merrill, 1972), pp. 24–32; and Hilary Putnam, "Reflections on Goodman's *Ways of Worldmaking*," *Journal of Philosophy*, 76 (1979), 603–618.

7. Nietzsche's simultaneous suspiciousness of and reliance on cognitive terms is well discussed in the opening chapter of John Wilcox, *Truth and Value in Nietzsche* (Ann Arbor: University of Michigan Press, 1974), to whose discussion I am generally indebted.

8. This argument is made in detail in my article "The Postulated Author: Critical Monism as a Regulative Ideal," *Critical Inquiry*, 8 (1981), 131–149.

9. More on this point can be found in my "Immanent and Transcendent Perspectivism in Nietzsche," pp. 477–486.

10. This view was originally and forcefully presented by Arthur C. Danto, *Nietzsche as Philosopher* (New York: Macmillan, 1965), chap. 3. Further references to this work in this chapter will be made parenthetically in the text. This view has been accepted, in various versions, by many other authors, including Daniel Brazeale, *Philosophy and Truth: Selections from Nietzsche's Notebooks from the Early 1870's* (New Jersey: Humanities Press, 1979), pp. xxxi–xxxviii; Ruediger Hermann Grimm, "Circularity and Self-Reference in Nietzsche," *Metaphilosophy*, 10 (1979), 289–305; and Wilcox, *Truth and Value in Nietzsche*.

11. Mary Warnock, "Nietzsche's Theory of Truth," in Malcolm Pasley, ed., *Nietzsche: Imagery and Thought* (London: Methuen, 1978), pp. 33–63, argues that these two views of truth create a serious conflict in Nietzsche's approach. More recently Richard Schacht, *Nietzsche* (London: Routledge and Kegan Paul, 1983), chap. 2, has tried to attribute both a correspondence and a pragmatist theory of truth to Nietzsche by distinguishing the domains to which each is intended to apply.

12. Danto, *Nietzsche as Philosopher,* pp. 86-87, discusses this idea in some detail.

13. This view is held by Grimm; see "Circularity and Self-Reference," p. 297.

14. Ernst Gombrich, *Art and Illusion* (New York: Pantheon, 1961), p. 63.

15. See the title essay in Gombrich's *Meditations on a Hobby-Horse* (London: Phaidon Press, 1963), pp. 1–11.

16. Quoted in Douglas Cooper, *The Cubist Epoch* (London: Phaidon Press, 1970), p. 33.

17. Sarah Kofman, *Nietzsche et la métaphore* (Paris: Payot, 1972), p. 187. Further references to this work in this chapter will be made parenthetically in the text.

18. I argue for this claim in "The Postulated Author," as well as in my "Writer, Text, Work, Author," in Anthony J. Cascardi, ed., *Literature and the Question of Philosophy* (Baltimore: The Johns Hopkins University Press, 1987).

19. Wayne Booth, *Critical Understanding: The Powers and Limits of Pluralism* (Chicago: University of Chicago Press, 1979), pp. 168–169.

20. Grimm, for example, in "Circularity and Self-Reference," argues that Nietzsche's view is refutable. Connecting it with his alleged pragmatism, Grimm concludes that "insofar as such a refutation . . . proved to be more useful, Nietzsche would prefer it to his own scheme" (p. 300). In a general discussion of perspectivism, Richard Rorty, who also thinks that the view is self-refuting, restricts its scope in order to avoid this problem and argues that perspectivist theories should be construed so as to apply only to first-order, "real" theories about the world and not to theories about such theories, like perspectivism itself. In this way the problem of self-reference is avoided; cf. his "Pragmatism, Relativism, and Irrationalism" in *Consequences of Pragmatism,* pp. 160–175. A general discussion of problems of self-reference in Nietzsche can be found in Pierre Klossowski, *Nietzsche et le cercle vicieux* (Paris: Mercure de France, 1969).

21. See Martin Heidegger, *Nietzsche,* trans. David Farrell Krell (New York: Harper and Row, 1979), I, 74.

3. A Thing Is the Sum of Its Effects

1. Walter Kaufmann, in *Nietzsche: Philosopher, Psychologist, Antichrist* (Princeton, N.J.: Princeton University Press, 1974), chap. 6, argues that the will to power represents an empirical generalization. According to Kaufmann, Nietzsche observed human behavior and saw that much of it can be explained if we assume that it is motivated by the quest for power. He then generalized this view to all human action and then to animal behavior. Eventually, he applied it to the universe as a whole. Kaufmann finds the psychological version of the view, at least in connection with human behavior, deeply illuminating, but he rejects outright the broader, cosmological, version (pp. 204–207). However, Maudemarie Clark has shown that there are very serious problems even with the psychological version, if we consider it as an empirical hypothesis ("Nietzsche's Doctrines of the Will to Power," *Nietzsche-Studien,* 12, 1983, 458–468). Her own view is that the will to power is a self-conscious "myth" (p. 461). A general discussion of the will to power can be found in Wolfgang Müller-Lauter, "Nietzsches Lehre vom Willen zur Macht," *Nietzsche-Studien,* 3 (1974), 1–60. The most extensive treatment is in Heidegger's two-volume *Nietzsche* (Pfullingen: Neske, 1961), parts of which have now appeared in English.

2. Martin Heidegger, *Nietzsche,* trans. David Farrell Krell (New York: Harper and Row, 1979), I, 7.

3. Kant had already expressed a view of matter as "moving power" in his *Metaphysische Anfangsgrunde der Naturwissenschaft,* and had been influential in this respect in Germany. Arthur C. Danto, *Nietzsche as Philosopher* (New York: Macmillan, 1975), chap. 8, discusses this text and gives some appropriate quotations. Once again, however, the theory of matter and reality in general as power can ultimately be traced back to Leibniz; cf. *Monadology,* secs. 61–62.

4. Ferdinand de Saussure, *Course in General Linguistics,* trans. Wade Baskin (New York: McGraw-Hill, 1959), p. 120. Further references to this work in this chapter will be given parenthetically in the text.

5. This view, along with its moral and psychological implications, appears often in Nietzsche; cf. *WP,* 293, 331, 333, 634; *Z,* IV, 19. It is discussed further in Chapter 5.

6. Similar statements can be found in *WP,* 135, 136, 531, 568, as well as in *GM,* I, 13.

7. This view can also be found in *WP,* 473, 519, 532. A clear discussion is in Richard Schacht, *Nietzsche* (London: Routledge and Kegan Paul, 1983), pp. 130–156.

8. See *WP,* 524: Consciousness "is only a means of communication: it is evolved through social intercourse and with a view to the interests of social intercourse—'Intercourse' here understood to include the influences of the outer world and the reactions they compel on our side; also our effect upon the outer world." It might be objected on Nietzsche's behalf that one should take into account his view that only a small part of our thinking is conscious (*GS,* 354; *BGE,* 3). Accordingly, this defense would continue, though consciousness develops along with our concept of the external world, the belief in the ego as "substance" may already be part of our unconscious, "instinctive," thinking. But Nietzsche, I think, construes instinctive thinking and acting (which he considers not primitive forms that underlie action and thought but sophisticated goals that must be pursued and mastered) as modes that specifically preclude the conscious differentiation between subject and object, doer and deed; cf. *WP,* 423; *Z,* II, 5; *BGE,* 213, and my discussion, Chapter 6.

9. Once again Leibniz's influence on Nietzsche is clear. Though of course Leibniz denies that any substance can act directly upon any other, he does believe that no substance changes by itself. He writes, for example, that "every change affects them all"; *Discourse on Metaphysics,* XV; cf. XIV.

10. I have made a case for this view in "Mythology: The Theory of Plot," in John Fisher, ed., *Essays in Aesthetics: Perspectives on the Work of Monroe C. Beardsley* (Philadelphia: Temple University Press, 1983), pp. 180–196. I apply the point to Nietzsche's case in Chapter 6.

11. Danto, *Nietzsche as Philosopher,* p. 219. Further references to this work in this chapter will be given parenthetically in the text.

12. Jacques Derrida, "Structure, Sign, and Play in the Discourse of the Human Sciences," in his *Writing and Difference,* trans. Alan Bass (Chicago: University of Chicago Press, 1978), pp. 280–281.

13. Jacques Derrida, "Signature Event Context," in *Margins of Philosophy,* trans. Alan Bass (Chicago: University of Chicago Press, 1982), p. 329. I discuss both inserted passages from Nietzsche in Chapter 6.

14. Michel Haar, "Nietzsche and Metaphysical Language," in David Allison, ed., *The New Nietzsche* (New York: Dell, 1977), p. 6.

15. Haar has pursued this question in his more recent article "La Critique nietz-schéene de la subjectivité," *Nietzsche-Studien*, 12 (1983), 80–110, esp. pp. 85–90.

16. Nelson Goodman, "The Way the World Is," in *Problems and Projects* (Indianapolis: Bobbs-Merrill, 1972), p. 24.

17. I have italicized the sentence beginning, "Actually . . ."

18. Gilles Deleuze, *Nietzsche and Philosophy*, trans. Hugh Tomlinson (New York: Columbia University Press, 1983), p. 6. Deleuze, however, believes that Nietzsche's thought ultimately involves a total emancipation from all traditional philosophical categories, and he seems to have influenced Haar in that regard.

19. It is a well-known fact that Nietzsche was hostile to Darwin and to what he took to be Darwin's views (see, for example, *BGE*, 13, 14, 253; *TI*, IX, 14; *EH*, III, 1; *WP*, 684, 685). But in fact a proper understanding of Darwin shows some remarkable parallels between his views and Nietzsche's. These are only now becoming evident. In the passage quoted in the text we saw Nietzsche apply his general theory of development to animal organs. Having stated that both the form and the meaning of everything is "fluid," he goes on to write: "The case is the same even *within* each individual organism: with every real growth in the whole, the 'meaning' of the individual organs also changes." Now, a major problem for evolutionary biology has been to account for the gradual evolution of organs that seem to have been useful only long after they must have begun developing. As Stephen Jay Gould has written, this problem has been resolved through the (inappropriately named) theory of pre-adaptation: "We avoid the excellent question, what good is 5 percent of an eye? by arguing that the possessor of such an incipient structure did not use it for sight," but for some other purpose instead ("The Problem of Perfection, or How Can a Clam Mount a Fish on Its Rear End?" in his *Ever Since Darwin*, New York: Norton, 1977, p. 107). Gould also writes that "the principle of pre-adaptation simply asserts that a structure can change its function without changing its form as such" (p. 108). But though he states his position in terms of structural continuity, his examples show that the structure does not remain the same over time but changes along with changes in function. The principle of pre-adaptation thus seems strikingly parallel to Nietzsche's views. This similarity is, in my opinion, only a small part of the connections between Nietzsche and Darwin, which should be studied systematically. These connections, however, do not include the view that the *Übermensch* represents a biological concept. It was in fact this early misreading of the *Übermensch* that caused Nietzsche to be generally suspicious of evolutionary thought.

4. Nature Against Something That Is Also Nature

1. Michel Foucault has given a careful treatment of Nietzsche's vocabulary concerning origin (*Ursprung*), descent (*Herkunft*), and emergence (*Entstehung*) in his important essay "Nietzsche, Genealogy, History," in his *Language, Counter-Memory, Practice,* ed. with an introduction by Donald F. Bouchard (Ithaca, N.Y.: Cornell University Press, 1977), pp. 139–164, esp. pp. 140–152; further references to this work in this chapter will be given parenthetically in the text. My only reservation about Fou-

cault's essay is that, perhaps inadvertently, it may give the impression that genealogy is a discipline with independent rules and principles that determine the objects with which it is concerned. In my own view, Nietzsche sees genealogy as a part of a larger enterprise in which he joins Paul Rée and the figures he discusses in *GM*, I, 1–3. Nietzsche does not, as Foucault does (pp. 152 ff.), contrast genealogy with history but insists that genealogy simply *is* history, correctly practiced.

2. It is usually assumed that Nietzsche has Herbert Spencer in mind here. I think that this is unlikely. When Nietzsche discusses Spencer (*GM*, I, 3), in indisputably negative terms, he contrasts Spencer's view, which he calls "much more reasonable" though "not for that reason more true," with the view of the nameless English psychologists to whom he refers in *GM*, I, 1–2. A more likely target for Nietzsche's polemic is, in my opinion, David Hume. David Hoy, in "Nietzsche, Hume, and the Feasibility of Genealogy," forthcoming in the *Proceedings of the Fifth Jerusalem Philosophical Encounter,* draws some interesting connections between Hume and Nietzsche but identifies Spencer as Nietzsche's only opponent.

3. Jean Granier, *Le Problème de la vérité dans la philosophie de Nietzsche* (Paris: Editions du Seuil, 1966), p. 502.

4. Nietzsche sometimes suggests that genealogy is his own invention (*GS*, 345). Yet, as I mentioned in note 1 above, in *GM*, I, 2, he describes the efforts of the "English psychologists" as "bungled" attempts at a "moral genealogy." This in turn suggests that he considers the enterprise in which Hume, Spencer, Rée, and himself are involved to be one and the same, the difference being that he succeeded where his opponents failed.

5. For some discussion of the genetic fallacy in connection with Nietzsche, see Hoy, "Hume, Nietzsche, and the Feasibility of Genealogy," p. 5.

6. In *GM*, I, 6, Nietzsche discusses the derivation of the terms *pure* and *impure* and warns against taking them, in their earliest occurrences, "too ponderously or broadly, not to say symbolically: all the concepts of ancient peoples were rather at first incredibly uncouth, coarse, external, narrow, straightforward, and altogether *unsymbolical* in meaning to a degree that we can scarcely conceive." This view contrasts sharply with the earlier argument of *On Truth and Lies in a Nonmoral Sense* to the effect that language is always at its origins metaphorical. This view, however, is often today identified as Nietzsche's final position on this issue. My own opinion is that this essay has been immensely overestimated.

7. For example, to Nietzsche's list of philosophers who never married (*GM*, III, 7) one could easily contrast another containing, among others, the names of Aristotle, Hegel, and Marx.

8. See the discussion in Gilles Deleuze, *Nietzsche and Philosophy,* trans. Hugh Tomlinson (New York: Columbia University Press, 1983), p. 5. Further references to this work in this chapter will be given parenthetically in the text.

9. Nietzsche writes, for example, "It may perhaps lie in some disease of the *nervus sympathicus,* or in an excessive secretion of bile, or in a deficiency of potassium sulphate and phosphate in the blood, or in an obstruction of the abdomen which impedes the blood circulation, or in degeneration of the ovaries, and the like" (*GM*, II, 15).

10. In the same section Zarathustra claims that there is no such thing as a will to life (see *TI*, IX, 14): "Indeed, the truth was not hit by him who shot at it with the word

'will to existence'; that does not exist. For, what does not exist cannot will; but what is in existence, how could that still want existence?" This view too can be traced back to Plato, *Symposium* 200a–204d, where it is argued that all desire is for what one does not already possess. Plato, however, does allow that one can desire to continue to possess what one possesses at the moment (200c–e).

11. In *GM*, II, 16, Nietzsche claims that the bad conscience and the feeling of guilt, which he considers a turning inward of aggressive instincts that were originally allowed to vent themselves on others, are "the serious illness that human beings were bound to contract under the stress of the most fundamental change they ever experienced—that change which occurred when they found themselves finally enclosed within the walls of society and of peace." This adds a new dimension to his crude explanation of suffering and anticipates not only Freud's pessimistic conclusions in *Civilization and Its Discontents* but also the very reasoning that led Freud to them.

12. Sarah Kofman, *Nietzsche et la métaphore* (Paris: Payot, 1972), p. 187.

13. Such a view, applied to other thinkers as well as to Nietzsche himself, can be found in Ben-Ami Scharfstein, *The Philosophers* (Oxford: Basil Blackwell, 1980).

14. Walter Kaufmann (in note 2 to his translation of *GM*, III, 24) seems to me to consider that this is Nietzsche's only reason for connecting science with asceticism: "This unconditional attitude, this refusal to question one point, is what seems objectionable to Nietzsche."

15. I have discussed these issues in more detail in "Can We Ever Quite Change the Subject?: Richard Rorty on Science, Literature, Culture, and the Future of Philosophy," *Boundary 2*, 12 (1982), 395–413.

5. This Life—Your Eternal Life

1. Quoted from Peter Fuss and Henry Shapiro, *Nietzsche: A Self-Portrait from His Letters* (Cambridge, Mass.: Harvard University Press, 1971), p. 74. The letter is dated June 28, 1883. The original, not easy to translate literally, is, "Das niemand lebt, der so etwas machen konnte, wie dieser Zarathustra ist," in *Nietzsche Briefwechsel: Kritische Gesamtausgabe*, Giorgio Colli and Mazzino Montinari, eds. (Berlin: de Gruyter, 1975–), III, 1, 386.

2. Such a treatment of the recurrence can be found in a number of recent authors: Arthur C. Danto, *Nietzsche as Philosopher* (New York: Macmillan, 1965), chap. 7; Walter Kaufmann, *Nietzsche: Philosopher, Psychologist, Antichrist* (Princeton, N.J.: Princeton University Press, 1974), chap. 11; Joe Krueger, "Nietzschean Recurrence as a Cosmological Hypothesis," *Journal of the History of Philosophy*, 16 (1978), 435–444; Arnold Zuboff, "Nietzsche and Eternal Recurrence," in Robert Solomon, ed., *Nietzsche: A Collection of Critical Essays* (Garden City, N.Y.: Doubleday, 1973), pp. 343–357. Bernd Magnus, "Nietzsche's Eternalistic Countermyth," *Review of Metaphysics*, 26 (1973), 604–616, and *Nietzsche's Existential Imperative* (Bloomington: Indiana University Press, 1978); and Ivan Soll, "Reflections on Recurrence," in Solomon, *Nietzsche*, pp. 322–342. Magnus and Soll, as we shall see, concern themselves with the possibility, rather than with the actuality, of the truth of this hypothesis. Further references to these works in this chapter will be made parenthetically in the text.

3. Tracy B. Strong, *Friedrich Nietzsche and the Politics of Transfiguration* (Berkeley: University of California Press, 1975), p. 261.

4. This point is well made by Danto, *Nietzsche as Philosopher,* p. 204; Kaufmann also discusses what he calls the "suprahistorical character" of this view, *Nietzsche,* pp. 319–321.

5. Danto, *Nietzsche as Philosopher,* p. 206. This criticism, accepted by Magnus, is also made by Krueger. A defense of Nietzsche against this charge has been offered by Marvin Sterling, "Recent Discussions of Eternal Recurrence: Some Critical Comments," *Nietzsche-Studien,* 6 (1977), 261–291, but only at the cost of attributing to Nietzsche a highly doubtful ontological theory.

6. Georg Simmel, *Schopenhauer und Nietzsche* (Leipzig: Duncker und Humblot, 1907), pp. 250–251; cf. Kaufmann, *Nietzsche,* p. 327. Soll suggests that a random recombination of states might avoid Simmel's criticism, but rightly concludes that Nietzsche's determinism does not allow such an interpretation of recurrence; "Reflections on Recurrence," pp. 327 ff.

7. The passage continues: "At least the Stoa has traces of it, and the Stoics inherited all of their principal notions from Heraclitus." This is clearly an overstatement. In any case, it is not clear what exactly Nietzsche thinks the Stoics took from Heraclitus, especially in view of the fact that he had written (much earlier, to be sure) that "Heraclitus has not escaped the 'barren minds'; already the Stoics reinterpreted him on a shallow level, dragging down his basically aesthetic perception of cosmic play to signify a vulgar consideration of the world's useful ends" (*PTG,* 7). Elsewhere Nietzsche gives a very negative picture of the view, which he attributes to the Pythagoreans, that "when the constellation of the heavenly bodies is repeated the same things, down to the smallest event, must also be repeated on earth" (*UM,* II, 2).

8. That Nietzsche may have thought of the recurrence as a cosmology is suggested by the fact that writers with whom he was familiar had argued for such a view, for example Heine (cf. Kaufmann, *Nietzsche,* pp. 317–319), and Schopenhauer, *The World as Will and Representation,* trans. E. F. J. Payne (Indian Hills, Colorado: Falcon's Wing Press, 1958), I, 273–274, 279. Nietzsche himself, as we saw in the preceding note, was willing to find the doctrine in Heraclitus, the Pythagoreans, and the Stoics. But apart from the qualifications mentioned there, we would still have to account for his notorious insistence on the radical novelty of the idea of the recurrence. Perhaps what he took to be novel is the psychological use to which he puts this cosmological idea.

9. These points are made by Soll, "Reflections on Recurrence," p. 323, and Magnus, "Nietzsche's Eternalistic Countermyth," p. 607.

10. Nikos Kazantzakis, *Asketike—Salvatores Dei* (Athens: Sympan, n.d.), pp. 49, 58. The translation is mine.

11. I am tempted to think that this is the only possible nonfatalistic reaction to the recurrence as a cosmology. It could be argued that the recurrence, so construed, only entails determinism, which does not in turn entail fatalism. But I think that the fact that an event has already occurred in the past makes its occurrence in the present necessary in a way in which the idea that human actions, like all events in the world, are caused by other events does not. Nietzsche, who accepts determinism, also claims that our beliefs and thoughts can function as causes of our actions (*KGW,* V, 1, 473).

12. Soll, "Reflections on Recurrence," p. 339. Soll's argument seems to presuppose a view of identity and continuity similar to that argued for more recently by Derek Parfit, "Personal Identity," in John Perry, ed., *Personal Identity* (Berkeley: University

of California Press, 1975), pp. 199–223. But Soll does not mark clearly the distinction between identity and continuity, and this misleads Sterling into an unwarranted criticism of Soll's view ("Recent Discussions of Eternal Recurrence," pp. 273–274). Zuboff argues that the recurrence is a matter of indifference because not only one's current life but a large number of possible alternatives to it as well will recur eternally ("Nietzsche and Eternal Recurrence," pp. 350–352). This seems very unlikely; cf. Krueger, "Nietzschean Recurrence," pp. 442–443; Soll, "Reflections on Recurrence," pp. 327–332.

13. Nietzsche's view has had a decisive influence on French existentialism, especially on Sartre; see *The Transcendence of the Ego,* trans. Forrest Williams and Robert Kirkpatrick (New York: Farrar, Straus and Giroux, 1957), pp. 73–74. For discussion, see John Wilcox, *Truth and Value in Nietzsche* (Ann Arbor: University of Michigan Press, 1974), pp. 114–126. Strong believes that the will to power and the recurrence are quite unconnected (*Nietzsche and the Politics of Transfiguration,* p. 261).

14. It may be argued that the rejection of the substantial subject, though it can lead to the idea that all of a person's actions are equally essential, does not lead to a thesis like (C) or (C'). That is, it might be true that if all my actions were equally essential to me, then I would have the same career in every possible world. But this would not imply that if my career had two or more successive phases in this world, each of which might in a sense constitute a distinct life, these phases would have to be exactly alike. But in reply to this objection we can ask how we are to understand the notion of a phase in this context. To consider the future occurrence a phase of my (total) life, we would have to have access to an enduring subject as the ground of this identification. But for Nietzsche the subject (the totality of my actions) disappears with my death. We could identify *me* as living again only if I were to be born again just as I was born this time, and to grow up just as I grew up, and so on. But from this it seems to follow that if I were to live again, I and the whole world (given the picture of the world I have been discussing) would have to be exactly as we have already been. We can therefore ascribe this view to Nietzsche simply on the basis of his denial of the substantial subject and without appealing to the stronger view that every part of a person's life necessitates every subsequent one, and that therefore a single part could recur only if it were preceded and followed by the very same parts that now precede and follow it.

15. A view of the recurrence not unrelated to the one I am presenting here is given, though with differences both in orientation and in emphasis, by Pierre Klossowski, *Nietzsche et le cercle vicieux* (Paris: Mercure de France, 1969). A relevant excerpt can be found in David Allison, *The New Nietzsche* (New York: Dell, 1977), pp. 107–120. An intentionally "metaphysical" version of "the will's aversion to time," construing it as the downgrading of the transient and as the effort to construct a timeless true world after all, is given by Heidegger, "Who Is Nietzsche's Zarathustra?" in Allison, *The New Nietzsche,* pp. 72–78. Heidegger develops this interpretation in great detail in his *Nietzsche* (Pfuleingen: Neske, 1961), I, 255–472.

16. Nietzsche often talks of the reinterpretation of the past, especially in connection with the notion of redemption, as its "destruction" or "annihilation"; cf. Z, I, 16; *GM,* II, 24.

17. This crucial theme appears often in Nietzsche's writings. Cf. Z, I, 18; Z, II, 7; *GM,* III, 16; and *WP,* 233, where he writes, "To be unable to have done with an experience is already a sign of decadence."

18. William Labov, "Narrative Analysis: Oral Versions of Personal Experience," in *Essays on the Verbal and Visual Arts: Proceedings of the American Ethnological Society* (Seattle: American Ethnological Society, 1966), pp. 37–39.

19. Gary Shapiro has presented a reading of the eternal recurrence that is diametrically opposed to mine: Shapiro construes the view as an attack on the very notion of narrative. According to Shapiro, both for Zarathustra and for Jesus as Nietzsche characterizes him in *The Antichrist*, "the totality of experience is sufficient unto itself and stands in no need of external explanations . . . The eternal recurrence is an antinarrative thought because it knows no isolated agents in the sequence of events, but only the interconnection of all events; it knows no beginning, middle, or end of the narrative but simply the continuous circle of becoming; and it tends to dissolve the mainstay of all narrative, the individual agent into the ring of becoming"; "Nietzsche's Graffito: A Reading of *The Antichrist*," *Boundary 2*, 9–10 (1981), 136; see also his "Nietzsche Contra Renan," *History and Theory*, 21 (1982), 218. He also discusses this subject in his unpublished manuscript "The Psychology of the Recurrence." Although I agree that Nietzsche envisages no isolated events of any sort, I can still insist that he does not thereby "dissolve" either agents or any other objects. Rather, as I have been arguing, he now sees them as complicated constructs, established precisely through narrative efforts.

20. This objection has recently been raised by J. P. Stern, *A Study of Nietzsche* (Cambridge: Cambridge University Press, 1979), pp. 120–121.

21. Just such a second-order view of the *Übermensch* is presented by Bernd Magnus, "Perfectibility and Attitude in Nietzsche's *Übermensch*," *Review of Metaphysics*, 36 (1983), 633–659, who discusses Stern's objection on pp. 638–639.

6. How One Becomes What One Is

1. This opposition, however, does not extend as far back as *The Birth of Tragedy;* see Chapter 2 above. I am still unconvinced by Paul de Man's otherwise brilliant attempt to show that the rhetoric of this work undermines the distinction between appearance and reality that is so central to its explicit argument; see his *Allegories of Reading* (New Haven: Yale University Press, 1980), pp. 79–102. Further reference to this work in this chapter will be made parenthetically in the text.

2. Nietzsche began writing *Ecce Homo* on his forty-fourth birthday, October 15, 1888, and finished it less than three weeks later, on November 4. During that time, and before his final collapse in January 1889, he also put together the text of *Nietzsche Contra Wagner* and of *Dionysos-Dithyramben*, but both works consist of already published material and involved no new writing.

3. The idea of becoming who one is had fascinated Nietzsche at least since his student years, as is indicated by a letter to Erwin Rohde dated November 3, 1867; see *Nietzsche Briefwechsel: Kritische Gesamtausgabe*, Giorgio Colli and Mazzino Montinari, eds., (Berlin: de Gruyter, 1975–), I, 2, 235. He had found these "solemn words" in Pindar's second *Pythian Ode*, l. 73: *genoi' hoios essi mathōn*, though he himself dropped the last word and along with it Pindar's reference to knowledge and, perhaps, specifically to the art of government. A recent discussion of this crucial and difficult passage in Pindar can be found in Erich Thummer, "Die Zweite Pythische Ode Pindars," *Rheinisches Museum für Philologie*, 115 (1972), 293–307.

4. Nietzsche makes a similar point in connection with willing in *WP,* 668, discussed in Chapter 3 above. A further complication is introduced by *WP,* 675.

5. A complex discussion of the relations between Nietzsche and Freud can be found in Paul Laurent Assoun, *Freud et Nietzsche* (Paris: Presses Universitaires de France, 1980), esp. pp. 169–186.

6. Nietzsche's approach also disposes of the following objection, raised by J. P. Stern, *A Study of Nietzsche* (Cambridge: Cambridge University Press, 1979), p. 116. Stern quotes the statement "Your true self . . . lies immeasurably above that which you usually take to be your self" from *Schopenhauer as Educator* (*UM,* III, 1). He identifies what we usually take to be the self with "the social . . . and therefore inauthentic self" and asks, "But is it not equally possible that 'your true self' may lie immeasurably below 'your usual self,' and that society, its conventions and laws may mercifully prevent its realization?" Nietzsche, however, does not believe that there can be an asocial or presocial self, or indeed that any self can exist independently of some sort of relation to other selves. He therefore does not believe that such a self (depending on one's sympathies) should or should not be repressed. Cf. Richard Rorty's reference to "the pre-Nietzschean assumption that man has a true self which ought *not* to be repressed, something which exists *prior* to being shaped by power," in "Beyond Nietzsche and Marx," *London Review of Books,* 19 February 1981, p. 6. In this context, one might allude to *Z,* I, 4, in which a distinction is drawn between the body, which Zarathustra identifies with the self *(das Selbst),* and the spirit, which he identifies with consciousness, with that which says "I" *(das Ich).* He then claims that the body uses consciousness for its own purposes: even "the despisers of the body," those who downgrade it and turn against it, are actually following the desires of their unconscious self, their own body. This may appear at first sight to recall the Freudian view. But the similarity does not seem to me to go any further. The issue is not whether Nietzsche distinguishes between consciousness and the unconscious, as of course he does (see Assoun, *Freud et Nietzsche,* pp. 170–179). The issue is whether he thinks that the unconscious self is to be identified with the real self and whether that is a stable reality underlying the apparent and transient aspects of conscious life. But this is not the case. On the contrary, Nietzsche thinks that the belief that they do have a stable self is precisely what turned the people he addresses into "despisers" of the body: "Even in your folly and contempt . . . you serve your self . . . your self itself wants to die and turns away from life" just because it "is no longer capable of what it would do above all else: to create beyond itself" (*Z,* I, 4). Both the conscious and the unconscious selves, which are related rather in the manner of part to whole, have a tendency toward continual change and development (*WP,* 659). There is therefore no question of *discovering* what one's true self is.

7. This ambivalence is reflected, but not discussed, in Harold Alderman's *Nietzsche's Gift* (Athens, Ohio: Ohio University Press, 1977). Alderman writes, for example, that "the Overman *is* the meaning of the earth . . . and yet we must also *will* that he shall be that meaning . . . Zarathustra's Prologue says, in effect, both that something *is* the case and that we ought to *will* it to be so" (p. 26). Elsewhere Alderman describes *Z,* I, 1 as "Nietzsche's statement of the conditions under which we may create—which is to say encounter—ourselves" (p. 35). Alderman does not discuss this problem explicitly, though at one point he writes that "to be oneself one must know one's limits; only thereby can one grow to meet—one's limits" (p. 126). This, in my

opinion, places too much emphasis on the discovery side of the view Nietzsche is probably trying to undermine (cf. *WP,* 495; *EH,* II, 9). By emphasizing the idea that one's limits are already established, Alderman seems to accept, along more individualistic lines, the Aristotelian interpretation to which I shall turn later in this chapter.

8. This idea appears in Nietzsche's notes, often in connection with the eternal recurrence. As I suggested in Chapter 5, it is quite compatible with taking the recurrence to be the continued existence of our always "unfinished" world; cf. *WP,* 639: "That the world is not striving toward a stable condition is the only thing that has been proved."

9. In connection with the discussion of truth, it is worth remarking that Nietzsche goes on in this passage to write of "the new psychologists" who accept these hypotheses and "precisely thereby . . . condemn themselves to *invention*—and—who knows?—perhaps to discovery" (*BGE,* 12).

10. Nietzsche's attacks on the concept of unity and other traditional "metaphysical" concepts is well documented, in a book influenced by Heidegger's reading of both Western philosophy and Nietzsche, by Eugen Fink, *Nietzsches Philosophie* (Stuttgart: Kohlhammer, 1960).

11. Descartes, *Meditation* II, ed. and trans. Elizabeth S. Haldane and G. R. T. Ross (New York: Dover, 1955), I, 153.

12. Ludwig Wittgenstein, *Philosophical Investigations,* trans. and ed. G. E. M. Anscombe (New York: Macmillan, 1953), sec. 18.

13. Amélie Oksenberg Rorty, "Self-Deception, Akrasia, and Irrationality," *Social Science Information,* 19 (1980), 920. Robert Nozick tries, on a much more abstract level, to account for the self as a "self-synthesizing" entity in his *Philosophical Explanations* (Cambridge, Mass.: Harvard University Press, 1981), pp. 71–114.

14. This passage is characterized by painterly and literary vocabulary (*vollschreiben, überpinseln, Zeichendeuter*—this last word being much more closely connected to the astronomical and astrological imagery on which Nietzsche relies here than Kaufmann's translation suggests) and should be congenial to those writers who want to locate in Nietzsche a serious insistence on the total absence of all "originary" unity. Nietzsche, I think, would agree that the unity in question cannot be given and that it is not there to be uncovered once all the "coats of paint" and the different "writings" have been removed: nothing would then remain over. But this agreement does not prevent him from wanting to *construct* a unity out of this "motley" *(bunt)* material; cf. *WP,* 259, 966. For contrasting views, see Stanley Corngold, "The Question of the Self in Nietzsche During the Axial Period (1882–1888)," *Boundary 2,* 9–10 (1981), 55–98, and J. Hillis Miller, "The Disarticulation of the Self in Nietzsche," *The Monist,* 64 (1981), 247–261. *BGE,* 215, with its allusion to Kant, is also relevant to my view: just as some planets, Nietzsche writes, are illuminated by many suns, sometimes by suns of different colors, "so we moderns are determined, thanks to the complicated mechanics of our 'starry sky,' by different moralities; our actions shine alternately in different colors, they are rarely univocal—and there are cases enough in which we perform actions *of many colors.*"

15. This view is denied by Stern, *A Study of Nietzsche,* who should be consulted on this matter; see his chap. 7, esp. p. 122 and n. 7.

16. There is only an apparent inconsistency between my statement and Nietzsche's view in *GS,* 367. In this passage Nietzsche distinguishes "monological art" from "art

before others" and claims that the most important distinction is between artists who look at their work in progress "from the point of view of the witness" and artists who have "forgotten the world." This distinction, however, must not be confused with the distinction between those who do and those who don't care what their public thinks. Rather, it is a question of which public one is addressing. The artists who "forget the world" still inspect their work and thus act as their own public.

17. Nietzsche's remarks on persons as hierarchical structures of desires and character traits interestingly prefigure the views of Harry Frankfurt, "Freedom of the Will and the Concept of a Person," *Journal of Philosophy,* 68 (1971), 5–20. Despite their many differences, the two views converge in that just as Nietzsche does not consider that every agent has a self, Frankfurt writes that not every human being need be a person: only agents who have certain desires about what their will should be are persons for him (p. 11). And just as Nietzsche considers that "freedom of the will" is not presupposed by, but attained through, agency, Frankfurt writes, "The enjoyment of freedom comes easily to some. Others have to struggle to achieve it" (p. 17).

18. Marcel Proust, *Remembrance of Things Past,* trans. C. K. Scott Moncrieff and Terence Kilmartin (New York: Random House, 1981), III, 915.

19. Aristotle, *Nicomachean Ethics* 6. 1, 6.

20. If my hypothesis is correct, Nietzsche, in seeing life as a work of art composed by each individual as it goes along in life (an idea which was very influential on Sartre's analysis of self-deception; *Being and Nothingness,* trans. Hazel Barnes, New York: Philosophical Library, 1956, pp. 55–70), can be placed within the great tradition that has been working out the consequences of the metaphor of the *theatrum mundi.* Nietzsche gives this tradition a secular turn, doing away with God and the angels as the audience for whom the world's drama is acted out (cf. *GM,* II, 7, 16, 23). This is once again ironic, for the tradition of the *theatrum mundi* can ultimately be traced back to none other than Plato (*Laws* 644d–e, 804c); cf. Ernst Curtius, *European Literature and the Latin Middle Ages* (Princeton, N.J.: Princeton University Press, 1953), pp. 138–144.

21. See Ronald Hayman, *Nietzsche: A Critical Life* (New York: Oxford University Press, 1980), p. 119.

22. The details of this argument can be found in my "Mythology: The Theory of Plot," in John Fisher, ed., *Essays in Aesthetics: Perspectives on the Work of Monroe C. Beardsley* (Philadelphia: Temple University Press, 1983).

7. Beyond Good and Evil

1. This has disturbed a number of Plato's commentators, notably F. M. Cornford, who, in his translation of the *Republic* (New York: Oxford University Press, 1945), renders the phrase *gennaion ti hen pseudomenous* simply as "a single bold flight of invention," and comments that Plato's "harmless allegory" should be compared "to a New Testament parable or the *Pilgrim's Progress*" (p. 106, n. 1). Yet Plato explicitly says that he wants all his citizens to accept this story as the literal truth (415d1–5). The aim of the story makes it impossible to take it as a parable or an allegory.

2. I would include in this class works as different from one another as Crane Brinton's *Nietzsche* (New York: Harper and Row, 1965), chaps. 4–5, and Gilles Deleuze's *Nietzsche and Philosophy,* trans. Hugh Tomlinson (New York: Columbia University

Press, 1983), chaps. 4–5. Both books have been, each in its own way, crucial to the interpretation of Nietzsche and his influence. But Brinton's overwhelming suspiciousness of Nietzsche seems to be counterbalanced by Deleuze's apocalyptic vision of a new world once, under Nietzsche's tutelage, the grip of dialectic and morality has been undone.

3. E. R. Dodds, *Plato: Gorgias* (Oxford: Clarendon Press, 1959), pp. 387–391, draws a number of parallels between Nietzsche and Callicles, but also makes some reasonable qualifications.

4. An illuminating account of Nietzsche's early views of morality, their relation to the positions of Kant and Schopenhauer, and Nietzsche's reasons for changing his approach is given in Maudemarie Clark's dissertation "Nietzsche's Attack on Morality" (Univ. of Wisconsin, 1977), pp. 17–107. I am not, however, convinced by Clark's view that in the *Genealogy* Nietzsche comes to think that morality is "indefinable."

5. It is significant that the notorious expression "master morality" (*Herren-moral*) does not ever appear in the *Genealogy*. The term appears only once in Nietzsche's published texts, in *BGE*, 260. The expression "noble morality" *(vornehme Moral)* occurs twice, in *GM*, 1, 10, and *A*, 24; cf. Clark, "Nietzsche's Attack on Morality," p. 114.

6. It is in this connection that Nietzsche mentions the "blond beast" that is supposed to lurk in all noble races. For the correct interpretation of Nietzsche's metaphor, which involves the lion and not the Aryan race, see Walter Kaufmann, *Nietzsche: Philosopher, Psychologist, Antichrist* (Princeton, N.J.: Princeton University Press, 1974), pp. 225–226, and Arthur C. Danto, *Nietzsche as Philosopher* (New York: Macmillan, 1965), pp. 169–170. Further references to these works in this chapter will be made parenthetically in the text.

7. Kaufmann, *Nietzsche*, p. 297, also writes: "He would like us to conform to neither and become autonomous." But Kaufmann gives no reason why Nietzsche would equate accepting a code of conduct with "conforming" to it in a sense that would preclude being autonomous. On the contrary, we have seen that Nietzsche is concerned to show that without codes and customs there can be no action whatsoever, let alone action that is noble and admirable. The serious question, therefore, concerns the particular code involved in each case.

8. This passage, as well as *GM*, I, 12, suggests that Danto's view that "Nietzsche was asking that we go *beyond* what we are, not *back* to what we were" (*Nietzsche as Philosopher*, p. 180) cannot be accepted without serious qualification. Though Nietzsche may not want us to go back to the specific *instance* of the type the nobles manifest, he may still want us to go back to the *type* itself.

9. This seems to be part of Danto's strategy. I think, however, that he may be too quick to argue that nothing in Nietzsche's theory commits him to approving of the barbarian (*Nietzsche as Philosopher*, p. 173). If the barbarian is a good instance of the type that Nietzsche praises, then Nietzsche also praises the barbarian.

10. Anton Chekhov, *Letters on the Short Story, the Drama and Other Literary Topics,* ed. Louis S. Friedland (New York: Minton, 1924), pp. 275–276.

11. Philippa Foot, "Moral Realism and Moral Dilemma," *Journal of Philosophy*, 80 (1983), 397.

12. We could always make sure that a portion of society would without question conform to a code of conduct by enslaving it. But such conformity would not be un-

conditional and would depend on the explicit imposition of the will of some members of that society on the rest.

13. These points are discussed in Kai Nielsen, "Nietzsche as a Moral Philosopher," *Man and World*, 6 (1975), 190–191.

14. A related reading of the *Übermensch* can be found in Bernd Magnus, "Perfectibility and Attitude in Nietzsche's *Übermensch*," *Review of Metaphysics*, 36 (1983), 633–659. Magnus defends his interpretation mostly on metaphilosophical grounds and not by the sort of considerations on which I rely here.

15. J. P. Stern, *A Study of Nietzsche* (Cambridge: Cambridge University Press, 1979), p. 117.

16. Martin Heidegger, *Nietzsche*, trans. David Farrell Krell (New York: Harper and Row, 1979), I, 125.

17. See M. S. Silk and J. P. Stern, *Nietzsche on Tragedy* (Cambridge: Cambridge University Press, 1981), chap. 1 and also chap. 7.

18. Despite my great admiration of and indebtedness to their work, these comments apply both to Martin Heidegger, "Who Is Nietzsche's Zarathustra?" in David Allison, ed., *The New Nietzsche* (New York: Dell, 1977), pp. 64–79, and to Gilles Deleuze, *Nietzsche and Philosophy*, trans. Hugh Tomlinson (New York: Columbia University Press, 1983), esp. chap. 5.

19. Hilary Putnam, *Reason, Truth and History* (Cambridge: Cambridge University Press, 1981), p. 216.

20. Even in the case of Vermeer, the text gives some indication that the narrator's point of view is not identical with that of Bergotte. The narrator mentions that Bergotte also saw in the painting, for the first time, "some figure in blue, that the sand was pink." This suggests that the beauty of the wall is after all a function of its interrelations with the other elements of the painting. The Vermeer incident is found in vol. III, pp. 185–186; the other passage occurs in vol. II, p. 558 of the C. K. Scott Moncrieff and Terence Kilmartin translation of Marcel Proust, *Remembrance of Things Past* (New York: Random House, 1981).

21. See Arthur Danto, *The Transfiguration of the Commonplace* (Cambridge, Mass.: Harvard University Press, 1981), chap. 4.

22. Some of the issues I have been discussing in this chapter are alluded to in Philippa Foot's "Nietzsche: The Revaluation of Values," in Robert Solomon, ed., *Nietzsche: A Collection of Critical Essays* (Garden City, N.Y.: Doubleday, 1973), pp. 157–168. Her view is much more negative than mine; cf. pp. 163, 168.

INDEX